The New International Relations of Sub-Regionalism

In the context of the end of the Cold War and the spread of globalism, sub-regions are attracting attention as new social units of international society that have never been observed before. In the "second wave" of regionalism that became active in the 1980s, a new regionalism that differed qualitatively from the old regionalism expanded globally. This "new regionalism" is characterized by multidimensionality, complexity, fluidity, and nonconformity; within it, we cannot overlook the fact that spaces on a new scale, such as sub-regions, are being formed in various parts of the world. The sovereign state system that has continued unbroken since the Westphalia Treaty is being transformed. Within this context, the increase in the number of sub-regions as new social units adds to the sense that we have arrived at a post-Westphalian international order.

This book focuses on the sub-region as a new social unit of international society. It is based on findings obtained through meticulous fieldwork and joint studies conducted over the past 10 years by about 20 researchers, primarily from Japanese universities and Chiang Mai University in Thailand. The sub-regions described here are mostly international cross-border spaces or units in the interior of a certain region; these include multiple states, states and parts of them, or more than two parts of states (often referred to as micro-regions). Such sub-regions have emerged in various parts of the world since the end of the Cold War. However, studies on sub-regions remain unexplored in the existing research on regionalism. The few studies that do exist mainly center on the economic aspects of sub-regions. In contrast, this book specifically examines the sub-regions in Asia (especially the Mekong region) and Europe from a political science and international relations perspective. The goal is to establish a new international relations by carving out a political angle of the sub-region, viewing it as a new social unit of international society, and attempting to shift the paradigm of conventional international relations. To understand the political dimension of a sub-region, this book chiefly focuses on three aspects: sub-regions and state strategies, bottom-up dimensions of sub-regions, and sub-regions and borders.

Hidetoshi Taga is Professor of Social Sciences at Waseda University, Japan

Seiichi Igarashi is Associate Professor in Graduate School of Social Sciences at Chiba University, Japan

Routledge Studies on Asia in the World

Routledge Studies on Asia in the World will be an authoritative source of knowledge on Asia studying a variety of cultural, economic, environmental, legal, political, religious, security and social questions, addressed from an Asian perspective. We aim to foster a deeper understanding of the domestic and regional complexities which accompany the dynamic shifts in the global economic, political and security landscape towards Asia and their repercussions for the world at large. We're looking for scholars and practitioners – Asian and Western alike – from various social science disciplines and fields to engage in testing existing models which explain such dramatic transformation and to formulate new theories that can accommodate the specific political, cultural and developmental context of Asia's diverse societies. We welcome both monographs and collective volumes which explore the new roles, rights and responsibilities of Asian nations in shaping today's interconnected and globalized world in their own right.

The Series is advised and edited by Matthias Vanhullebusch and Ji Weidong of Shanghai Jiao Tong University.

China and EU
Reform and Governance
Edited by Jing Men and Annika Linck

Sustainable Development Goals in the Republic of Korea
Edited by Tae Yong Jung

Access to Higher Education: Refugees' Stories from Malaysia
Lucy Bailey and Gül İnanç

The New International Relations of Sub-Regionalism
Asia and Europe
Edited by Hidetoshi Taga and Seiichi Igarashi

Find the full list of books in the series here: https://www.routledge.com/Routledge-Studies-on-Asia-in-the-World/book-series/RSOAW

The New International Relations of Sub-Regionalism
Asia and Europe

Edited by
Hidetoshi Taga and
Seiichi Igarashi

LONDON AND NEW YORK

First published 2019
by Routledge
2 Park Square, Milton Park, Abingdon, Oxon OX14 4RN

and by Routledge
711 Third Avenue, New York, NY 10017

Routledge is an imprint of the Taylor & Francis Group, an informa business

© 2019 selection and editorial matter, Hidetoshi Taga and Seiichi Igarashi; individual chapters, the contributors

The right of Hidetoshi Taga and Seiichi Igarashi to be identified as the authors of the editorial material, and of the authors for their individual chapters, has been asserted in accordance with sections 77 and 78 of the Copyright, Designs and Patents Act 1988.

All rights reserved. No part of this book may be reprinted or reproduced or utilised in any form or by any electronic, mechanical, or other means, now known or hereafter invented, including photocopying and recording, or in any information storage or retrieval system, without permission in writing from the publishers.

Trademark notice: Product or corporate names may be trademarks or registered trademarks, and are used only for identification and explanation without intent to infringe.

British Library Cataloguing-in-Publication Data
A catalogue record for this book is available from the British Library

Library of Congress Cataloging-in-Publication Data
Names: Taga, Hidetoshi, 1949– editor. | Igarashi, Seiichi, 1972– editor. | Taga, Hidetoshi, 1949– Toward a new analytical framework of subregions.
Title: The new international relations of sub-regionalism : Asia and Europe / edited by Hidetoshi Taga and Seiichi Igarashi.
Description: New York : Routledge, 2019. | Series: Routledge studies on Asia in the world | Includes bibliographical references and index.
Identifiers: LCCN 2018025633
Subjects: LCSH: Regionalism—Asia. | Regionalism—Europe. | Regionalism (International organization) | International relations. | Transnationalism. | International cooperation.
Classification: LCC JZ5333 .N48 2019 | DDC 327.5—dc23
LC record available at https://lccn.loc.gov/2018025633

ISBN: 978-1-138-09325-6 (hbk)
ISBN: 978-1-315-10695-3 (ebk)

Typeset in Galliard
by codeMantra

Contents

Foreword   vii
GLENN D. HOOK

Notes on contributors   xi
Preface   xv

Introduction: new critical perspectives for sub-regions/sub-regionalism   1
HIDETOSHI TAGA AND SEIICHI IGARASHI

PART I
Theoretical Reflections   25

1 Toward a new analytical framework of sub-regions: cross-scale regional governance   27
 HIDETOSHI TAGA AND HIDEO KOJIMOTO

PART II
Sub-Regionalism in Asia   51

2 Small states' strategies in the Mekong region: perspectives from Laos   53
 YUJI MORIKAWA

3 Alternative Mekong regionalism from the perspective of regional hegemony and civil society   71
 SEIICHI IGARASHI

4 Civil society vs. GMS states in terms of infrastructure and hydropower development projects   107
 KOSUM SAICHAN AND HIROSHI KOMATSU

5 Changing borderland local communities with
   development of the GMS program   124
   EKAMOL SAICHAN

6 The Mekong region and changing borders: a focus
   on the CBTA and BCPs   160
   TETSU SADOTOMO AND KENJI NAKAYAMA

PART III
Sub-Regionalism in Europe   181

7 Normative politics in the European Union's external
   actions: the case of ENI Cross-Border Cooperation   183
   YOICHIRO USUI

8 Sub-regionalism in the border regions between the
   EU and Russia   197
   KAZU TAKAHASHI

9 The parallel evolution of functional macro-regions and
   cross-scale regional governance as emerging political
   instruments in the North Sea Region   213
   HIDEO KOJIMOTO, YOSHITAKA OTA, AND ANN BELL

   Conclusion: future challenges in the study or
   sub-regions/sub-regionalism   226
   HIDETOSHI TAGA AND SEIICHI IGARASHI

   Index   233

Foreword
Glenn D. Hook

In *The New International Relations of Sub-Regionalism*, a group of social scientists from mainly Japan and other parts of East Asia offer an empirically rich, theoretically informed and incisive examination of how sub-regional projects are changing the political, economic and social landscape of two key centres of the global political economy: East Asia and Europe. The editors, two prominent Japanese scholars, Hidetoshi Taga and Seiichi Igarashi, have brought together contributors who are able to offer a range of critical perspectives that have grown out of their long years of research on regionalism. While their empirical fieldwork means that the authors have crossed the boundaries of many different states, sub-regions and regions during their years of engagement in the field, the book takes as its particular foci the Mekong sub-region and sub-regions in Europe. The book offers a distinctive, non-Eurocentric interdisciplinary approach to the question of sub-regionalism, adding, especially in the East Asia chapters, a nuanced understanding of the complex nature of sub-regional activities. The team should be congratulated on publishing their work as an edited volume in English.

The framework used to illuminate how space is being reconfigured on different spatial scales, from regionalism on the micro- level to the sublevel and on to the macro level, makes a distinction between sub-regions and sub-regionalism. While the distinction between a region as geographic space and regionalism as a political project can be found in earlier research on regionalism, what is noteworthy about the approach adopted here is the move away from a focus on the state as the quintessential participant in regionalism to examine substate and non-state actors as well. Particularly rewarding is the attention the book pays to the soft spaces of sub-regionalism and to the role of substate as well as non-state actors. While not ignoring the role of the state, the authors view sub-regions flexibly, involving a multitude of actors and different scales of governance. Where states are the focus, this includes small states such as Laos, which has been playing an important role in promoting sub-regionalism. In this sense, the authors are not on a positivist mission to analyse sub-regions in terms of size, scope or institutionalization but rather adopt a constructivist approach in order to illuminate how the boundaries to sub-regions can change as these entities are socially constructed as 'action spaces' (p. 7) in the context of interacting at the state, substate and non-state levels.

The main aim of the book is to examine sub-regions with a particular view to the dynamics of their politics, exploring the similarities and differences between the politics of sub-regions in Europe, where institutionalization is advanced, as illustrated by the European Union (EU), and in East Asia, where sub-regionalism has developed without much institutionalization, as seen in the book's detailed examination of different aspects of the Greater Mekong Sub-region (GMS). In the EU, issues of governance have tended to be viewed through the prism of multilevel governance, whereas in the sub-regional spaces of East Asia, the politics of governance revolves around a fluid range of actors as stakeholders rather than as top-down decision makers representing the state. We see this in the fascinating detail of how the everyday lives of the people are interwoven into the fabric of the legal separation between states implied by the sovereign territorial state's imposition of national borders dividing one from the other. The rich empirical data produced by the authors show how stakeholders in border areas, as in the case of the border region between Vietnam and Myanmar, are able to exploit dual borders, where the everyday life of the local people in the subnational regions is intertwined through the use of unofficial routes across the territorial borders of the state. The interweaving of people's lives across national borders is a quintessential feature of the Mekong sub-region, where borders are not viewed simply as legal barriers but also as a transnational space of interaction. Here the local inhabitants take advantage of border crossings, linking together their everyday lives in separate sovereign states. These links are facilitated by the Cross-Border Transport Agreement (CBTA), which is helping to knit together space across national boundaries in a way to create action spaces.

As far as sub-regions in Europe are concerned, the volume makes a valuable contribution to our understanding of the various roles that actors play in the development of regionalism outside of intra-EU cooperation as well as of the different levels of involvement within the EU. This is evident in the case of the fisheries policy in the North Sea Region; in the case of the United Kingdom (UK), a substate political authority in one of its constituent countries, the Aberdeenshire Council of Scotland, plays a crucial role in regional governance, along with subnational actors in Denmark and Norway. Meanwhile, as far as the Euro-regions outside of the EU are concerned, we find that these areas are able to facilitate the entry of states into the EU, as seen when the Upper and Lower Prut River Euro-regions performed this function prior to Romania's entry into the EU. But there is a normative, not simply institutional, aspect to how the EU operates, as seen in the transfer of normative frameworks of understanding from within the EU to non-members. This is illustrated by the EU's efforts to institutionalize cross-border cooperation between substate and non-state actors.

While the evidence presented shows how the EU's role in disseminating norms to non-members is crucial in maintaining an 'arc of stability' around the EU, the recent decision of UK to leave the EU following a national referendum in June 2016 and the decision of the Catalonian government to hold a referendum and declare independence from the Spanish state in October 2017, despite the steadfast opposition of the central government and the constitutional court, highlight how regionalist projects face challenges from inside as well as outside in terms of governance. That said, thanks to the authors' focus on a range of actors, including substate and non-state actors, not just the state, we are able to come to a much deeper understanding of the complex interaction taking place on different spatial scales as sub-regionalist projects stimulate the emergence of new international relations in East Asia and Europe, as are emerging in Europe in the wake of the political use of referenda as tools of governance.

In this way, the contributors to *The New International Relations of Sub-Regionalism* make a welcome contribution to our understanding of regionalism in East Asia and Europe. The volume adds rich empirical analysis to the literature and can be expected to help to invigorate the debate on the analysis of the different levels of regionalism emerging around the world.

Glenn D. Hook is emeritus professor of the University of Sheffield. He was formerly the Toshiba International Foundation Anniversary Research Professor in the Politics and International Relations of Japan in the School of East Asian Studies. His latest publication is *Environmental Pollution and the Media: Political Discourses of Risk and Responsibility in Australia, China and Japan* (Routledge, 2017).

Notes on contributors

The editors

Hidetoshi Taga is a professor at Waseda University, School of Social Sciences. He graduated from Waseda University's School of Law in 1973 and also earned his M.A. there in 1975. In 1981, he completed the coursework for the doctoral program in law at the same university. Later that year, he obtained an assistant professor position at Niigata University's Faculty of Law. He became a professor there in 1987. In 1996, he took on a professor position at Waseda University's School of Social Sciences and served as the dean from 2008 to 2012. He specializes in international relations and peace studies. His main publications are *Asian Community* (co-authored, 2013), *A New Frontier of International Relations* (co-authored, 2010), *Sub-Regionalism in the European Union and the East Asian Community* (co-edited, 2006), *Designing an East Asian Community, Volume 1* (co-authored, 2007), *International Comparison of Regionalism* (co-authored, 2005), *Actors and Transformation of the International Community* (edited, 1999), and *Cross-border Experiment* (edited, 1992).

Seiichi Igarashi is an associate professor at Chiba University's Graduate School of Social Sciences. He graduated from Keio University's Faculty of Letters in 1994. He earned his M.A. and Ph.D. from Waseda University's Graduate School of Social Sciences. He became a research associate at Waseda University's School of Social Sciences in 2002; a post-doctoral research fellow of the Japan Society for the Promotion of Science (JSPS) in 2005; an assistant professor at Waseda University's Faculty of Social Sciences in 2008; a researcher for the global Centers of Excellence (COE) program at Kyoto University in 2010; and a lecturer at Chiba University's Faculty of Law and Economics that same year. He specializes in international relations and Asian studies. His main publications include *New Regionalism and Civil Society in East Asia* (2018), *Military, Political Power, and Civil Society in Developing Countries* (co-authored, 2016), *Transformation of the Intimate and the Public in Asian Modernity* (co-authored, 2014), *The Modern Global System and Neoliberal Globalism* (co-authored, 2014), and *A New Perspective on Democratization and Civil Society* (2011).

The contributors

Ann Bell is a member of the North East Scotland College Regional Board. She chairs the Human Resources Committee and is vice chair of the Governance Steering Group. She was marine adviser to the North Sea Commission and director and executive secretary to the North Sea Regional Advisory Council. In 2003, she received a Most Excellent Order of the British Empire (MBE) from Queen Elizabeth II for services to the fishing industry and communities.

Hideo Kojimoto is a professor at Nihon University's College of Law. He earned his M.A. in sociology from the University of Essex's Department of Sociology and his Ph.D. from Waseda University's Graduate School of Social Sciences. He specializes in EU area studies, the study of international marine policy, and international politics. His main publications include *A Macro Region of the EU* (2014) and *Transformation of International Actors and Identities* (2000).

Hiroshi Komatsu is a research fellow at the Center for Relational Studies on Global Crises at Chiba University. He earned his M.A. and Ph.D. from Waseda University's Graduate School of Social Sciences. He specializes in international relations in East Asia and modern Okinawan politics. His primary publications include *For and Against Reversion of Okinawa to Japan* (2015) and *Revisiting Japan's Security from Okinawa* (co-authored, 2015).

Yuji Morikawa is a professor at Nagasaki University's School of Global Humanities and Social Sciences. He earned his M.A. and Ph.D. from Waseda University's Graduate School of Social Sciences. He specializes in international relations in East Asia. His main publications include *A New Political Dynamics for Regional Formation in East Asia* (2012) and *Regional Order in East Asia after World War II and Cold War* (co-authored, 2012).

Kenji Nakayama is an associate professor at Soka University's Faculty of Law. He earned his M.A. and Ph.D. from Waseda University's Graduate School of Social Sciences. He specializes in international relations in East Asia and peace studies. His primary publications include *A Study of Endogenous Governance and Transnational Actors in Northeast Asia* (2015) and *An Introduction and Reference for Asian Regional Integration* (co-authored, 2013).

Yoshitaka Ota is a research assistant professor at the University of Washington's School of Marine and Environmental Affairs and director at the Nereus Program, an interdisciplinary ocean research initiative. He completed his M.Sc. and Ph.D. in anthropology at the University College London. His most recent publications include *Committing Social Responsible Seafood in Science* (2017) and *A Rapid Assessment of Co-benefits and Trade-offs among Sustainable Development Goals in Marine Policy* (2017).

Tetsu Sadotomo is a professor at Nihon University's College of Law. He earned his M.A. from Nihon University's Graduate School of Law. He specializes in international relations and peace studies. His recent research interests include the Mekong River Basin countries as a sub-region of East Asia. His main publications include *International Relations* (co-edited, 2013) and *Designing the East Asian Community* (co-authored, 2006).

Ekamol Saichan is a member of the Steering Committee of the Regional Center for Sustainable Development (RCSD) at Chiang Mai University. He earned his M.A. from Thammasat University in 1973 and 1977, respectively. He also earned his M.A. from the Institute of Social Studies in The Hague, the Netherlands. His chief publications is *20 Years of Greater Mekong Sub-region (GMS)* (co-authored, 2011).

Kosum Saichan is a guest lecturer at Chiang Mai University's Political Economy Graduate Program in the Faculty of Social Sciences. She earned a doctorat de 3e cycle in political science from the University of Poitiers in France. She specializes in Southeast Asian politics. Her main publications include *Implementation of European Union Immigrant Integration Policy* (2017) and *Politics and Regional Integration in Greater Mekong Sub-region* (2014).

Kazu Takahashi is a professor at Yamagata University's Faculty of Literature and Social Sciences. She earned her M.A. in international relations at Tsuda. She specializes in international relations theory and East European studies. Her main publications include *Evolving Power Politics and Resistance* (co-authored, 2012) and *How Did Eastern Europe Change under the Process of EU Integration?* (co-authored, 2010).

Yoichiro Usui is a professor at the Niigata University of International and Information Studies' Department of International Studies. He earned his M.A. in research from the University of Leeds' Department of Law in the United Kingdom. He specializes in EU politics. His main publications include *The Normative Politics of the European Union* (edited, 2015) and *Normative Politics in EU Environmental Governance* (2013).

Preface

The official, full-fledged start of this research dates back to 2005. In that year, researchers from 12 Japanese universities (Hirosaki University, Yamagata University, Chiba University, Toyama University, Kagawa University, Niigata Prefectural University, Kagoshima Prefectural College, Seijo University, Toyo Eiwa University, Niigata University of International and Information Studies, Nihon University, and Waseda University) came together to form a "sub-region research group." Later, due to several career movements, Teikyo University, Meiji University, Nagasaki University, University of Shizuoka, and Soka University joined the group. Since then, we have continued to undertake collaborative surveys and research with assistants and students from these universities as well as scholars from Chiang Mai University in Thailand. The group's members presented the empirical results of their research, primarily focusing on comparisons between East Asian sub-regions such as the Greater Mekong Sub-region (GMS) and various micro- and sub-regions under the authority of the European Union (EU) at group meetings held twice per year.

The principle aim of the group is to vigorously and empirically examine sub-regions that have conventionally been neglected by others studying international relations (IR). The sub-region is a "new social unit" and/or a "new social experiment" that has been observed in many corners of the world and contains diverse findings that compel us to revise conventional IR theories. This understanding serves as the background for the current volume, *The New International Relations of Sub-Regionalism*. Those who contributed to the book were recruited from the sub-region research group, primarily based on the strength of their broad knowledge in their respective fields. Each contributor was asked to take into account the new perspectives proposed in the introduction when writing their individual chapters.

In producing this volume, Mr. Simon Bates, editor at Routledge, lent us a tremendous amount of support. We met him for the first time in Tokyo in September 2014, where he showed great interest in our idea to suggest new theoretical and empirical perspectives of IR focusing on the sub-region, as suggested by researchers in Japan and Asia. He patiently waited for one-and-a-half years until we applied for peer review, encouraging us throughout that process. We would like to express our deepest gratitude to him as well as to Mr. Tan ShengBin, editorial assistant at Routledge, whose swift attention to details during the editorial process provided helpful comments and support. We would like to thank Ms. Assunta Petrone, project manager at codeMantra, for helping to proofread our work. In addition, we would like to thank Ms. Kei Igarashi, assistant administrator of the Graduate School of Social Sciences at Chiba University, who carried out a detailed proofreading of the entire manuscript.

This book is supported by the Japan Society for the Promotion of Science (JSPS) Grant-in-Aid for Scientific Research (B) (Grant No. 18402017, FY2006-FY2008, Sub-Regions in the EU and East Asian Community: Building a Model for International Cooperation in Regional Governance), JSPS Grant-in-Aid for Scientific Research (B) (Grant No. 21402016, FY2009-FY2011, Multi-Level Governance in a Global Age: Comparison of Sub-Regionalism in the EU and Asia), JSPS Grant-in-Aid for Scientific Research (B) (Grant No. 25301012, FY2013-FY2015, Research into Sub-Regional Governance in East Asia: The Formation of the Greater Mekong Sub-Region), and JSPS Grant-in-Aid for Scientific Research (B) (Grant No. 16H05700, FY2016-FY2019, Multi-Layer Sub-Regions and New Security Architecture in East Asia).

Hidetoshi Taga
Seiichi Igarashi

Introduction
New critical perspectives for sub-regions/sub-regionalism

Hidetoshi Taga and Seiichi Igarashi

The upsurge of sub-regions in the second wave of regionalism

In the context of the end of the Cold War and the spread of globalism, sub-regions are attracting attention as new social units of international society never before observed. In the "second wave" of regionalism that became active in the 1980s, a "new regionalism," which differed qualitatively from the "old regionalism," expanded globally. "New regionalism" is characterized by multi-dimensionality, complexity, fluidity, and nonconformity (Söderbaum 2003: 1), and within it, we cannot overlook the fact that spaces on a new scale, such as sub-regions, are being formed in various parts of the world. The sovereign state system that has continued unbroken since the Westphalia Treaty is being transformed,[1] and within this context, the increase in the number of sub-regions as new social units adds to the sense that we have arrived at a post-Westphalian international order.

Previously, Nye defined a region as "a limited number of states linked by a geographical relationship and by a degree of mutual interdependence" (Nye 1968: xii). This definition, which regarded only a region consisting of multiple states as a region, clearly reflected the international conditions of those times. Currently, there are attempts to adopt a broader and more flexible definition that overcomes territorial factors and geographical realities. For example, Fawcett stated as follows:

> We need to refine regions to incorporate commonality, interaction and hence the possibility of cooperation. From another perspective, regions could be seen as units or "zones," based on groups, states or territories, whose members display some identifiable patterns of behavior. Such units are smaller than the international system of states, but larger than any individual state; they may be permanent or temporary, institutionalized or not. Another approach likens a region to a nation in the sense of an imagined community: states or peoples held together by common experience and identity, custom and practice.... Most regions that identify themselves, or are identified by others, as such share some or all of these characteristics, though often

in different quantities and combinations. Regions, though, do not need to conform to state boundaries. They may comprise substate as well as suprastate and trans-state units, offering different modalities of organization and collaboration.

(Fawcett 2004: 432)

However, even in this definition, there remains little recognition of sub-regions whose scale is smaller than that of an average-sized state.

From the geographical perspective, the sub-regions described here are generally international cross-border spaces or units in the interior of a certain region, which include (1) multiple states, (2) states and parts of states, or (3) more than two parts of states. With regard to term (1), when a sub-region includes many states, it is designated a macro-region. We can alternatively term (3) a micro-region or a cross-border region. Conventional research into regionalism has focused exclusively on (1), but this book focuses on (2) and (3). These definitions have an affinity with the European context, where the European Union (EU) defines sub-regions according to its regional policy. For example, in INTERREG IIIB, states and parts of states ((2), called sub-regions) are a policy area, while in INTERREG IIIA, the space formed from parts of states ((3), called micro-regions) is a policy area (Figures I.1 and I.2). The microregions of (3), which are the closest spaces to the lives of local residents, can be described as the connection of living areas that are separated by national borders.

While defining sub-regions in this way, the physical size of the spaces, institutional levels, and territoriality are not decided *a priori*. In terms of physical size, sub-regions around the world have a range of sizes; moreover, their sizes are constantly changing. With regard to the level of institutionalization, explicit systems, for example, international mechanisms such as INTERREG, do not always exist in sub-regions, as is evident from non-European case studies. Even INTERREG has gradually been institutionalized, mainly through the deepening regional integration of the EU. As for territoriality, there are not only formal sub-regions defined by states and international institutions, but also informal ones driven by companies and other non-state actors that do not have definite territoriality. These informal sub-regions do not necessarily have clear boundaries based on national borders or local units. According to the constructivist perspective, regions are spaces that are socially constructed and recognized by a variety of actors; therefore, they are likely to change.

Although it did not use the concept of a sub-region, research on sub-regions began at the start of the 1990s, mainly focusing on local economic zones, such as Europe's Baltic Sea region and the Indonesia-Malaysia-Singapore Growth Triangle (IMS-GT) (Figures I.1 and I.3) (Yuan 1991; Sandberg 1992; Joenniemi 1993; Thant, Tang, and Kakazu 1995). Subsequently in Europe, upon the fullfledged introduction of INTERREG, which uses sub-regions as a policy instrument, research employing sub-regions as case studies instantly began to blossom (Anderson, O'Dowd, and Wilson 2003; Kramsch and Hooper 2004; Leibenath, Korcelli-Olejniczak, and Knippschild 2008; Smallbone, Welter, and Xheneti

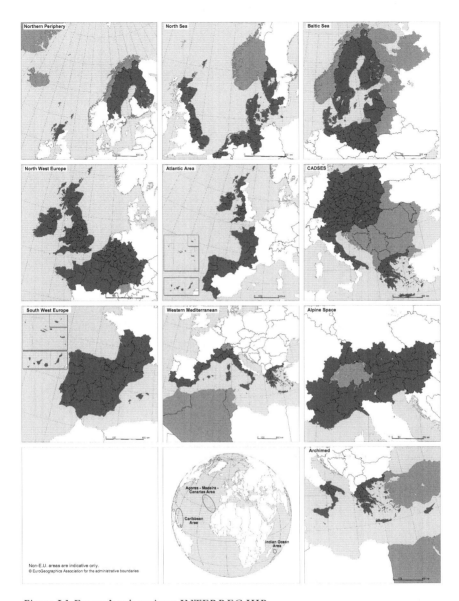

Figure I.1 Europe's sub-regions: INTERREG IIIB
Source: Created by the authors based on http://ec.europa.eu/regional_policy/archive/interreg3/images/pdf/int3b_uk_a4p.pdf, accessed October 13, 2017.

Note: INTERREG of the EU territory is in a darker shade of gray. INTERREG of the non-EU territory is in a lighter shade of gray.

2012; Stokłosa and Besier 2014). On the other hand, while there have been attempts to research sub-regions outside of Europe, in many cases, these studies only elucidated one aspect (often the economic or developmental aspect) (Breslin and Hook 2002; Sasuga 2004; Söderbaum and Taylor 2008; OECD 2009), and

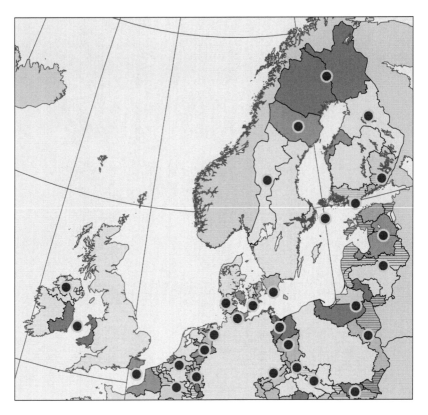

Figure I.2 Europe's sub-regions: INTERREG IIIA
Source: http://ec.europa.eu/regional_policy/archive/interreg3/abc/voleta_north_en.htm, accessed October 13, 2017.

little research has been conducted on either the theoretical or political aspects of these regions. However, regardless of this delay in research, cross-border spaces called sub-regions have been formed in various parts of the world, particularly since the end of the Cold War (Table I.1). In the process of forming each of these sub-regions, the engagement of a variety of actors could be observed. From this empirical fact, it is necessary to recognize that "regionalism" constitutes the ideas, identities, and ideologies related to a regional political project in which these various actors are involved.[2] Regionalism is not always led by states because not only states, but also various non-state actors aim to realize different visions of a region, and conflict can therefore occur regarding how the region should be constructed (Schulz, Söderbaum, and Öjendal 2001: 254–256; Igarashi 2018: 49–51).

Why has the study of regionalism in international relations and international political science up to the present time not demonstrated sufficient interest in the phenomenon of sub-regions? Moreover, why have sub-regions been more or less marginalized as a subject of analysis in the mainstream of international political theory?

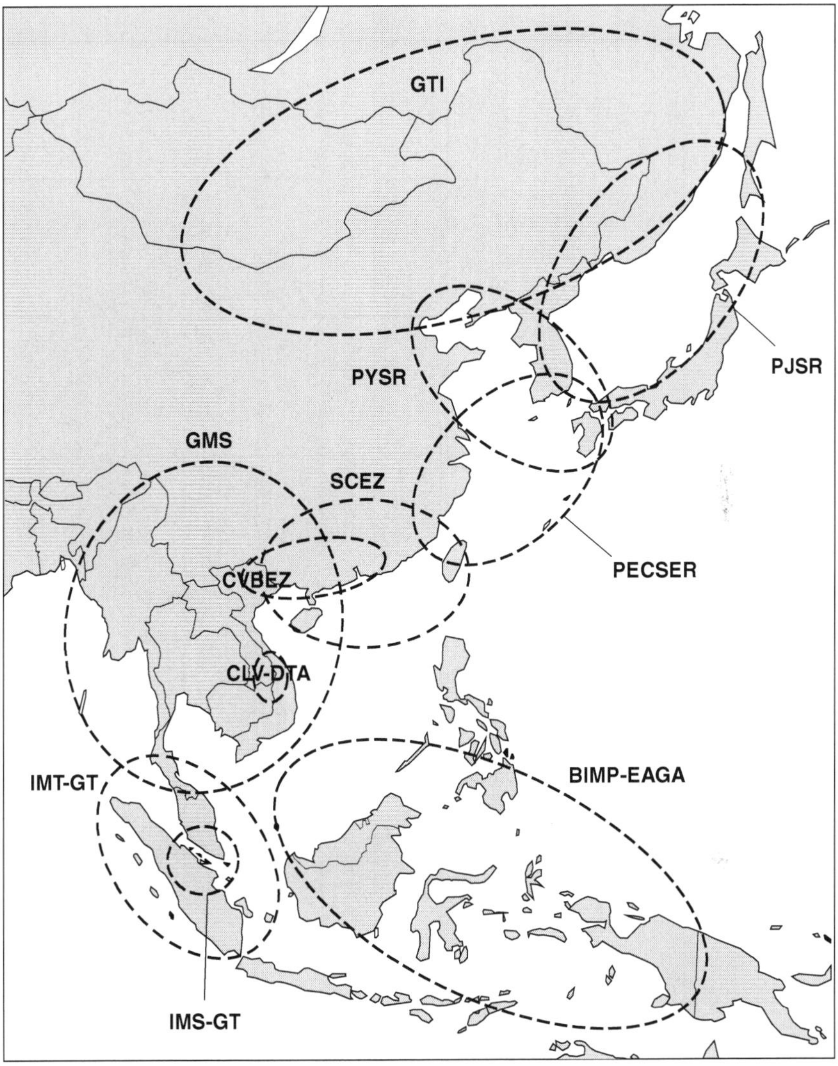

Figure I.3 Asia's local economic zones

Source: Created by the author. The source of the map is http://www.freemap.jp/itemimages/asia/kouiki2/thumbnail.png, accessed June 10, 2015.

Note: GTI=Greater Tumen Initiative; PJSR=Pan-Japan Sea Region; PYSR=Pan-Yellow Sea Region; PECSER=Pan-East China Sea Economic Region; GMS=Greater Mekong Sub-region; CVBEZ=China-Vietnam Border Economic Zone; SCEZ=South China Economic Zone; IMT-GT=Indonesia-Malaysia-Thailand Growth Triangle; IMS-GT=Indonesia-Malaysia-Singapore Growth Triangle; BIMP-EAGA=Brunei Darussalam-Indonesia-Malaysia-Philippines East ASEAN Growth Area.

Table 1.1 The main sub-regions in international society

Region	Name	Year	Advocate
Europe	Baltic Sea Region	1992	Central government
	North Sea Region	1989	Local government
North America	Pacific North West Economic Region (PNWER)	1991	Local government
	Detroit-Windsor	1999	Local government
	San Diego-Tijuana		
Asia	Indonesia-Malaysia-Singapore Growth Triangle (IMS-GT)	1989	Central government
	Pan-Yellow Sea Region (PYSR)	1991	Local government
	Greater Mekong Sub-Region (GMS)	1992	ADB
	Quadrangle Economic Zone (QEZ)	1993	Central government
	Indonesia-Malaysia-Thailand Growth Triangle (IMT-GT)	1993	Central government
	Brunei Darussalam-Indonesia-Malaysia-Philippines East ASEAN Growth Area (BIMP-EAGA)	1994	Central government
	Pan-Japan Sea Region (PJSR)	1994	AJSRS
	South Asia Sub-Regional Economic Cooperation (SASEC)	1997	Central government
	Cambodia-Laos-Vietnam Development Triangle (CLV-DT)	2004	Central government
	Greater Tumen Initiative (GTI)	2009	UNDP
Africa	Maputo Development Corridor (MDC)	1996	Central government
	Zambia-Malawi-Mozambique Growth Triangle (ZMM-GT)	2000	UNDP

Source: Created by the authors.

Note: Blanks in the year and the advocate column indicate that the information is unavailable. AJSRS=Association for the Japan Sea Rim Studies.

First, if viewed from the perspective of political science, an indicator that a region is relevant for analysis is the presence of a regional institution there, which is recognized as an actor in international society. However, apart from in the part of Europe in which INTERREG operates, many sub-regions do not have such an institution. To borrow the words of Schmitt-Egner, there are geographical limitations to sub-regions as "action units" that possess a regional mechanism (Schmitt-Egner 2002: 181). Of course, this is not to deny the possibility that in the future, sub-regions will experience a "spillover" into political areas or develop into "institutionalized political systems," as described by Hettne and Söderbaum (Hettne and Söderbaum 1997: 462–468).[3] That said, when approaching non-European case studies that have a low institutional level, it is necessary to understand sub-regions as informal "action spaces," arising from the activities not only of states but also of various non-state actors from the perspective of political geography.

Second, the majority of sub-regions that are widely recognized in international society are oriented toward economics and development, with the exception of Europe's sub-regions, which have developed cooperation in various areas without being biased toward economics, and consequently tend to be excluded as subjects of analysis by political scientists. In reality, however, many sub-regions are closely associated with the political strategies of sovereign states. Furthermore, even in sub-regions that are formed spontaneously, once the sub-region itself has been formed, we cannot overlook the possibility that it will affect the sovereign states system or the regional order. We are particularly interested in the long-term peace-building function of sub-regions. Impasses in relations between states can be eliminated by sub-regions. If these sorts of political dynamics have not been understood in existing international relations or the study of regionalism, this can only be described as academic negligence.

Achievements of sub-region research

With our own research we have undertaken the task of filling in these gaps in the previous research and uncovering the new political dynamics of sub-regions. The starting point for our sub-region research was studies on the Pan-Japan Sea Region as a sub-region in Northeast Asia, which was advocated by the Association for the Japan Sea Rim Studies. We worked to uncover at an early stage the ways in which the formation of sub-regions such as the Pan-Japan Sea Region differs from conventional regionalism, which is initiated by sovereign states, and how the formation of sub-regions has the potential to transform the sovereign state system (Taga 1997). We particularly focused upon the role of local governments as international actors. We have understood this formation of regions on a new scale to be an effective means of making a breakthrough in overcoming the tension-prone relations between Northeast Asia's sovereign states (Taga 2002). In the process of analyzing economic, political, and cultural aspects, we arrived at the concept of a "water catchment area" as a formative element of the Pan-Japan Sea Region. Focusing on the location of "water," which since ancient times has

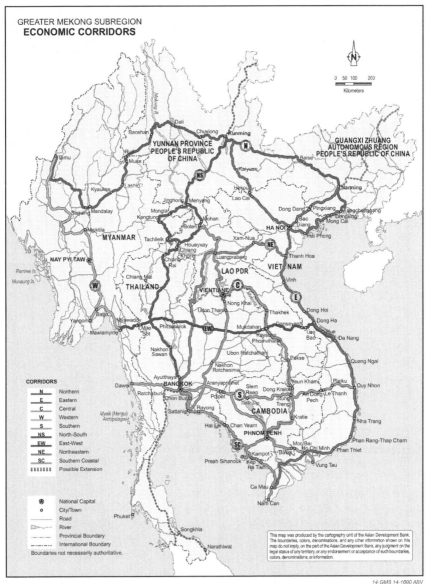

Figure I.4 Map of the Greater Mekong Sub-region (GMS)
Source: https://www.adb.org/sites/default/files/publication/29387/gms-ecp-overview-2015.pdf, accessed December 7, 2017.

been the source of community formation, we came to recognize the ways in which regions are formed without being limited by national borders. Based on the findings of our research on the Pan-Japan Sea Region, we next focused on the Greater Mekong Sub-region (GMS) (Figure I.4), another Asian sub-region formed in a shape that crosses Northeast and Southeast Asia.[4]

In existing studies, various sub-regions model themselves upon a Europe in which further regional integration occurs under the EU, but in Asia, such phenomena have emerged independently in places like the GMS, despite the absence of an overarching organization like the EU. Furthermore, while the construction of sub-regions is often in each nation's interest, there has been a bottom-up dynamic from non-state actors such as civil society networks, which are usually thought of as undeveloped. Based on this perspective, our research, which focused on Asian sub-regions in comparison with Europe, set a goal of analyzing the role of sub-regions—not only as a useful tool for addressing problems where national interests collide, but also as an arena in which various non-state actors are involved—and considering their contribution to the regional and international order. In so doing, we have made an ambitious attempt not only to overcome the limits of contemporary international relations theory but also to modify the existing Eurocentric and state-centric study of regionalism.

At first, we focused on the importance of the role played by various-scale cross-border regional cooperation in sub-regions within the post-Cold War international system. By gaining insight into the manner in which such cooperation functions, not only in Europe but also in East Asia, we empirically demonstrated that sub-regions can be found operating in many parts of the world without the development of an overarching governing structure between the countries concerned, as in the EU. This approach is in contrast to those who think that the EU integration process will inevitably lead to various-scale cross-border regional cooperation connecting parts of more than two states to each other. In East Asia, these sub-regions have emerged freely and exhibit no formal hierarchies or systemic roles.

On the basis of this research, further study was conducted on governance in sub-regions in various areas, including the GMS, which sought to clarify the mechanisms of cross-border cooperation within sub-regions. This demonstrated the absence of a hierarchy both horizontally, within geographical space, and vertically, in the decision-making process. More specifically, we can say with confidence that there is no hierarchy between states and their regions in this decision-making process, and this form of governance in regional cooperation develops by incorporating these regions as stakeholders, in effect making them "policy containers." This provides an empirical correction of the issue of allocating authority between the regional body, the state, and the sub-region, which in Europe is seen to be a question of multi-level governance (MLG).[5]

The results of our research to date have clarified that sub-regions have special features that emerge more or less independently. Conversely, the results also show cases in which the formation of a sub-region has not been to the advantage of each of the states concerned and where cross-border cooperation has strained relations between countries. Thus, our purpose in the future is to ascertain what changes sub-regional cooperation could or could not induce in the regional and international order, and thereby analyze both the impact of sub-regions on regional and international order, and their mutual influence.[6] Answering this question is one of the aims of our research on the efficacy of sub-regions, which will lead to a reconsideration of international relations between Asian states that are unable to resolve their tangled relationships.

Regarding the empirical investigations on which we placed much value, the most important discovery of our research has been the wealth of traditional cross-border activities that differ from those offered under the "maintenance of order" through border management practices based on the sovereign state system. These activities are largely a separate phenomenon from modern highway construction. Generally, within an hour by car from large border-crossing points, with modern customhouses and large flows of goods, there exist border points where crossing is only permitted to "locals." Despite some variation, we found this phenomenon occurring from Myanmar to Vietnam. There also exist the unofficial and traditional crossings of various ethnic groups living on both sides of the border. It is assumed that the authorization of people's traditional border-crossing activities and a life sphere that extends across borders occurs throughout the GMS. It appears as if governance in the borderlands occurs at two levels, and national borders seem to have two purposes. As is often said, patronages emerge where there are regulations, and the duality of borders will emerge according to the circumstances. Supplementary research was conducted in crossing the border between Myanmar and northern Thailand twice, suggesting that the phenomenon is even more apparent here (Taga 2007).

Through this intensive research, it is clear that there is a need for more "microscopic" studies of the situation at the border. On one hand, in Europe during the Cold War, there was little crossing of the borders between the communist and capitalist states. On the other hand, Asian borders were secretly crossed daily by people bearing goods over the mountains, even during periods of blockade and closed borders resulting from political tensions. In Asia, this history and tradition of people's border-crossing activities and life spaces across national borders has been maintained to the present day, and attention must be given to this phenomenon in our contemporary age of sub-regionalism. Through these field surveys, we have become strongly aware of the need to understand sub-regions as the connection of people's living areas.

Furthermore, we have acknowledged that borders are changing from objects of exclusion to drivers of cooperation, to which the sub-regional developments within regions add momentum. While, in international politics, borders and borderlands are implicated as drivers of tension directly related to territorial issues, we have discovered a means of viewing them from a different perspective. This constitutes the significance of examining the border-crossing activities of people and lifeworlds that traverse national borders from the perspective of sub-regions. These empirical facts encouraged us to conduct new research on the relationship between changes to national borders and the formation of sub-regions. As described in the following section, a major difference between our research and existing border studies is that we have attempted to understand national borders in terms of their interaction with the new spaces of sub-regions.

Toward new perspectives

Based on the aforementioned research, in order to question the efficacy of sub-regions, including informal and nonhierarchical sub-regions, this book encompasses four perspectives. The first is an analysis of how the sub-region is related to state strategy. The second examines the role of non-state actors who are involved from the bottom-up and the dimension of the sub-region's undercurrent. The third is related to the relationship between sub-regions and national borders. The fourth develops a non-Eurocentric and interdisciplinary approach.

Sub-regions and state strategies

The activities of sub-regions have varying degrees of fundamental autonomy; however, it must be noted that they are closely connected to state strategy and, in this respect, the sub-regions of East Asia are no exception. For example, in Japan's latest Comprehensive National Development Plan, the development of regions integrated by the sea, that is, Tohoku with the Far East, Hokuriku with the Pan-Japan Sea, and Kyushu with East Asia as water catchment areas, has been earmarked as essential for Japan's future growth. It is not unusual for the Comprehensive National Development Plan to discuss issues beyond the nation's territory. If the starting point is indeed national territory, then routes in and out of the country must be mentioned. It is characteristic of this specialty that developing this idea involves not specific spots but areas.

From China's perspective, pursuing the development of a new communications infrastructure within the GMS creates the illusion of reviving the tributary roads that were a part of the historical tributary system of China. For China, the GMS, in which China shares land borders with neighboring countries, is an extension of the intimate sphere. For Japan, strengthening regional cooperation with the GMS and Northeast Asia will allow it to serve as a counterweight to China, whose influence over its neighbors is huge. Therefore, through a comparative analysis of both the harmonious and contrasting relations between the effects of a national strategy and the autonomous governance of sub-regions, our study will clarify the role and functions of cross-border regional cooperation in international society.

To explain this type of relationship between sub-regions and sovereign states, a new theoretical approach is required. With regard to this point, Swe and Chambers emphasized the importance of taking a postclassical realism analytical viewpoint for GMS case studies. Postclassical realism is similar to neorealism in that it also emphasizes the self-serving behavior of states based on material factors. However, postclassical realism and neorealism differ insofar as neorealism emphasizes the possibility of conflict, short-term state goals, and military security, while postclassical realism stresses the probability of conflict, long-term goals, and economic capacity, and advocates three factors (technology, geographic proximity, and international economic pressure) as affecting the likelihood of conflict (Brooks 1997). When considering the actions of states that are involved in GMS from this perspective, we can interpret them as having several possible meanings. China's prioritization of long-term economic benefit over short-term security, the intervention of outside powers such as Japan and the United States (US), and the formation of a border economic zone led by Thailand indicate that states are aiming to maximize their economic power (Swe and Chambers 2011).

This kind of state-level perspective has been neglected in both existing European and non-European research. For example, in Europe, the process of increased regional integration within the EU's cross-border regional cooperation occurs together with its extension into Eastern Europe. Cross-border cooperation (CBC) on the external borders of the EU, a key priority both in the European Neighbourhood Policy (ENP) and in the EU's strategic partnership with Russia, can be reconsidered in the context of state strategies. In addition, in Europe, "scales-struggles" have developed among the supranational organizations, states, and local governments over the distribution of political resources. By scrutinizing such characteristics of the sub-regions, it might even be possible to explore the implications of pressing for modifications on the mainstream of international relations theory.

Bottom-up dimension of sub-regions

In governing and forming sub-regions, non-state actors such as local governments and non-governmental organizations (NGOs), as well as nation-states and various international organizations, play important roles. Within the macro-regions modeled in the 1960s, such as the EU, there developed a variety of sub- and micro-regions, brought about at multiple levels, which centered on relations not only between states but also among local administrative bodies, NGOs, and international organizations large and small. In particular, under Europe's INTERREG program, local governments have acquired a new identity as international actors and can be seen as the driving force behind the formation of sub-regions. In Asia, it is generally thought that non-state actors remain undeveloped in comparison to Europe. However, if examined at length, it is clear that in Asia too, such actors have already been more or less involved in the policy processes of sub-regions. For example, civil society actors who are concerned with the problems of market-driven and development-driven regionalism or sub-regionalism are already undertaking various activities (Igarashi 2011, 2018), and these activities may be even more active than those in Europe. Similarly, in Asia, which has lagged behind in terms of democratization, the perception remains strong that CBC by local governments is undeveloped, but in actuality, it is developing incrementally.[7] Therefore, interpretations based only upon a state-based paradigm are not useful in analyzing this development.

The role of civil society has been of interest to the New Regionalism Approach (NRA) presented by Hettne and Söderbaum, which aims to overcome the existing state-centric mainstream theory. The NRA has called the current form of regionalism in various parts of the world a "neoliberal regionalism," which is reverential to economic globalization; further, the NRA has been considering civil

Introduction: new critical perspectives 13

society actors as a dynamic force to resist this regionalism (Mittlelman 2000: 47–48, 116). There is very little disagreement that many of the sub-regionalisms around the world are also of the "neoliberal" or "market-oriented" types. However, regardless of its presentation of this sort of new analytical perspective, the NRA has still only conducted a few empirical analyses on civil society. In addition, its research on sub-regions themselves is nearly nonexistent.

Research on local governments, which has been neglected by the NRA, is progressing in Europe. However, MLG, which is the typical framework for analyzing European regionalism, establishes the theoretical assumption that the respective actors play roles in the hierarchy to which they belong (Marks 1993). Therefore, this framework cannot ascertain the actual situation: namely, that it is not the case that the actors in each hierarchy are active only in the hierarchy to which they belong and that, in reality, they are, active outside of their own hierarchy. For example, local governments are building direct relations with the EU and are playing an important role not only as cross-border actors but also as cross-hierarchy actors (Kojimoto 2005: 9–10). MLG does not fully understand the actual situation, in which local governments have become "actors that go beyond the type of actor who proceeds only along the basic policy implemented by the EU and states and have started to be active as important 'international cooperation actors' who are establishing a 'grand design for regional and international cooperation' " (Kojimoto 2003: 34).

When we direct our attention to the undercurrent of sub-regions, it should be considered that in East Asia, through the normalization of cross-border-migration, state borders become a gateway to expanding friendship rather than exclusion. One of the key findings obtained from our various rounds of fieldwork is that in East Asia, where the formation of a regional grouping between states had been stymied, there are a series of traditional unofficial border crossings between the states concerned in addition to the more visible formal border crossings. This demonstrates that we must clarify how East Asia's contemporary borders have been formed while simultaneously seeking to uncover the historical events behind the formation and proclamation of these states, their borders, colonization and independence, and the movement of peoples. It is clear that describing the phenomenon of border-crossing as pores of a balloon is not only equivalent to a topological fault, but also a failure to describe the essence of the phenomenon. Through clarification of these bottom-up dimensions, it will be understood that the meaning of international order becomes quite different from how it is generally comprehended when one examines it from the perspective of the sub-region. In addition, cross-border migration accompanied by the development of sub-regions transforms local communities, especially those near borders.

Sub-regions and borders

We are beginning to understand this sort of transformation of national borders in terms of its relation to the new spaces or social units of sub-regions. We can alternatively describe this as the relations between sub-regions (surfaces) of various scales that are complexly intertwined and overlap with national borders (borderlines).

Researchers in conventional border studies have been interested in the changes to national borders themselves and in the actors involved therein (Wastl-Walter 2011; Wilson and Donnan 2012: 964). However, the formation of regions of various scales as new social units is relativizing national borders by linking the many spaces that are separated by these borders while also raising the issue of territoriality. However, as before, political geography and political science are interested predominantly in organizations, governances, or actors, and have basically neglected territorial aspects (Chilla, Evrard, and Schul 2012).

If, as stated by Sack, we consider territoriality to be constructed from social and human elements, and the product of a social context (Sack 1986: 30), then we should regard it as closely related to the existence of the formation of new spaces that are created through the movements of and contact between people and their relations. The formation of various sub-regions is nothing other than the disintegration of a perception of reality that assumes territoriality based on the framework of sovereign states, the relativization of national borders, and a process for building a new territoriality. The growth of various actors other than states, as stated by Ruggie, brings about the unbundling of territoriality (Ruggie 1993: 165) and as a result advances its reconstruction. The sub-regions that appear in this process can also be described as cross-border reterritorialization (Popescu 2008).

For example, historically, extraterritorial acts have been routinely repeated via informal methods, and as a result, in some cases, national borders have come to be mere façades in actual terms. These sorts of borderlands, where the borders are easily crossable, are often redefined as *de jure* regional spaces from policy perspectives and are granted a new territoriality. In addition, the formation of new regions further promotes the relativization of national borders. At the very least, this characterizes the border economic zones that are dotted around the Mekong region. In the case of Europe, *de jure* space-formation pressure from "above" acts more strongly. The Euroregion is a means of territorially organizing and formalizing previously unstructured cross-border regional and local spatial interaction (Popescu 2011: 607).

The boundaries of the new sub-regions are sometimes clearly demarcated by boundaries that are established by policy, as in Europe. However, in many cases outside of Europe, the boundaries are unclear, particularly in the case of micro-regions of parts of states. It is not always true that these regions have been institutionalized. Even so, the new sub-regions, as more autonomous spaces, possess potentially political natures in their relations with public authorities or higher regions. Although the formation of the new territoriality of sub-regions advances the relativization of national borders, sub-regions have become contested spaces because they are separated by national borders. This is because the various actors have different value systems and norms, and they promote changes in the awareness and identities of the people and actors involved.

Relativization of Eurocentric approach

The existing study has relied upon a European model that has an overarching structure in the EU and is not visible in other regions, and has attempted to generalize the unique experience of the EU to the rest of the world. However, the autonomy and specificity that sub-regions possess as new social units cannot be fully understood by using the theoretical frameworks (e.g., MLG) that have emerged from Europe. In particular, the formation of micro-regions reflects the reality of the lives of local residents. Even when the formation of the upper region is not progressing, it still advances voluntarily and informally. MLG, which was originally focused on formal regions of a top-down type, tends to overlook this sort of diversity and fluidity of sub-regions. In order to understand the functions of sub-regions that have not been institutionalized and the diverse aspects of sub-regions that differ according to region, it becomes essential to jettison Eurocentric teleological ideas.

In addition, it is obvious that there is a need for an exhaustive comparative analysis of what is different regarding the variance between Europe and East Asia. It would also be desirable to investigate from an interdisciplinary perspective that incorporates the social sciences, law, and history to address why such phenomena have emerged. While in Europe the change in the meaning of borders has occurred at the level of the general population, in East Asia, the conventional meaning of borders has been preserved and, in recent years, gradually recognized. Here, there is a need to examine the issue of identity. It is vital that the literature on sub-regionalism and MLG considers the variety of actors who, underpinned by various identities, attempt to cross the border.

A related point is that while the NRA aims to achieve non-Eurocentrism, its emphasis on the actual regionalization process and the various actors therein has established regions other than Europe as subjects of analysis; further, it has actively turned its attention toward conducting research on regions where governance is underdeveloped, and boundaries are unclear. Its subject of analysis is not only the "formal regionalism" of regional organizations between states and regional systems but also the "informal regionalism" by non-state actors. However, as described earlier, the NRA has not yet addressed the problems of its analytical blind spots and lack of empirical research and is still at the initial stage of research into sub-regions.

Therefore, by placing the Asian model and GMS at the center of comparison and addressing analytical blind spots in the existing research (such as civil society movements and the identities of local governments, and the relations between sub-regions and borders), we attempt to overcome the European bias and connect our research to the establishment of a new analytical perspective for research on sub-regions. What is important in this respect is not specializing in economics but instead employing a variety of academic disciplines—including political science, sociology, international political science, international relations, law, history, and regional studies—and adopting an interdisciplinary approach to the phenomenon of sub-regions. This approach will eventually enable us to produce a general model that is not restricted by the existence in Europe of the unique international organization that is the EU, and has greater relevance for development of the regional management of large-scale cross-border regional cooperation elsewhere in the world.

The aims and contributions of the book

This book recognizes the new analytical perspective described earlier and, while focusing on sub-regions, aims to develop a new academic field within regionalism research. Ideally, this will, in turn, connect to the goal of constructing an alternative international relations, with the new phenomenon of sub-regionalism as the "scaffold." This book is structured with an awareness of the following five perspectives.

The first is the importance of thorough empiricism. There is no method other than empiricism to understand the actual situation in sub-regions that are changing significantly. We have acquired a Grant-in-aid for Scientific Research and other financial aid for 17 years without interruption and have been holding research meetings and conducting field surveys on an average of twice per year. A number of vital and new research issues emerged from this research, one of which was the existence of traditional unofficial cross-border contacts separate from state-level cross-border regions in East Asia. Another issue is the unique development of GMS as a sub-region, quite unlike the development found within Europe. We attempt to incorporate into the model not only the official discourse between states as used in research on free trade agreements (FTAs) and the like, but also the unofficial realities that will be clarified through continued overseas fieldwork in these borderland regions. Moreover, tireless fieldwork has also been undertaken on European borders, including around the North and Baltic Seas, between France and Germany, and in the Czech Republic and Italy, and these efforts to grasp the true situation regarding such constantly changing European borders serve as resources for modeling and comparative analysis. All of the groups of case studies taken up by the chapters in this book are supported by empirical facts that can only be discovered through these sorts of continuous field observations.

The second perspective, which is related to field surveys, concerns the interaction between sub-regions and national borders. Changes to national borders promote the formation of sub-regions, but the converse is also true. The particular areas of interest covered in this book relate to the relationship between reterritorialization, which is the formation of sub-regions, and changes to national borders; further, it analyzes through microscopic observations how these changes are transforming the perceptions of people, actors, identities, and social relations.

The third is the perspective of sovereign states in sub-regions research. As we have proceeded with the sub-regions research, it has become increasingly clear to us that sub-regions are connected to the phenomena of interest in the state-centric rationalist approach, such as cooperation, conflict, and confrontation between sovereign states in realism and neoliberal institutionalism. More specifically, whether sub-regions are subjects or objects, spontaneous phenomena, or artificial phenomena, we attempt to research their implications in terms of international relations (the sovereign states system, the regional order, and the international order) in the spaces of sub-regions themselves. Existing research has largely ignored this point.

The fourth perspective is the various non-state actors involved in the formation of sub-regions. However, it is difficult to state that either existing European or non-European research has empirically verified, to a satisfactory extent, the roles of local government and civil society actors as non-state actors in sub-regions. When the focus is placed on non-state actors, while also observing the region's informal aspects (or, to borrow the words of Fawcett, "soft regionalism"),[8] a social-constructionist perspective must be adopted in order to understand the region as a "social construction" created by various actors. This book provides the perspective necessary to understand sub-regions as new international social units in which these new actors operate. This viewpoint, together with the second one, also encourages us to explore the possibility of the autonomy of sub-regions and to ask whether they can change the sovereign states system and regional order.

The fifth perspective is the pursuit of a cross-referencing, interdisciplinary approach. In regionalism research, there has often been a strong tendency to rely on the assumption of a "turning point" that Europe should aim for. Our research group, consciously moves away from this sort of attitude, by asking the question "What do we (Asia) have that they (Europe) do not have?" but not its opposite and addressing this question through a comprehensive discussion from a gathering of Asian researchers on Asia and Europe. The chapters, therefore, that focus on Europe also use various findings obtained from Asian studies and the fieldwork on the GMS. This book intentionally attempts to reverse the usual idea through its focus on Asian case studies by researchers in various fields and use of case studies on Europe for comparative purposes.[9] While striving to promote a productive dialog between non-European and European research, this book aims to construct a foothold for the construction of non-Eurocentric regionalism research.[10]

The structure of the chapters is as follows. In the first part (Chapter 1), theoretical reflection is conducted from new perspectives gained through our collaborative research. In the second part (Chapters 2–6), the Mekong region is adopted as a case study of an Asian sub-region. In the third part (Chapters 7–9), Europe's sub-regions are considered for the purposes of comparison with the Asian case studies.

In Chapter 1, Hidetoshi Taga and Hideo Kojimoto present their methodology for explaining how the formation of sub-regions can activate a "politics among scales." They do so by adopting a "cross-scale regional governance model" approach, in combination with political geography, to decipher how the formation of sub-regions can activate "politics among scales." This chapter considers, from a theoretical perspective, the competition between supranational, state, and regional authorities over the distribution of political and economic resources within EU macro-regions, offering an alternative analytical perspective to the MLG model.

Chapter 2 deals with the relations between sovereign nations, sub-regions, and multilateralism. The formation of the Mekong region is closely and complexly related to each of its nation's strategies, and, in addition, the changes to the regional order due to the formation of the GMS are considered. Here, Yuji Morikawa particularly focuses on the national strategies of Laos and seeks to answer the questions of how small states survive in the international order through the Association of Southeast Asian Nations (ASEAN) integration and the GMS project, and what role the Mekong region has played. This chapter comprises an analysis of the interaction between small states and sub-regions, which is not explained by existing mainstream theories.

In Chapter 3, the focus is placed on transnational civil society, which is attracting attention as a non-state actor. In the Mekong region, various cooperation frameworks are being formed, but "neoliberal sub-regionalism," which emphasizes the market and development initiated by the state ("state-centric sub-regionalism"), are predominant. In this regard, civil society actors are focused on the negative impacts or overlooked problems resulting from "neoliberal sub-regionalism" and "state-centric sub-regionalism." Furthermore, while forming a framework that crosses national borders, they have developed various activities to embody "alternative Mekong regionalism" from "below." The activities of these civil society actors are considered empirically by Seiichi Igarashi, who uses a new critical regionalism approach, based on the NRA as well as neo-Gramscianism, to understand them as a counter-hegemony in opposition to the dominant hegemony of "state-centric and neoliberal sub-regionalism."

Chapter 4 examines the specific roles of civil society in the Mekong region, focusing on certain cases. GMS states have strategies to attract foreign direct investment, mainly based on the implementation of new investment laws and regulations; however, in financial support for large-scale developments, if local residents feel dissatisfaction or deception, the investment risks for enterprises increase. It is difficult to create successful projects by providing inappropriate compensation or by plundering or exploiting land, labor, water resources, and forestry; however, many large-scale projects in GMS countries nevertheless result in explicit or implicit human rights abuses, without sufficient consideration being given to environmental impact. Major examples include the Dawei Special Economic Zone project in Myanmar and the hydropower dam projects being implemented by several GMS states. In this chapter, Kosum Saichan and Hiroshi Komatsu consider this through a detailed examination of civil society activities that have been conducted, with the aim of protecting local residents' human rights and the natural environment from these developmental projects.

Chapter 5 addresses the transformation of local communities in the borderlands, which is progressing as an undercurrent in the Mekong region. Ekamol Saichan explores some advantages and disadvantages of the cross-border economy in the Mekong region. Local communities have developed positive perceptions due to the improvement in their lives, that is, the growth and variety of the local economy, personal security, higher income, modern transportation, more daily life facilities, and engagement with the outside world. However, some also have negative perceptions. Villagers attributed improvements in their living standards to changes in laws and policies, changes in access to roads and other services, and the expansion of nonagricultural work. Ekamol Saichan explores these problems, which not only persist in border areas but are also among the most worrying social problems associated with the opening up of borders.

Chapter 6 examines the transformation of national borders caused by the development of sub-regions. It focuses in particular on the implementation of the Cross-Border Transport Agreement (CBTA) and the recent conditions at border-crossing points (BCPs) in the GMS. The CBTA is an important initiative, not only for promoting the cross-border transportation of goods and people among the contracting countries but also for creating the regional space referred to as the GMS, which comprises cross-border sub-regionalism. Through on-site surveys, which were primarily conducted by Tetsu Sadotomo and Kenji Nakayama, this chapter aims to describe and discuss the realities of the border transformations promoted by the establishment of the CBTA system. The academic findings obtained through this fieldwork, which relate to some of the BCPs in the North-South and East-West Economic Corridors, offer a resource for all research at the sub-regional level. In particular, the authors aim to use detailed fieldwork experiences to learn about the changes to, and relations between, sub-regions and national borders.

Chapter 7 focuses upon the strategic implications of CBC in EU external border areas, which has been carried out as part of the ENP using European Neighbourhood Instruments (ENI). This cooperation is called ENI CBC and is supplemented with Macro-Regional Strategies (MRS). Yoichiro Usui examines a crucial problem of this policy, which is that ENP has been oriented solely toward socioeconomic dimensions, despite the fact that it should essentially be a part of EU security policy because target countries of this policy have been politically vulnerable. However, on the basis of this understanding, this chapter will show that although it has been essentially socioeconomic and has had a small fund, ENI CBC has significant implications for normative politics of the EU in its external actions.

Chapter 8 provides a case study comparison of GMS and the sub-regions in Eastern Europe, where realistic national strategies are strongly emerging. In this chapter, Kazu Takahashi focuses on the Euroregion in which, alongside the eastwards expansion of the EU, a boundary is increasingly being established between the EU and Russia, paying particular attention to the boundary between Russia and Ukraine. In this region, decentralization is not progressing, and the activities of its residents are limited; thus, the states remain the dominant actors. The author considers whether this Euroregion, as a tool of the EU's expansion strategy, in the future will come to an end alongside the end of the expansion of the EU or whether it can acquire autonomy as an independent regional movement.

In Chapter 9, Hideo Kojimoto, Yoshitaka Ota, and Ann Bell consider the North Sea Region (NSR) as an arena for regional governments as they work to achieve and maximize their political agendas through participation in sub-regional governance. The government of Aberdeenshire is one of the main regional actors in the North Sea Commission (NSC), which is the political network of regional governments in the North Sea Rim. Aberdeenshire has systemically applied a strategy of "jumping scale," while INTERREG and the Regional Advisory Council in the North Sea have become the vehicles that enable the realization of these regional government agendas. The authors conclude that the form of sub-regional governance in the NSR is a "regional government-led cross-scale governance model." This is one of the three models of cross-scale regional governance introduced in Chapter 1 by Taga and Kojimoto.

The volume's conclusion reaffirms the findings obtained in each of the previous chapters and summarizes the significance of this book in existing international relations and regionalism studies. In order to further advance the research on sub-regions, the conclusion will present future tasks, such as the effect that the Brexit and the US's unilateralism have on sub-regions; transnational cooperation among local governments in the Mekong region; various scaled sub- and micro-regions formed in East Asia; and the security function of sub-regions, a political dynamic that was not given sufficient coverage in this book.

Notes

1 The author, focusing upon the Japan Sea Rim as a case, foresaw the phenomenon of the dismantling of the sovereign state as early as the early 1990s (Taga 1991).
2 Söderbaum gives a definition of regionalism close to this one (Söderbaum 2003: 7).
3 Hettne and Söderbaum introduce the new concept of "regionness" (Hettne and Söderbaum 2000: 462–468). For them, regions are nothing other than the process that achieves constantly evolving transformations. This is an "imagined community" with a territorial basis. From this understanding, Hettne presented the concept of "regionness" as a framework for comparative analysis rather than as a stage theory. This regionness is divided into five levels. The first level is regional spaces or regions as a geographical unit. Regions are basically separated by physical boundaries and have ecological features. This level corresponds to regions such as North America, Central Asia, and the Indian subcontinent. This is a "proto region," and at this level, there is the slight development of trans-local relations. The second level is regions as social systems. While the spread of trans-local relations between human populations that were previously isolated can be observed, the sovereign state system is also being established. However, at this level, interstate relations are still characterized by a balance of power, and the regionness level remains low to the extent that it can even be described as anarchic. In terms of security, a feature of this level is the regional "security complex." Nineteenth-century Europe is a typical example of this, while today, Northeast Asia corresponds to this level. The third level is regions as a regional society. At this level, exchanges and interactions between states and non-state actors occur in various fields, such as politics, culture, and economics. However, even at this level, states remain the only dominant actors, as they did before. In the event that a more formal type of cooperation is carried out, a region becomes defined by the member countries of regional organizations and therefore can be termed a "formal region." The fourth level is regions as regional communities. Here, the organizational framework promotes the convergence of societal communication and values, and behavior in the region as a whole, and a transnational civil society is formed. At this level, the relations between "formal regions" defined by states and "de-facto regions"

that play the role of a transnational civil society are mutually strengthened. In the field of security, this level corresponds to Deutsch's pluralistic security community. ASEAN can be described as being at the initial stage of this level. The fifth level is regions as institutionalized political regimes or "regional states." They have a clear identity as actors, have the functions of actors, have legitimacy and a decision-making structure and consequentially have reached the ultimate level of "regional state." This process is similar to the one by which sovereign states are formed. Important areas for regional intervention at this level are conflict resolution and welfare, and this fifth level corresponds to the level of the EU.
4 The GMS, as described here, refers to the region determined as a policy domain by the Asian Development Bank (ADB). According to the ADB, the GMS is a natural economic area bound together by the Mekong River, covering 2.6 million square kilometers, with a combined population of approximately 326 million. It is comprise of Cambodia, Laos, Vietnam, Myanmar, Thailand, and the Yunnan province and Guangxi Zhuang Autonomous Region of China.
5 The Japan Society for the Promotion of Science (JSPS) Grant-in-Aid for Scientific Research (B) (Grant No. 21402016, FY2009-FY2011, Multi-Level Governance in a Global Age: Comparison of Sub-Regionalism in the EU and Asia).
6 With regard to this point, the latest research by Hensengerth verifies a case study of the relations between China and Vietnam in terms of GMS which developed from the promotion of national interests and is gradually changing into an independent actor that can influence relations between states (Hensengerth 2009).
7 For example, in Thailand's Mukdahan province and Laos' Savannakhet province, local governments are cooperating in the field of disease (Long 2011).
8 Fawcett strictly distinguishes between "the hard regionalism" of pan- or sub-regional groups formalized by interstate arrangements and organizations, and the "soft regionalism" of promoting a sense of regional awareness or community (Fawcett 2004: 433).
9 On this point, the approach of our research is clearly different to that of the NRA, which simply denies Eurocentricity (Hettne 2003).
10 In recent years in regionalism research, there has been a need for a productive dialogue between European and non-European research (Warleigh-Lack and Van Langenhove 2010; Söderbaum and Sbragia, 2010; Murray 2010; Fawcett and Gandois 2010; Malamud 2010; Warleigh-Lack and Rosamond 2010). However, despite such requests, as before, no progress has been made in the dialogue between the two sides.

References

Anderson, James, Liam O'Dowd, and Thomas M. Wilson (eds.) (2003) *New Borders for a Changing Europe: Cross-Border Cooperation and Governance*, London: F. Cass.

Bøås, Morten, Marianne H. Marchand, and Timothy M. Shaw (2003) "The Weave-World: The Regional Interweaving of Economies, Ideas and Identities," in Fredrik Söderbaum and Timothy M. Shaw (eds.) *Theories of New Regionalism: A Palgrave Reader*, Basingstoke: Palgrave Macmillan, pp. 197–209.

Breslin, Shaun, and Glenn D. Hook (eds.) (2002) *Microregionalism and World Order*, Basingstoke: Palgrave Macmillan.

Brooks, Stephen G. (1997) "Dueling Realisms," *International Organization*, 51 (3): 445–477.

Chilla, Tobias, Estele Evrard, and Christial Schulz (2012) "On the Territoriality of Cross-Border Cooperation: 'Institutional Mapping' in a Multi-Level Context," *European Planning Studies*, 20 (6): 961–980.

Fawcett, Louise (2004) "Exploring Regional Domains: A Comparative History of Regionalism," *International Affairs*, 80 (3): 429–446.
Fawcett, Louise, and Helene Gandois (2010) "Regionalism in Africa and the Middle East: Implications for EU Studies," *Journal of European Integration*, 32 (6): 617–636.
Hensengerth, Oliver (2009) *Regionalism in China-Vietnam Relations: Institution-Building in the Greater Mekong Subregion*, London: Routledge.
Hettne, Björn (2003) "The New Regionalism Revisited," in Fredrik Söderbaum and Timothy M. Shaw (eds.) *Theories of New Regionalism: A Palgrave Reader*, Basingstoke: Palgrave Macmillan, pp. 22–42.
Hettne, Björn, and Fredrik Söderbaum (2000) "Theorising the Rise of Regionness," *New Political Economy*, 5 (3): 457–472.
Igarashi, Seiichi (2011) "The New Regional Order and Transnational Civil Society in Southeast Asia: Focusing on Alternative Regionalism from below in the Process of Building the ASEAN Community," *World Political Science Review*, 7 (1): 1–31.
Igarashi, Seiichi (2018) *New Regionalism and Civil Society in East Asia: Hegemony, Norm, and Critical Regionalism Approach*, Tokyo: Keiso Shobo (in Japanese).
Joenniemi, Pertti (ed.) (1993) *Cooperation in the Baltic Sea Region*, Washington, DC: Taylor & Francis.
Kojimoto, Hideo (2003) "Cross-Border Wide-Area Management Plan (Grand Design) and the Roles of Local Governments: A Case of the 'Nor Vision' in the North Sea Coastal Region," *Council of Local Authorities for International Relations Forum*, 169: 31–35 (in Japanese).
Kojimoto, Hideo (2005) "An Attempt to Construct a 'Cross-Border Wide-Area Management' Model as an EU Regional Policy Analytical Framework: Research on the Reorganization of Spaces in the Euroregion to Illustrate the Baltic Sea Grand Design VASAB2010 and INTERREG IIC," *Studies in Humanities: Social Sciences*, 14: 1–37 (in Japanese).
Kramsch, Olivier, and Barbara Hooper (eds.) (2004) *Cross-Border Governance in the European Union*, London: Routledge.
Leibenath, Markus, Ewa Korcelli-Olejniczak, and Robert Knippschild (eds.) (2008) *Cross-Border Governance and Sustainable Spatial Development: Mind the Gaps!*, Berlin: Springer.
Long, William J. (2011) "Cross-Border Health Cooperation in Complicated Regions: The Case of the Mekong Basin Disease Surveillance Network," in G. Shabbir Cheema, Christopher A. McNally, and Vesselin Popovski (eds.) *Cross-Border Governance in Asia: Regional Issues and Mechanisms*, New York: United Nations University Press, pp. 93–121.
Malamud, Andrés (2010) "Latin American Regionalism and EU Studies," *Journal of European Integration*, 32 (6): 637–657.
Marks, Gary (1993) "Structural Policy and Multilevel Governance in the EC," in Alan Cafruny and Glenda Rosenthal (eds.) *The State of the European Community*, New York: Lynne Rienner, pp. 391–410.
Mittlelman, James H. (2000) *The Globalization Syndrome: Transformation and Resistance*, Princeton, N.J.: Princeton University Press.
Murray, Philomena (2010) "East Asian Regionalism and EU Studies," *Journal of European Integration*, 32 (6): 597–616.
Nye, Joseph S. Jr. (1968) *International Regionalism: Readings*, Boston, MA: Little, Brown.

Organisation for Economic Co-operation and Development (OECD) (2009) *Trans-Border Urban Co-operation in the Pan Yellow Sea Region*, Paris: Organisation for Economic Co-operation and Development.

Popescu, Gabriel (2008) "The Conflicting Logics of Cross-Border Reterritorialization: Geopolitics of Euroregions in Eastern Europe," *Political Geography*, 27 (4): 418–438.

Popescu, Gabriel (2011) "Transcending the National Space: The Institutionalization of Cross-Border Territory in the Lower Danube Euroregion," in Doris Wastl-Walter (ed.) *The Ashgate Research Companion to Border Studies*, Farnham: Ashgate, pp. 607–624.

Ruggie, John Gerard (1993) "Territoriality and Beyond: Problematizing Modernity in International Relations," *International Organization*, 47 (1): 139–174.

Sack, Robert David. (1986) *Human Territoriality: Its Theory and History*, Cambridge: Cambridge University Press.

Sandberg, Mikael (ed.) (1992) *Baltic Sea Region Environmental Protection: "Eastern" Perspectives and International Cooperation*, Stockholm: Almqvist & Wiksell International.

Sasuga, Katsuhiro (2004) *Microregionalism and Governance in East Asia*, London: Routledge.

Schmitt-Egner, Peter (2002) "The Concept of 'Region': Theoretical and Methodological Notes on its Reconstruction," *Journal of European Integration*, 24 (3): 179–200.

Schulz, Michael, Fredrik Söderbaum, and Joakim Öjendal (2001) "Key Issues in the New Regionalism: Comparisons from Asia, Africa and the Middle East," in Björn Hettne, Andras Inotai, and Osvaldo Sunkel (eds.) *Comparing Regionalisms: Implications for Global Development*, New York: Palgrave, pp. 234–276.

Smallbone, David, Friederike Welter, and Mirela Xheneti (eds.) (2012) *Cross-Border Entrepreneurship and Economic Development in Europe's Border Regions*, Cheltenham: E. Elgar.

Söderbaum, Fredrik (2003) "Introduction: Theories of New Regionalism," in Fredrik Söderbaum and Timothy M. Shaw (eds.) *Theories of New Regionalism: A Palgrave Reader*, Basingstoke: Palgrave Macmillan, pp. 1–21.

Söderbaum, Fredrik, and Ian Taylor (eds.) (2008) *Afro-Regions: The Dynamics of Cross-Border Micro-Regionalism in Africa*, Uppsala: Nordiska Afrikainstitutet.

Söderbaum, Fredrik, and Alberta Sbragia (2010) "EU Studies and the New Regionalism: What Can be Gained from Dialogue?," *Journal of European Integration*, 32 (6): 563–582.

Stokłosa, Katarzyna, and Gerhard Besier (eds.) (2014) *European Border Regions in Comparison: Overcoming Nationalistic Aspects or Re-Nationalization?* New York: Routledge.

Swe, Thein, and Paul Chambers (2011) *Cashing in Across the Golden Triangle: Thailand's Northern Border Trade with China, Laos, and Myanmar*, Chiang Mai: Mekong Press.

Taga, Hidetoshi (1991) "An Approach to the Japan Sea Rim Studies," *Journal of Law and Politics*, 23 (3–4): 334–353 (in Japanese).

Taga, Hidetoshi (1997) "Asian Subregionalism as Social Units: Change inside and outside," a paper submitted to the International Conference on Comparative Regional Studies, held at Tohoku University, Sendai, Japan.

Taga, Hidetoshi (2002) "Tasks and Efforts by Non-State Actors: Towards North East Asia Cooperative Regional Society," a paper submitted to the Northeast Asia Intellectuals' Solidarity (NAIS) Conference held in Incheon, South Korea.

Taga, Hidetoshi (2007) "Flow of Chinese More Visible than Flow of Yen," *International Herald Tribune/The Asahi Shimbun*, May 28, 2007.

Thant, Myo, Min Tang, and Hiroshi Kakazu (eds.) (1995) *Growth Triangles in Asia: A New Approach to Regional Economic Cooperation*, Oxford: Oxford University Press.

Warleigh-Lack, Alex, and Luk Van Langenhove (2010) "Rethinking EU Studies: The Contribution of Comparative Regionalism," *Journal of European Integration*, 32 (6): 541–562.

Warleigh-Lack, Alex, and Ben Rosamond (2010) "Across the EU Studies-New Regionalism Frontier: Invitation to a Dialogue," *Journal of Common Market Studies*, 48 (4): 993–1013.

Wastl-Walter, Doris (ed.) (2011) *The Ashgate Research Companion to Border Studies*, Farnham: Ashgate.

Wilson, Thomas M., and Hastings Donnan (eds.) (2012) *A Companion to Border Studies*, Chichester, West Sussex: Wiley-Blackwell.

Yuan, Lee Tsao (ed.) (1991) *Growth Triangle: The Johor-Singapore-Riau Experience*, Singapore: Institute of Southeast Asian Studies.

Part I
Theoretical Reflections

1 Toward a new analytical framework of sub-regions
Cross-scale regional governance

Hidetoshi Taga and Hideo Kojimoto

Introduction

When political scientists confront problems that cannot be resolved with the conceptual tools at their disposal, they often turn to approaches from other disciplines; referred as a "turn." Constructivists adopted the concept of identity from sociology as a turn to explain the changing natures of actors involved in globalism. This sociological turn served as a critique of the static analysis, by which the identities of actors embedded in a rigid state hierarchy were a given and enduring constant. It also enabled a dynamic analysis that provided for a transformation of actors' identities.

In the late 1990s, political scientists broadened their focus to include the international political decision-making processes that subsumed the notion of governance, which utilized a governance turn (Inoue 2003a; 2003b). This shift in analysis of governance led to a review of the political decision-making processes and introduced an analytical framework that brought new norms to international political science.

It can be said that a scalar turn is taking place using the expertise of political geography.[1] In this scalar turn, political scientists have not only served up a critique of power relationship analyses that focus on the state scale but have also begun to turn their attention to the power relationships among scales. These three *turns* have posed a direct challenge to existing research frameworks based on the once-uncontested concept of the sovereign state system and provide critical verification of the relativization of the state itself.

The emergence of sub-regions and scalar transformations

A scale-based pluralistic regional understanding

Massey has referred to spaces as *power geometry*, the compression of time and space that induces spatial structural changes, so that the distribution of power in any given space is continually undergoing change (Massey 1993: 61). In the midst of these changing power structures, new relationships arise between individual actors, and existing relationships are transformed. As a result, the space becomes a complex web of dominant and subordinate relationships. As these environmental changes unfold, space is socially reconstructed, and new scales, such as sub-regions, are created.

Swyngedouw has argued that in the midst of these changes, scale mobilization, domination, and generation become core issues for a social space, and that at each scale, strategies are developed to accommodate the struggle for scale domination as well as to exclude certain actors from participating in activities at specific scales (Swyngedouw 2004: 147). In processes uploaded to the supranational scale, and processes generated at or downloaded to the sub-regional scale, struggles among actors for domination reoccur, just as Swyngedouw indicated they would. At the same time, each actor in the region invests its intentions with the objective of forming a complex governance arrangement worthy of its description as a power geometry.

Before continuing, we would like to examine what scale is, and the geographic discussions that revolve around scale. For a detailed description of scale itself, see the explanation by Smith, who initiated the discussion of building scales in the field of geography (Smith 2000). Smith organized scale into three broad categories: cartographic scale, methodological scale, geographical scale. Cartographic scale corresponds to a reduced scale on a map. Methodological scale is an operational scale used by researchers to set a specific research objective, such as a regional population survey. Geographical scale, unlike the cartographic or methodological scales, is a scale that indicates the dimensions of a specific region. In this chapter, geographical scale will be used, and we will offer an explanation of what a scale can express in the emergence of sub-regions.

Yamazaki has defined geographical scale as "a unit of space formed through a specific social process" (Yamazaki 2010: 112). For example, it can be said that units that represent new European political spaces have been formed through the integrative processes of the European Union (EU). Yamazaki made the following observation about the relationship between politics and scale:

> What is important in thinking about the relationship between scale and politics is that the politics of adjustment of interests or execution of power does not always deploy the same scale to the base, and constitutes mutual interaction and deployment between differing scales.
> (Yamazaki 2010: 121, translated by the authors)

From the perspective of political science, it can be said that Yamazaki's definition points to a re-scaling of the state that causes the dis-embedding of a supranational entity, such as the EU, the individual member states of the EU, and other authorities in the government hierarchy, and removes them from a particular scale or system, allowing the various actors in the political space of the sub-region to go beyond the regional scale in order to make adjustments to their agendas or to exercise power or influence.

Political science and political geography

Why is there a need to bring a political geography perspective into a discussion of governance in the field of international politics? The reasons for doing so are threefold. First, the concept of region, which has been discussed *a priori* in the international political science field, requires an elaboration of its geographical attributes, using political geography methodologies. By identifying how a region forms, we can clarify what attributes determine the scale of a new sub-region. By doing so, the governance characteristics and nature of the disputes that emerge in the sub-region can be clarified. Second, after studying the attributes of a region, a boundary can be demarcated. Demarcation of the boundary and consideration of the meaning of that boundary can then be put to use to clarify the range of applications suitable for sub-regional norms and rules. Third, the scale concept is useful for considering power relationships in new regions such as sub-regions.

Regional governments that have been embedded within a state hierarchy have begun using a political instrument called "jumping scale" to become involved in rule- and budget-making proposals at the supranational level. Thus, using a political geography perspective facilitates theoretical analyses of power sharing and power migration at scales apart from the state.

Before the transformations in the role of the state, the three contributions of political geography attribute boundary and power sharing (at various levels) as the starting point for the arguments and theoretical approaches of scholars working in the field of international politics. However, the emergence of the sub-regional scale has led to wholesale changes in how the state functions and is viewed as a policy container, the significance of national borders as boundaries for policy formation and implementation, and the role of state scale as a unified governance scale. The transformation of the meaning of national territory in regional policy, and particularly how this transformation of meaning has altered how national territory is used as an instrument of governance, also results in a change in the attributes of the instruments shared by sub-regional actors. Together with this attribute change, the meaning of boundary is also changing. In addition to the transformation of the meaning of horizontal attributes and boundaries, we must also consider the change in perpendicular power sharing between scales. For these reasons, any analysis of sub-regional governance using political science or international relations theory must be done within a political geography framework.

Regarding the relationship between political geography and political science, O'Loughlin has commented that while the concepts of territoriality and traditions of place have not yet been utilized as analytical tools by political scientists, political geographers have readily applied the logic and approaches of political science to their own field (O'Loughlin 2000). Political geography is an academic field that uses spatial articulation to clarify all types of power and the interactions between power loci. With this in mind, it can be argued that political scientists must shift their focus to regional phenomena that cannot be contained within the transnational social spaces defined by the sovereign state.

Even before these changes were beginning to occur, transnational economic space or transnational social space was beginning to exceed the state's governing capacity, and norms were being adjusted based on market and civil society principles. As a result, the formation of regional agreements was also beginning to proceed in a cross-party manner, often emerging to embrace globalization or in resistance to globalization. However, the emergence of new spaces at the sub-regional scale in the international community has given rise to the need to reread political spaces, moving away from changes in the territoriality of states in which the concept of national territory is the focal point.

State re-scaling and struggles between scales

State transformation in Europe

The Second World War brought great devastation to Europe. After the war, great pains were taken to consider how to embed peace into Europe's interstate political space. This was also the beginning of the re-scaling operation that relativized how the individual states, from a supranational level, dealt with territory, sub-state actors, and non-state systems. The resulting birth of the European Coal and Steel Community (ECSC) in 1951 can be considered the beginning of the restructuring of Europe's political space.

With the almost fifty-year integration process that has followed, it is noteworthy that in the *European Governance: White Paper*, prepared in 2001 by the European Commission, regional governments were, for the first time, officially designated as important actors involved in the shared governing of Europe (CEC 2001). This acknowledgement offered hints that Europe was moving toward a multi-dimensional regional understanding of scales beyond the single state-centered scale. In other words, it was the beginning of a move away from a solitary, rigid understanding of space, in which the EU is a *Europe of the States*, toward a multi-dimensional understanding of a *Europe of the Regions* that includes a shared existence with members of the Committee of the Regions (CoR). This multi-dimensional spatial interpretation is now being factored into all areas of EU regional policy implementation.

Although there is a growing awareness of this form of power sharing between scales, a number of issues have begun to emerge as a result of the lack of congruence between the EU, EU member states, regional authorities, and other governance levels. In the North Sea and the Baltic Sea Regions, the management of fishery resources, the resolution of environmental issues, and the tackling of regional emergencies have been discussed as issues that must be handled between scales. Since the existing hierarchical framework was centered on the state, problems that affected trans-border areas had not been dealt with effectively. To meet these challenges, the meaning of political space was reconsidered through the establishment of the sub-region. Just as Cox illustrated the importance of shared governance between scales (Cox 1998), the sub-region has appeared to represent the beginning of cross-scale regional governance, a format that includes actors at other levels. A cross-scale regional governance framework serves as a contrast to a multi-level governance (MLG) analytical framework (hereafter, MLG), which is a rigid multi-level sharing format centered on the state.

Struggles between scales

Sub-regions are characterized by their overlapping, nonexclusive territories and the fact that they can change shape. However, at this time, no democratic system of governance has been devised to represent sub-regions.[2] Therefore, a new decision-making process, one that supersedes the existing hierarchy of related regional actors, is needed. At the same time, environmental non-governmental organizations (NGOs), university research institutions, fishery-related organizations, oil and gas industries, labor unions, and other actors operating under different agendas and norms need to come together in horizontal and other *meta-governance* processes that go beyond functions and issues (Jessop 2004).

As a result of the creation of sub-regions with new regional governance scales, a new system is needed for adjusting the anarchic power relationships within these regions. Furthermore, the absence of territorial governance actors that fit precisely within the sub-regional scale has prompted a political adjustment at locations where actors are able to engage in horizontal governance activities and have also led to a shift in the normative formation and structural creation between states that had previously been targeted for analysis by political scientists working in international politics.

This spells the end of political science research that has been based on the premise of a monopoly of state power under the sovereign state system. This means that any new methodology that goes beyond the state scale will pose challenges for political scientists. Today, it appears that we are approaching new regional policy paradigms and research opportunities that seek a new form of regional governance that can go beyond the state system (Brenner 1999). This involves the emergence of a new political awareness that fits within an analytical framework of a struggle between scales, a framework that differs from those used to understand international politics, such as the Marxian struggle between classes or the struggle between developed countries and developing countries found in the world systems theory of Wallerstein. This, therefore, represents a paradigm conversion in the field of international politics.

EU macro-regions and soft spaces

EU macro-regions and macro-regionalism

It has been mentioned briefly that a legacy of regional governance is being formed in the European sub-regions through the INTERREG program (See also Kojimoto, Ota, and Bell, Chapter 10). These European "sub-regions" experienced a major turning point when the DG Regio of the European Commission decided to introduce a comprehensive and holistic policy called the "macro-regional strategy" as a coordinating program for the sub-regions and used the term "macro-region" for this particular sub-region, which then became part of the EU vernacular. EU macro-regional strategies have now become cross-sectoral and have evolved into a comprehensive cross-scale policy framework for spatial planning, environmental, transport, and competition policies. These strategies represent a new grand design for promoting regional planning. In the discussion of the EU macro-regions that follows, we will use "sub-region" in the broad sense when referring to soft spaces, and "macro-region" in the narrow sense when referring to a regional policy unit of the EU.

Since the EU Strategy for the Baltic Sea Region (EUSBSR) went into effect in 2009, macro-regional strategies have been adopted in rapid succession in the Danube, the Alps, and the Adriatic Sea and Ionian Sea regions. These existing trans-border regions, or macro-regions, are becoming official EU policy implementation units.

The EU defines a macro-region as "an area including territory from a number of different countries or regions associated with one or more common features or challenges" (Samecki 2009). The phrase, "one or more common features or challenges," does not adequately represent the comprehensive character of a macro-region. Rather, in the case of each macro-region, the areas that are included share a common historical background, including past relations that may be both cooperative and antagonistic.

The EUSBSR is the world's first official macro-regional strategy, with a platform to solve regional problems and to apportion the resources to be allocated toward its various functions. The EUSBSR encompasses the Baltic Sea rim area that contains portions of eight EU member states. The strategy identifies four key challenges:

- To enable a sustainable environment;
- To enhance the region's prosperity;
- To increase accessibility and attractiveness;
- To ensure safety and security in the region.

Prior to the EUSBSR, issues concerning the Baltic Sea were dealt with not only by multi-layered intergovernmental institutions such as the Council of the Baltic Sea States (CBSS), the Helsinki Commission (HELCOM), and the Nordic Council but also by interregional or cross-border cooperative bodies such as the Union of the Baltic Cities (UBC), the Baltic Sea Commission (BSC), and the B7 Baltic Islands Network. Although these groups or networks have each grappled with Baltic Sea issues, a new policy instrument was required after the fifth enlargement of EU territory, when the Baltic Sea was placed under the umbrella of the EU as an inland sea.

Own circumstances of the EU macro-regions

Since the beginning of the implementation of EU macro-regional strategies, the terms "macro-regionalization" and "macro-regionalism" have also come into use and are the subject of extensive research (Bialasiewicz, Giaccaria, Jones, and

Minca 2012; Kern and Gänzle 2013). Bialasiewicz, Giaccaria, Jones, and Minca conclude that this is nothing more than a trend toward a "'EU'rope" re-scaling and argue that an accurate analysis of this transition has yet to appear (Bialasiewicz, Giaccaria, Jones, and Minca 2012).

It is true that macro-regionalization or macro-regionalism is a new research subject. The problem here is that current research on the EU generalizes this phenomenon by positioning the creation of macro-regions as an EU-ized process, or, in other words, as a hasty attempt to conduct politics within or about established scales (McCarthy 2005: 750). By doing so, individual situations are handled in isolation, without examining the context in which they were created. Questions that need to be asked are "why was a new region created at this time and why for this particular place?" Another issue that has been completely overlooked is how the formation of new scales has led to the spread of a "politics among scales" (McCarthy 2005: 732). There must be reasons for forming macro-regions and for involving certain groups of actors to participate in the establishment of these regions. It is understood that these include areas that can be set in a generalized model and that these are areas that require additional explanations and a careful handling of their individual characteristics.

It is important to keep in mind that this macro-regional creation process is related to the geographies of the respective regions, the historical processes that played a role in their creation, and the positioning of and relationships between existing member states. Therefore, attempts to understand these processes require an analysis of each macro-region's circumstances. In other words, many researchers have been captivated solely by the new phenomenon of macro-regional strategies from the perspective of EU-ization and have lost sight of what led to the establishment of macro-regions. In the sections that follow, we will examine the three patterns of the cross-scale regional governance model.

Validity of the soft spaces concept

The soft spaces concept was developed by Allmendinger and Haughton in order to promote a discussion on the emergence of new scales (Haughton and Allmendinger 2008; Allmendinger and Haughton 2009; Allmendinger and Hughton 2010; Haughton, Allmendinger and Oosterlynck 2013; Allmendinger, Chilla, and Sielker 2014; Allmendinger, Haughton, Knieling, and Othengrafen 2015; Allmendinger, Haughton, and Shepherd 2016). It is a useful concept for explaining macro-regions and the re-scaling of states. So, what is soft space?

Allmendinger and Haughton have furthered the conversation about state re-scaling in relation to space planning, which involves the initiation of various actors' participation in the re-scaling of their own strategies and policies (Allmendinger and Haughton 2009: 619). In addition, it is argued that state re-scaling involves the breaking down of spatial boundaries that are fixed in law, and the creation of a new space (Allmendinger and Haughton 2009: 619). This new space is a soft space. Soft spaces have spatial overlaps and supplant existing

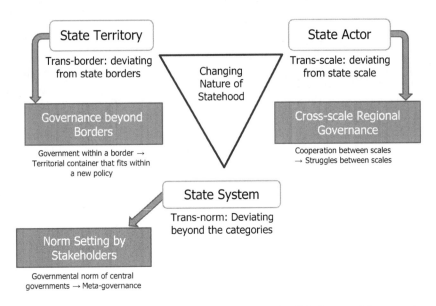

Figure 1.1 Re-scaling the state: transforming international political space while preserving the state concept.
Source: Prepared by the authors.

legal and official scales, such as state territories. In contrast, hard spaces are fixed and hierarchical.

What is important here is that soft space is not a concept that is antithetical to hard spaces, but rather serves as a complement to them (Heley 2013: 1329). In this sense, hard spaces and soft spaces can be regarded as a methodology that helps facilitate an understanding of the processes of state re-scaling and the establishment of sub-regions (Figure 1.1). At the same time, the original meanings of hard and soft spaces span a spectrum of characteristics, including flexibility, resilience, and sensitivity, which are also relevant to the analysis of regions. Using this spectrum, we can more clearly see which individual macro-regions, such as the Baltic Sea Region, the North Sea Region (NSR), and the Danube Region, are soft-based and which are hard-based. This spectrum can also help clarify the place-based characteristics of individual macro-regions and enable the verification on an axis of how development processes have differentiated over time (Table 1.1).

Comparison of hard and soft spaces

To further understand soft spaces, let us verify their characteristics in comparison with hard spaces. First, with regard to range, hard spaces assume the form of a legal jurisdiction. At the same time, there are certain places where power is associated with legal jurisdiction. Here, the territorial governance actor, in regard to

Table 1.1 Comparison of hard and soft spaces

	Hard Spaces	Soft Spaces
Range	Legal jurisdiction and its hierarchy	Zones, such as lifestyle zones natural geographic zones, economic zones, environmental zones, resource distribution zones, and their multiple layers and overlaps
Boundary relationship with adjacent regions	• Non-overlapping, exclusive • If overlapping, there are struggles (territorial problems)	• Overlapping also exists • If overlapping, promote territorial cohesion
Main actors	Territorial governance system actors	Territorial governance system actors, functional actors, issue-oriented actors
Responsibility	• Hard jurisdiction and clear jurisdictional division of hierarchical places • Vertical place-sharing MLG	• Application of the responsibility concept itself is impossible • Unclear adjustments by stakeholder conferences • Place-sharing within the same scale Cross-scale Regional Governance
Adjustment method (resource allocations for example)		
Institution-making process	Formal	Informal
Governing process	Democratic process based on elections to establish the government	Need for meta-governance
Scale	Institutional	Neo-liberal (Haughton et al. 2013)
Topic	State scaling	Spatial rescaling + State rescaling

Source: Prepared by the authors.

multi-layered regional jurisdictions, is responsible for policy assignments within the existing political hierarchy. This is an MLG pattern in which multiple layers of governing authority are distributed among levels. As a method of governance, MLG optimizes administrative institutions located among hierarchically overlapping jurisdictions as well as public administrative functions. So, what about boundaries? For example, a boundary is when a hard space is adjacent to another hard space, neighboring countries, for example; they are both at the same scale, and the boundary does not overlap and is mutually exclusive. If the borders were to overlap, the actors with jurisdiction over the hard spaces would very likely clash, as is seen in territorial disputes.

Meanwhile, natural geographic zones, ecological zones, as well as economic zones, would be considered soft spaces. Unlike hard spaces, these can also include adjacent soft spaces that overlap. In the EU macro-regions, these have been designed intentionally as such and play a role in promoting EU territorial cohesion when they engage in mutually beneficial good governance practices. Negotiations over the setting of boundaries then become part of the political process and the possibility arises that there will be conflict over how a boundary is drawn or in deciding what will be encompassed in the space. Territorial governance actors, functional actors, and issue-oriented actors participate in such negotiations. Since each actor is negotiating under different behavioral norms, meta-governance, which requires adjustments between participating bodies, becomes necessary. At the same time, adjustment patterns related to political resources between scales take the form of cross-scale regional governance.

These comparisons show that since territorial governance actors, especially states, are the main actors in hard spaces, hard spaces are characterized by their close relationships with other territorial governance actors. In these hard spaces, democratic processes based on elections are used to form governments, and a rigid jurisdictional range is used to define the boundaries, with responsibility for individual internal locations determined by a clear jurisdictional division of hierarchical places. Here, the preconditions needed for state re-scaling are clearly nested in state policy or behavior.

In contrast, it is impossible to apply the concept of MLG responsibility in soft spaces since, over the course of negotiations between concerned actors, the power sharing between vertical levels is reset. At the same time, the adjustments that occur in the negotiations in stakeholder meetings, which serve as meta-governance-type platforms, go beyond state re-scaling and create new scales.

Discussion: the cross-scale regional governance model

Critiques of the multi-level governance (MLG) analytical model

Along with the emergence of a macro-regional approach, approaches to the power geometry of the areas have also changed. The relationships between territorial governmental actors have been rearranged from a hierarchically embedded structure to a heterarchical structure, and the creation of new modes and rules are required for actors to govern within these new policy containers. Therefore, in order to distribute the management of regional resources among actors within macro-regions, a new system of governance is required (Table 1.2).

The MLG model has been used to analyze multi-layered political compartmentalization and policy coordination between scales. This includes both Type I and Type II models (Marks and Hooghe 2004). However, even if the latter model is quite successful in explaining cooperative governance arrangements, it does not serve as a definitive framework for explaining the creation of macro-regions and the struggles between actors from each scale in these macro-regions. Cross-scale regional governance is defined as a style of policy coordination between actors who were once embedded in a multi-layered hierarchical structure who have now moved to a cross-scale dynamic that also includes struggles between scales. Since there is no single jurisdictional political entity within a macro-region, actors participate in the governance of the macro-region by moving outside of their respective realms, such as a regional authority shifting out the jurisdiction of the region.

The MLG analytical model is limited in that it only identifies political compartmentalization. As Swyngedouw has noted, space is a socially constructed phenomenon that develops in conjunction with "the mobilization of scale, the occupation of geographical scale, and production of scale" (Swyngedouw 2004: 147). The power geometry among actors is altered through the emergence of the macro-regional scale and the progression of the functional utilization of this scale. The MLG model lacks a representation of the dynamics of politics among scales and inadequately represents the constructive trans-scale articulations of power sharing. The scale is not a given, and the establishment of a new scale leads to the reconstruction of scale dynamics.

As Marks, Hooghe, and Blank have pointed out, the MLG model in Europe has changed not through institutional or system-making processes, but through political decision-making (Marks, Hooghe, and Blank 1995: 24). Even the MLG Type II analytical model did not consider scale dynamics; rather, it only explained the multi-layered governmental system and policy development processes. In the process of mobilizing and occupying a new scale, actors are not only responsible for influencing the process of constructing the scale but are also affected, in turn, by changes in the nature of the other actors involved. This dynamic is the core concept behind the cross-scale regional governance model.

The macro-regional approach leads to a change in the style of governance, wherein actors, being embedded into each scale, are able to move out of these scales in order to deal with transnational issues that would be difficult to solve through a single state. Within the MLG structure, not only are the actors embedded into a particular scale, but the scales themselves are also tightly embedded into a hierarchical structure wherein the central governments of the member states still possess power.

Table 1.2 State re-scaling through fluidity of soft spaces

	Soft Spaces (broad definition)	① ⇑	Soft spaces - formative period (narrow definition)	② ⇑	Hardening of macro-region
Relationship with other scales	Aggregations of hard spaces between states Hierarchical		Heterarchical		While not quite a hierarchy, it is a fixed relationship
	Three scales of government space in the same place		Meta-governance space as one more negotiation scale within the same place		Three scales of government space + pseudo-government space in the same place (does not pass through a democratic process)
	Transition from MLG space to non-MLG space		Discursive Space, Negotiation Space, Meta-Governance Space		Financial Resource Exchange Space, Actual Space
Visible reality			Stakeholder conference		Comprehensive EU Macro-Regional strategy

Source: Prepared by the authors.

Notes
① Hollowing out: The role of the state is hollowing out and coming to be shared with other actors.
② Filling in (Jones, Goodwin, Jones, and Pett 2005): New roles are filling in the new scales.

Three types of the cross-scale regional governance models

In EU regional policy, the EU commission has tried to accelerate trans-border interactions among regional authorities and to accelerate EU integration by relativizing state borders. These trans-border activities also helped establish mutual trust. However, although these activities enhanced the solidarity of transregional networks for regional authorities in the new macro-regional scale, the establishment of the new scale led to problems for the networks. This process illustrates the emergence of trans-scale actors and the mechanisms that generate "jumping scale."

Here, our analytical framework distinguishes the existing multi-layered structure within the scales of MLG from the actors embedded in these scales. Along with the increased relativization of state borders, state policy containers have begun to lose efficiency and legitimacy in the field of EU regional policy. Regional authorities have started to cooperate with the EU Commission and the EU Parliament using the sub-regional commissions under the Conference of Peripheral and Maritime Regions of Europe (CPMR) and the CoR as proxies.

The end product of the compartmentalization of Europe is marked by the following features: the EU scale has gathered supranational and functional legitimacy, member states have maintained their gate-keeping role of reallocating EU funds, and regional authorities continue to function as clients to their central governments. Through the state re-scaling process, the macro-region has emerged as an intermediate unit between the EU level and the regional level. In terms of the core constituent unit, the EU as the "Europe of the States" was transformed into "Europe of the Europe," then "Europe of the Regions" before becoming "Europe of the Macro-Regions." This emergence of a multi-scalar Europe has vitalized the politics among scales, with the regional level becoming the new core element of Europe.

The ability of EU member states to serve as jurisdictional policy containers has diminished as transnational policy issues have arisen and the state's functional role over regional policy has come to be concentrated at a supranational level. States, as single actors, no longer monopolize the process of decision-making for the macro-region. This thereby marks the end of politics within the scale of states.

The governance pattern created during the process of creating a macro-region can be classified into three cross-scale regional governance models: the state-led model, the regional government-led model, and the supranational institution-led model (Table 1.3). Examples of these models include the state-led model, found in the Baltic Sea Macro-region, where the state actively promotes cooperation in the region under the auspices of the Nordic Council; the regional government-led model of the North Sea Macro-region, where regional government networks such as the North Sea Commission play a leading role; and the supranational institution-led arrangement in the Danube Region, where the EU has institutionalized the framework used to create other macro-regions.

Table 1.3 Macro-regionalism: cross-scale regional governance model pattern

Pattern	State-led Type	Regional Government-led Type	Supranational Institution-led Type
Macro-region	EU Strategy for the Baltic Sea Region (EUSBSR)	EU Strategy for the North Sea (Autonomous Strategy)	EU Strategy for the Danube Region (EUSDR)
Year implemented	2009	Not yet implemented	2011
EU member state	8	7 (plus 1 Non-member State)	9 (plus 5 Non-member States)
Related grand design	VASAB2010	NorVision	VISION PLANET
Regional policy program	INTERREG Baltic Sea Program, etc.	INTERREG North Sea Program, etc.	INTERREG Middle Europe + Southern Europe spaces, etc.
Existing international frameworks (Environment)	Helsinki Commission	OSPAR Commission	Danube Commission
Lead actor	Council of the Baltic Sea States (CBSS) Nordic Council	North Sea Commission (NSC)	European Commission for Regional Policy

Source: Prepared by the authors.

The state-led model, the regional government-led model, and the supranational institution-led model are positioned on a continuum for the softening of hard spaces and the hardening of soft spaces. A macro-regional space that has once been softened will again be transformed into a space that has the characteristics of a hard space in the process of re-scaling that occurs when it is incorporated into the EU system.

The state-led model is a model in which a state that originally was a hard space territorial governance actor takes the lead in forming a macro-region. It may at first appear strange that a body that was once a state would lead a state re-scaling. However, with the hollowing-out of state functions in its region, the Baltic Sea Macro-region becomes a good example of this model. In the Baltic Sea Macro-region, states actively participate in the formation of macro-regional governance arrangements and, at their own initiative, have made efforts to facilitate the formation of the macro-region. Even if the grouping of states after the establishment of a macro-region appears to be the same as before, strategic re-selections of state identities were performed. This is called "the changing same."

The regional government-led model incorporates the soft characteristics generated during the macro-region formation process. The objective of the regional governments is to prioritize decentralization. Here, the regional government aspects of the CoR's and the CPMR's moves in the direction of soft spaces can be seen.

Meanwhile, in the formative period of the aforementioned process, the cross-scale regional governance supranational institution-led model lacks the softening of hard spaces and serves as a model only for the latter half of the process. If we skip past the first half of this process, we can examine the European Commission's stance toward hard spaces.

EU-ization is a process of the re-hardening of a space that has been softened. Therefore, in the North Sea Macro-region, where hardening is not considered a good thing, the adoption of a macro-region strategy that uses the discourse of hardening does not appear to be making any headway. When a regional government-led model region such as the North Sea is softened, the centrifugal force emanating from a state or supranational power becomes operative, and if this power is too strong, returning to a re-hardening step becomes difficult. In a state-led model region such as the Baltic Sea, the state actor maintains a balance between centrifugal and centripetal forces, and previously hollowed-out functions are re-injected into the macro-region in a form that ensures the even balance of these two forces. In the supranational institution-led model found in the Danube and related macro-regions, centripetal forces pushing toward the supranational level make a strong appearance during hardening. As can be seen, macro-regionalization is not a simple concept, in that the softening and hardening processes must include an analysis of the background of each individual macro-region, and as a result the simple application of EU-ization is clearly not enough to explain everything.

Politics among scales and jumping scale

Actors embedded in the existing multi-level hierarchy use jumping scale to the new scale of macro-regions, thereby elevating their attempts to maximize their own groups' interests to the supranational level. Over the course of the Baltic Sea Macro-region's governance formation, countries along the Baltic Sea coast jumped over the old East-West security arrangements to the supranational level to ensure that their disputes became EU-shared issues. Member states led jumping scale, which led to macro-regional governance and could be called *state-led-type jumping scale*. Meanwhile, in the case of the North Sea Macro-region, regional governments along the North Sea coast jumped their disputes over North Sea ocean resources to the supranational scale, so these disputes became an EU issue. Here, regional governments led the jumping scale to create macro-regional governance, and this could be called *regional government-led-type jumping scale*, and this difference is classifiable.

In the Danube Macro-region, environmental problems related to the spatial planning of river catchment areas were handled by the European Commission. Since these environmental disputes had been brought to the EU level from the beginning, there was no resort to politics among scales using jumping scale. However, at the outset, regional policy measures failed to yield results at the level of the INTERREG CADSES (Central European Adriatic Danubian South-Eastern European Space) Macro-region, leading to a dispute over the introduction of a new scale, and unless an agreement could be reached between scales by the states and regional governments, an effective regional policy will not be obtained (Graute 2008). The Danube Macro-region has many more definitive regional characteristics than the old CADSES, and disputes are much better articulated. Whether *supranational institution-led cross-scale regional governance* in the Danube Macro-region can be implemented successfully or not will depend on the sharing of experiences and knowledge by the types of regional governance actors that have made progress in other macro-regions.

The changing natures of the state

De-embedding and the changing three natures of the state

This examination of the changes that have occurred with the formation of macro-regions and emergence of jumping scales leads us to the stage for an investigation of the process of state re-scaling and re-embedding in each scale (Sawa and Minamino 2006; Sawa 2010). What is important here is not the continuation or the extinguishing of the state but rather the dissection of the nature of the state, an investigation of what has changed in the nature of the state or what has not changed (Figure 1.1). We must ask what kinds of transformations have occurred in the nature of the state due to the processes by which diverse scales have appeared. On this point, an even deeper understanding of cross-scale regional governance in the creation of macro-regions is a prerequisite.

Going *beyond borders* in such a macro-region does not stop at changes in the horizontal power balance between states but also induces deviations beyond the scale that bring on changes in the vertical power balance between regional actors. This *beyond scale* is established when the power configurations that were previously dominated by the state are supplemented by the power inputs of such various regional governance actors as supranational organizations or regional governments. In addition, this supplementary power evokes changes in the power balance between meta-governance actors. As a result, the possibilities for stakeholder participation have been enhanced, generating deviations from the previous actions and agendas of involved actors that help strike a balance between government, market, and civil society norms.

Deviating from state borders

With the extension and institutionalization of EU regional policy, the enlargement of the supranational entity has led to the emergence of complex issues that straddle national borders. For example, in the North Sea, the depletion of cod and other ocean resources and environmental pollution problems along shipping routes have raised new issues for discussion at venues where states are no longer able to wield effective policy instruments. This represents the first of the three deviations—*deviating from state borders*. Put simply, problems that straddle and spread quickly across national borders find the territories of each individual state to be too small and not effective, and cannot be dealt with effectively by individual states, confined as they are to their national territories. On the other hand, the EU covers an extensive amount of territory that it is too large and cumbersome to tackle trans-border issues. However, the use of a new scale, the macro-region, as the instrumental conduit to deliver the policies needed to cope with these issues, is able to fill the gap between the state scale and the supranational scale. These and other related cross-border issues cannot be fixed merely by having the regional authorities of adjacent trans-border territories sign agreements of cooperation, while maintaining their presence within a state-controlled national framework. A policy instrument that straddles important connections or water catchment areas that span three or four countries is needed. Furthermore, these need not be groupings that cover all of a state's territory, although parts of its territory can be included, depending on the issue and policy.

Deviating from scale embedding

The macro-region has been proven to be an effective domain for jumping scale by actors who wish to take their disputes to a different scale. Actors therefore select macro-regions as domains for resolving disputes. However, there is no single regional administrative actor with jurisdiction over the macro-region itself. In other words, a macro-regional actor that would be a perfect body to wield the necessary policy instrument does not exist. With the impetus from *deviating from state borders*, and the beginnings of new scales, the significance of cultural exchanges and cooperation between neighboring regional authorities has grown. In other words, regional governments that were previously embedded in state hierarchies as actors under state jurisdictions, and passively followed the state's foreign policies, must now develop strategies for independent and beyond-border activities. Rather than clarifying who is governing a region, and in what way, and rather than compartmentalizing static regional actors as in MLG, it is now necessary to see that regional actors are becoming involved at more than one scale.

The governance situation in the macro-regions is complex and sometimes even chaotic, with administrative actors from supranational, state, and regional levels embedded in a multi-level hierarchy, forming horizontal relationships in order to participate in heterarchical governance. Of the *three deviations*, this is the second: *deviating from scales*. When one looks at the dynamic between the regional governance actors in *deviating from scales*, the state actor does not exist as a solitary and absolute power, but rather is simply one actor actively attempting to adjust or coordinate a macro-regional power structure.

Deviating beyond categories

The third deviation is *deviating beyond categories*. This deviation looks at the state as a regional actor and its limitations therein. In macro-regions, a comprehensive transfer of policy functions is often needed in such areas as environmental policy, fisheries policy, transport policy, competition policy, and other policies that are relevant to the macro-region. When these functional policy transfers are made, the macro-region and its stakeholders become invested in these various policy areas. However, although regional representatives are involved in the governance and problem-solving processes that tackle these prioritized issues, these issues are likely be those, like environmental problems, that continue for generations or those that elicit normative clashes between the various actors. In these cases, forming a consensus among the diversity of participating actors is often problematic. At this point, policy adjustments become impossible under the norms of civil society, as these issue-oriented identities are attuned to governmental action norms that place the highest priority on the rights and benefits of the demos (Taga 1999). When governance formats with differing adjustment mechanisms for actor norms, such as governments, markets, or civil society, appear, the formation of a new, independent norm for the macro-region becomes necessary. An adjustment pattern that promotes stakeholder participation is a process that achieves results based on the assumption of responsibility for initiating dialogue or offering explanations. Only the norms differ. Specialist groups with the respective action norms also participate in this process.

Conclusion

The macro-region as a download destination: re-allocation and re-embedding

The EU integration process is a state re-scaling process as well as a power reallocation process. In other words, when the *three deviations* occur, state re-scaling is promoted, and state power is uploaded to the mega-region, the EU.

However, governance based on this upload does not mean that state re-scaling has ended; rather, the power uploaded to the mega-region is negotiated between political spaces and falls into a scale that has been subdivided, becoming the actual policy introduction body. The first download destination is the hierarchical MLG space that preserves the state hierarchy, while the other download destination is the heterarchical disruptive cross-scale regional governance space.

The process for moving EU regional policy funds to states within state territories, such as in Objective 1 of the EU regional policy, appears at first glance to be the same as the policy implementation procedure in the existing MLG. However, this corresponds to implementation of EU regional policy, and the result is that the hierarchical MLG is judged to be effective as a download destination. In other words, when confronted with a choice between the hierarchical MLG and the disruptive cross-scale regional governance, we must clearly understand that among the changeable selections, the result was the selection the unchanging side (the changing same).

As for the disruptive cross-scale regional governance space, as discussed earlier in this chapter, there are heterarchical policy spaces such as macro-regions. What is decisively different about the hierarchical space when compared with the heterarchical space is the relationship between the actor and scale. In the hierarchical space, the de-embedded state actor, as shown earlier, is re-embedded in MLG. Meanwhile, in the heterarchical space, an actor is re-embedded into a new scale, such as the macro-region. This is due to the aim for greater efficiency and optimization in the implementation of a policy objective when it is uploaded to the mega-region as a policy decision. This is a response to the question of why a policy that had been downloaded to a region and uploaded to the EU is then moved to a macro-region and not to a state. Only the heterarchy of the macro-region provides political effectiveness to the jumping scale.

Re-scaling the state enables the participation in a new governance arrangement by actors that have been de-embedded, and the maintenance of governance that has developed in relation to a separate scale, as well as the maintenance of a multiple-activity identity. This is the reality of an EU region, and a space where multiple governances are shared. If MLG returns as a re-embedding destination, there are cases where it may also be re-embedded in cross-scale regional governance.

Future issues and future predictions: possibility as a tool for analysis of the cross-scale regional governance model

The cross-scale regional governance model as an analytical framework focuses on the formation of an EU macro-regional governance arrangement, a *new scale*, and dynamically revises and develops the existing governance analysis framework. When the cross-scale regional governance model is used, *changes in the power structure between actors* through jumping scale, for example, emerges as a logical and useful analytical tool. In addition, the macro-regional development process consists of three models—the *state-led*, the *regional government-led*, and the *supranational institution-led*—and the macro-region creation process that had hitherto been difficult to tell apart from other creation processes, could now be readily explained. In the future, the development process for all macro-regions can be expected to include cross-scale political negotiations. The three models clarify the emergence and characteristics of the macro-region, and the actors involved in macro-regional governance have been made clearly aware of the disputed points and are aware of the new rules.

In this chapter we have argued that EU Studies emerged as a critique of existing state-system research, However, since EU Studies researchers have concentrated on the arguments at a supranational scale, they have failed to grasp some of the realities that have emerged within the evolving EU polity and has dimmed the critical research perspective necessary to grasp and analyze these changing realities. This research method thus reached a dead end, until a path for escaping the stalemate was achieved with *politics among scales*, an analytical framework in which the EU supranational scale has been relativized with other scales. As a result, EU Studies are now promoting regional governance research that looks at the governance issues, policies, and strategies that emerged after state re-scaling. The rereading of transnational or cross-border political space from the perspective of the macro-regional scale that has been raised in this chapter will lead to research that brings *politics among scales* into the field of vision and takes into consideration everything from global scales to the EU as a mega-region as well as the micro-regional scale. We are confident that this will stimulate and enrich the international political science debates that will follow.

The rejection of the given

In the projects which have been conducted for this book, we have been engaged in a comparative study of sub-regions in East Asia and the EU from the perspective of drafting a grand design, and here, with a degree of self-criticism, we would like to offer our view as to what has been missing in conventional comparative studies of these two regions. First of all, conventional discussions have taken the sub-region as a given and as a consequence have not paid attention to a constructivist aspect that the sub-regional scale has historically contained. In other words, even in the East Asian region, we should have started our research with the question "what kind of scale should be applied to sub-regions such as Northeast Asia or the Japan Sea Rim Region?" The fact that we have used these scales as a given indicates that the validity of our study could be questioned.

Second, in sub-region studies of East Asia, the major challenge has traditionally been how to extricate ourselves from the following curse: "Because there is a EU polity in Europe that serves as the object of comparison, generalizations that can be applied to East Asia are difficult." This, in other words, is the curse of "EU integration theory" for researchers working on East Asian sub-regions. However, if we continue to let ourselves be trapped by the question of the "EU polity," there will be no progress in our research. If we do not disaggregate our analysis of the EU polity to space, institutions, and actors rather than trying to capture the EU polity as a whole, there will be no progress in sub-regional studies. In fact, in the North Sea Macro-region in Europe, we see the region is not simply made up of the sovereign territories of the EU member states. This is evident when one looks at the involvement of regional authorities from Norway, a non-EU member state, in the formation and affairs of the region, and the complexity found in the Barents Sea Macro-region due to the involvement of Danish Greenland and the Faeroe Islands, which have opted out of the EU. Without examining the dynamism through which macro-regional scale is constructed and the processes by which the scale is constructed, it is no longer possible to generalize based on the existence of the "EU polity."

As the decline of one scale often suggests a decline in political power that corresponds to that scale, the emergence of a new scale can indicate the birth of new political power that has adapted to it or the revival of an old actor with a new identity (Paasi 2002). Also, taking into account that the EU has been utilizing the North Sea Macro-region and various cross-border regions that cannot be accommodated in "the state's nest" or "the state hierarchy" as policy vessels for new problem-solving, it is meaningful to analyze international politics using the scale as a new analytical framework drawing from analytical concepts of political geography.

It is very likely that the forms of governance in sub-regions in Asia are different from those in Europe due to different historical circumstances. We can therefore not set the scope of a sub-region without discussing the constructive process.[3] In studying the East Asian region, the discussion of a distinctive or unique Asian scale and the analysis of the process of forming these scales will be indispensable. What is also needed in studying the East Asian region is more attention to the possibility of a completely different model from the MLG analytical framework based on cooperation among actors, something like a cross-scale regional governance analytical framework based on opposition among actors.

Acknowledgements

Prof. Victor Lee Carpenter of Hirosaki University has helped us with English proofreading and Ms. Naoko Sato of Aomori Chuo-Gakuin University tidied up figures. We would like to thank both of them.

Notes

1 Discussions with Professor Yuichi Kagawa of the University of Shiga Prefecture and Professor Takashi Yamazaki of Osaka City University have deepened our understanding of political geography and helped to educate us about the documentation related to this theme. We use this note to express our gratitude.
2 Caution is required regarding the point that macro-regions are not always nested nicely inside the EU region.
3 Kang's critical paper on the needs for new analytical framework helped to foster our views on the comparative aspects on the sub-regions from the perspective of the international security studies (Kang 2003).

References

Allmendinger, Phil, and Graham Haughton (2009) "Soft Spaces, Fuzzy Boundaries, and Metagovernance: The New Spatial Planning in the Thames Gateway," *Environment and Planning A*, 41 (3): 617–633.

Allmendinger, Phil, and Graham Haughton (2010) "Spatial Planning, Devolution, and New Planning Spaces," *Environment and Planning C: Government and Policy*, 28 (5): 803–818.

Allmendinger, Phil, Tobias Chilla, and Franziska Sielker (2014) "Europeanizing Territoriality—Towards Soft Spaces?," *Environment and Planning A*, 46 (11): 2703–2717.

Allmendinger, Phil, Graham Haughton, and Edward Shepherd (2016) "Where is Planning to be Found?: Material Practices and the Multiple Spaces of Planning," *Environment and Planning C: Politics and Space*, 34 (1): 38–51.

Allmendinger, Phil, Graham Haughton, Jörg Knieling, and Frank Othengrafen (eds.) (2015) *Soft Spaces in Europe: Re-negotiating Governance, Boundaries and Borders*, London: Routledge.

Bialasiewicz, Luiza, Paolo Giaccaria, Alun Jones, and Claudio Minca (2012) "Re-scaling 'EU'rope: EU Macro-regional Fantasies in the Mediterranean," *European Urban and Regional Studies*, 20 (1): 59–76.

Brenner, Neil (1999) "Globalisation as Reterritorialisation: The Re-scaling of Urban Governance in the European Union," *Urban Studies*, 36 (3): 431–451.

Commission of the European Communities (CEC) (2001) European Governance: A White Paper, COM (2001) 428 final (Brussels: CEC, 25 July 2001), European Commission, Brussels.

Cox, Kevin R. (1998) "Spaces of Dependence, Spaces of Engagement and the Politics of Scale, or: Looking for Local Politics," *Political Geography*, 17 (1): 1–23.

Graute, Ulrich (2008) Director of the Joint Technical Secretariat, INTERREG IIIB CADSES Neighbourhood Programme. Interview by authors. Transcript. Portorož, Slovenia, June 2, 2008.

Haughton, Graham, and Phil Allmendinger (2008) "The Soft Spaces of Local Economic Development," *Local Economy*, 23 (2): 138–148.

Haughton, Graham, Phil Allmendinger, and Stijn Oosterlynck (2013) "Spaces of Neoliberal Experimentation: Soft Spaces, Postpolitics, and Neoliberal Governmentality," *Environment and Planning A*, 45 (1): 217–234.

Heley, Jesse (2013) "Soft Spaces, Fuzzy Boundaries and Spatial Governance in Post-devolution Wales," *International Journal of Urban and Regional Research*, 37 (4): 1325–1348.

Inoue, Yuji (2003a) "'Governance Turn' in European Integration Studies and International Relations Approaches," *Journal of Law and Politics*, 195: 57–100 (in Japanese).

Inoue, Yuji (2003b) "'Governance Turn' in European Integration Studies and International Relations Approaches (2)," *Journal of Law and Politics*, 197: 97–128 (in Japanese).

Jessop, Bob (2004) "Multi-level Governance and Multi-level Metagovernance," in Ian Bache and Matthew Flinders (eds.) *Multi-level Governance*, Oxford: Oxford University Press, pp. 49–74.

Jones, Rhys, Mark Goodwin, Martin Jones, and Kevin Pett (2005) "'Filling in' the State: Economic Governance and the Evolution of Devolution in Wales," *Environment and Planning C: Government and Policy*, 23 (3): 337–360.

Kang, David C. (2003) "Getting Asia Wrong: The Need for New Analytical Frameworks," *International Security*, 27 (4): 57–85.

Kern, Kristine, and Stefan Gänzle (2013) 'Macro-regionalisation' as a New Form of European Governance: The Case of the European Union's Strategies for the Baltic Sea and the Danube Regions (ISL Working Papers; 2013:3), Department of Political Science and Management, University of Agder.

Marks, Gary, and Liesbet Hooghe (2004) "Contrasting Visions of Multi-level Governance," in Ian Bache and Matthew Flinders (eds.) *Multi-level Governance*, Oxford: Oxford University Press, pp. 15–30.

Marks, Gary, Liesbet Hooghe, and Kermit Blank (1995) *Integration Theory, Subsidiarity and the Internationalisation of Issues: The Implication for Legitimacy*, EUI Working Paper RSC No. 95/7, San Domenico: European University Institute.

Massey, Doreen (1993) "Power-geometry and a Progressive Sense of Place," in Jon Bird, Barry Curtis, Tim Putnam, George Robertson, and Lisa Tickner (eds.) *Mapping the Futures: Local Cultures, Global Change*, London: Routledge, pp. 60–70.

McCarthy, James (2005) "Scale, Sovereignty, and Strategy in Environmental Governance," *Antipode*, 37 (4): 731–753.

O'Loughlin, John (2000) "Responses: Geography as Space and Geography as Place: The Divide between Political Science and Political Geography Continues," *Geopolitics*, 5 (3): 126–137.

Paasi, Anssi (2002) "Place and Region: Regional Worlds and Words," *Progress in Human Geography*, 26 (6): 802–811.

Samecki, Pawel (2009) "Macro-regional Strategies in the European Union," discussion paper presented at the EU Baltic Sea Strategy Ministerial Conference on the EU Baltic Sea Strategy, Stockholm, September 18, 2009.

Sawa, Munenori (2010) "The Process of Spatial Reorganization in India due to Globalization: Focusing on De-territorialization and Re-territorialization," *Japanese Journal of Human Geography*, 62 (2): 132–153 (in Japanese).

Sawa, Munenori, and Takeshi Minamino (2006) "Changes in an Indian Village Involved in Globalization: De-territorialization and Re-territorialization of a Rurban Village in the Bangalore Metropolitan Area," *Japanese Journal of Human Geography*, 58 (2): 125–144 (in Japanese).

Smith, Neil (2000), "Scale," in R.J. Johnston, Derek Gregory, Geraldine Pratt, and Michael Watts (eds.) *The Dictionary of Human Geography, 4th edition*, Oxford: Blackwell Publishing, pp. 724–727.

Swyngedouw, Erik (2004) "Scaled Geographies: Nature, Place, and the Politics of Scale," in Eric Sheppard and Robert B. McMaster (eds.) *Scale and Geographic Inquiry: Nature, Society, and Method*, Oxford: Blackwell, pp. 129–153.

Taga, Hidetoshi (1999) "Deep Layers of Social Units in the International Community," in Hidetoshi Taga (ed.) *Transformation of the International Community, and Actors*, Tokyo: Seibundo, pp. 395–427 (in Japanese).

Yamazaki, Takashi (2010) *Politics, Space, Location: Toward a 'Political Geography'*, Kyoto: Nakanishiya Shuppan (in Japanese).

Part II
Sub-Regionalism in Asia

2 Small states' strategies in the Mekong region
Perspectives from Laos

Yuji Morikawa

Introduction

The rise of China has brought increased prominence to international politics in East Asia in the context of an international order exhibiting signs of a power shift, notably in relation to the ongoing relative decline in what had been the hegemonic influence of the USA. At the same time, the Association of Southeast Asian Nations (ASEAN) has taken a central position within international relations in Southeast Asia, where the multilateralism exemplified by ASEAN, Japan, China, and South Korea (ASEAN+3) has spread rapidly since the 1990s. Whereas the character of international relations in East Asia increasingly focused on China and other large states, in the context of international politics accord with the realist claims of H. J. Morgenthau and E. H. Carr as prescribed by power and national interest, the multilateralism of Southeast Asia constitutes a liberal relationship. Within the context of these two contrasting visions of international relations in East Asia, countries looking to nationalism as a basis for their respective existences constitute an extremely complicated system.

In this chapter, I consider the role of small states in the complex system of Southeast Asia and Indochina as one of its constituent sub-regions. Focusing on the role of small states in international relations within discussions of the dynamics of relations among large states, I clarify the formation of sub-regions by examining the role of Laos in regional formation. I also discuss the challenge of strengthening regional cooperation through an analysis of the subjective role played by small states as they have responded actively to the regionalism advocated by ASEAN, which, especially since the 1990s, has worked to deepen and expand cooperative relationships with the broader Asian region.

From buffer state to agent of regional formation

Indochina after the end of the Cold War saw the inception of a variety of regional cooperation frameworks, most notably the Greater Mekong Sub-region (GMS) Economic Cooperation Program organized by the Asian Development Bank (ADB), that positioned this area as a kind of representative sub-region in East Asia that was anticipated to blossom as a new unit within the international social order.[1] The current mushrooming of overlapping regional frameworks that involve the participation of large states from outside the region has engendered a continuing situation in which common norms (and the ideological bases on which they are grounded) have little substance. This situation, as well as the absence of any systematic analyses of the regional setting, has further complicated interpretations of the positioning of the group of states consisting of Cambodia, Laos, Myanmar, and Vietnam (CLMV), and of the sub-region within the regional order.

The transformation of the region by cross-border development, to use a conventional spatial analogy, constitutes a process of both quantitative and qualitative transformation in terms of the transformations, encroachments, and combinations that accompany expanded mutual exchanges of people and materials. As a dynamic chronotope, the process may be interpreted as the pluralization of identities in which history is fused with memory. Given its complex classification as a chronotope interlacing a temporal axis for apprehending the attributes of the state in their historical context, with a spatial axis showing regional expansion, the formation of a sub-region by Laos and the other countries of the Mekong River delta in mainland Southeast Asia (Indochina), as the site of GMS development projects, ASEAN regionalism, and an increasingly unified market after the Cold War, could be regarded as the states' establishment of new boundary lines.

From the 1960s to the present day, many of the small states that exist in this heavily stratified region have been immersed in the processes of nation-building and economic development in a thoroughly postcolonial context and simultaneously engaged in the formation of a new region through interstate cooperation. The formation and transformation of regions engendered by the movements of various cross-border international relations actors is also a phenomenon that increases unity across the wider region while relativizing the existence of the state. In an effort to free itself from the structural position of relying on an external power for security as a pre-Cold War "buffer state" (Pholsena and Banomyong 2005)[2] or as a state serving as an "intermediate zone in the balance of powers" (Stuart-Fox 2005), Laos has been actively involved in cooperative efforts aiming at regional development and ASEAN regional integration.

The process of this spatial transformation entails (i) a political will oriented toward "state formation" that defines boundaries and maintains neutrality, and (ii) the process of strengthening political ties with neighboring countries through development aid and cooperation that will lead to regional formation. This process of chronotope transformation, moreover, also entails the process of simultaneous determination by states' authority of state and regional boundaries in the operation of the two opposing vectors of state *integration* and *relativization*. The transformation of this complex regional space is manifested in the aggregate form of Laos's international relations (Morikawa 2014).

Laos has an area of 236,800 square kilometers, which is equivalent of that of the UK. Its population was estimated to 6.49 million inhabitants in 2015 with a density of 27 habitants per square kilometers (the lowest in ASEAN states).

Although there are abundant natural resources and hydroelectric potential of Mekong, Laos has the characteristics of a poor and small economy. In 2015, the Human Development Index (HDI) was 0.586, the same level as that of Cambodia, and was ranked 138th out of 188 countries and territories.[3] Laos is geographically not small, but in terms of international politics, it is a small power.

In the context of Laos's international context, the transformation of identities linked to history and memory and touching the borders of all countries involved in the GMS is characterized by both its aspect as a "marginal state" heteronomously determined through relations with neighboring states via their mutual boundaries (Oba 2004) and the aspect in which it acts autonomously to redefine those boundaries. Accordingly, the crux of this paper is to clarify the role of Laos as an actor in the formation of a *regional order* from the standpoint of both a "marginal state" and the autonomy of a small state.

The state formation process of Laos as a small state proceeding under the dynamics of integration and relativization, as described earlier, is embedded in international relations that take the form of a multilayered network consisting of multiple development cooperation frameworks, and it is reasonable to ask whether the connectivity of the entire region has increased in a complicated fashion (Morikawa 2014). State formation in Laos has also become one and the same with regional formation that is also linked to the process of ASEAN regional integration and has proceeded in a complex network of policy cooperation through individual bilateral relationships with (i) China and other neighboring states; (ii) Vietnam, with which Laos had enjoyed a "special relationship" since the establishment of the country in 1975; and (iii) Thailand, on which Laos is strongly dependent in terms of its society, culture, and economy. Because the USA gave Thailand strong military support during the Vietnam War, Laos's historical perspective made Thailand appear aggressor. However, relations between Laos and Thailand have clearly improved since the end of the Cold War. Now freed of geopolitical and ideological hostility (Pholsena and Banomyong 2005: 59), Thailand is the largest trading partner for Laos in 2015.[4] The relations between the two neighbor states have improved since the end of the Cold War.

Thus, while it is certain that networks within the region are being formed in a multilayered fashion, in terms of whether this has led to the cultivation of unity as a unit of international society, we can only describe the process as being incomplete. Even now, in functional and institutional terms, a move exists to deepen multilateral partnerships centered on ASEAN to form an "East Asian" region through negotiations among the governments of each nation. However, this "East Asian" regional concept, which was born out of a process aiming toward regional cooperation while taking the structure of a "reverse hub-and-spoke system" (Yamamoto 2007) with the small-state federation of ASEAN at the core of the network, sits in opposition to an "Asia-Pacific model" that involves the participation of the USA. Thus, in the background of this international relations context, the dynamics of traditional international politics that are engaged in the search for power and benefit are operating, even as they contribute to the increase of global economic interdependence (Morikawa 2012).

56 *Yuji Morikawa*

Many previous studies on Asian regional formation and the international order have placed their analytical focus on interstate relationships, primarily in relation to the large states. Using the extent of sovereign power as the sole standard, Laos and the other small states comprising the group of other institutionally transitional nations that have joined ASEAN since the end of the Cold War tend to be regarded, in the context of international relations, as entities that are *acted upon*. However, the fact that East Asian international relations and regional formation focused on ASEAN are not solely the product of so-called "power politics" is clear, even without looking to ASEAN as an example. In studies of regionalism around the world, it is impossible to ignore the presence of behavioral principles and norms among small states that are attempting to prescribe a new model for international relations. Accordingly, I will aim to juxtapose aspects of the behavioral principles of small states such as Laos with the traditional dynamics of international politics that regard profit and power as variables in line with the contexts of regional formation. In doing so, I will discuss Laos's relationships with the large states and other states in the region to consider the challenges for regional formation, sustainable development, and the maintenance of security using a theoretical chronotope-based approach that draws on both spatial and temporal analyses.

The concept of "small states" as methodology

The concept of "small states"

The Lao People's Democratic Republic (PDR), from the latter half of the 1980s, has pursued a growth strategy through "new economic mechanisms" (from 1986) that aim for the partial introduction of a market economy under what is in political terms a one-party socialist regime. Laos's shift to a market economy, although beginning with policy reforms to state-owned enterprise, is unrolling comprehensive economic and structural reforms that aim to introduce a free market. These economic liberalization measures also reflect the contradictory policy of successfully accomplishing a solely economic institutional transition from a planned economy to a market economy while simultaneously ensuring the survival of socialism as the state ideology. While doggedly maintaining economic development that is reliant on outside forces and a firm commitment to neutrality in foreign relations might be seen as ways of overcoming this contradiction, these are also challenges of the utmost difficulty for LDC-type small states such as Laos.

The political and economic history of the Lao PDR since its establishment in 1975 has broadly been divided into three separate periods (Table 2.1) (Amakawa 2005; Pholsena and Banomyong 2005) corresponding to an initial period of *building the socialist state* (Period 1, from 1976), a second period of *economic reform* (Period 2, from 1986 to 1997), and a third period of economic development (Period 3, from 2003) (Amakawa 2005). Economic reforms that have been gradually implemented in Laos over these three periods have been inextricably linked to flashpoints in international relations in mainland Southeast Asia (from the First Indochina War to the Cambodian–Vietnamese War). In the midst of this economic reform process, especially in the phase from Period 2 when the Laotian economy began to take off and stabilize, by deepening its reliance on China with the normalization of relations between China and Russia (1992) and its accession to ASEAN, Laos has sought to both escape its position as a buffer state constituted by its primary bilateral relationships and pursued a process of state integration while at the same time contributing to regional formation linked to ASEAN integration. In this chapter, I propose a new scheme for prioritizing the history of Laos's international relationships. The aforementioned Periods 1–3, a time of state integration aimed at building an economic base for national integration and state formation by the People's Revolutionary Party (1976–2003). Furthermore, the era from 2004 when China refreshed its regional policies and began providing overseas aid and direct investment in earnest (2004–2015). The adjustments made to relations with China, which have been

Table 2.1 Historical timeline of Laotian international relations

[Period 1] "Building the socialist state"
1975	Establishment of the Lao People's Democratic Republic and the dictatorial regime of the People's Revolutionary Party
1976	Special relationship with Vietnam
1979	Break-off of relations with China

[Period 2] "Economic reforms"
1986	Market-based economic reforms
1988	Normalization of relations with Thailand
1989	Restoration of relations with China
1991	Chinese Premier Li Peng's official visit to Laos
1991	Establishment of new Constitution (addition of Article 16 "New Economic Management Mechanisms")
1992	Treaty of Amity and Cooperation between Thailand and Laos
1992	Launch of Asian Development Bank- Greater Mekong Sub-region (ADB-GMS)
1994	Treaty on Amity between Russia and Laos (an "ordinary relationship")
1995	Mutual assistance between Laos and Cambodia
1996	ASEAN Mekong River Basin Development Cooperation (AMBDC) Conference
1997	Accession to ASEAN

[Period 3] "Economic development" / "Regional integration strategies"
2000	Initiative for ASEAN Integration (IAI)
2003	Laos–China Leader's Summit
2004	First Cambodia–Laos–Vietnam (CLV) Summit
2006	Eighth Congress of the Lao People's Revolutionary Party (LPRP); "National development centered on economic development"
2009	Objective set to graduate from Least Developed Country (LDC) status by 2020
2011	Ninth LPRP Congress; "7th 5-year plan (2011–2016)"
2017	Tenth LPRP Congress; "Vision 2030"

Source: Created by the author.

overly one-sided in the context of sub-regional formation. Among these periods, it is in the phase from Period 3 onward that Laos has developed its autonomy as an international relations actor while aiming at both ASEAN integration and sub-regional formation.

In the following, as key analytical concepts, I touch on "small states," "buffer systems," and "regional formation."

While small states of small powers are states whose conditions of survival are governed by the trends of large states (their conceptual opposites), their absolute definition has been regarded as difficult. R. L. Rothstein defines small states as states that are fundamentally dependent on the institutions, processes, and development of other countries for their own national security, stipulating their character as states that have no choice but to give up even their independence.[5] Countermeasures available to small states as a means of resisting power politics are broadly divided between ways for countries to isolate themselves from international relations in pursuit of neutrality and the strategy of accepting federations and coalitions among states. The formation of alliances, which is representative of the latter method, is the outcome of changing the balance of power within the international system. From a realist viewpoint, while small states seek to form alliances against the rise of hegemonic states, rather than building an international order to establish a balance of power on their own, they instead form alliances whenever they recognize threats to their own national security.[6] This is also what might be called a "passive state" strategy. Even from the standpoint of liberalism, which privileges international institutions, small states that are unable to bear the burden of institutional costs will be reliant on an international order constructed by the leadership of large, even hegemonic states.

Many small states have experienced setbacks when pursuing alliance strategies and neutrality strategies, in particular.[7] Nevertheless, although the superiority of large states in the international order remains a fact, globalization in the context of East Asia has effected a deepening of national interdependence, primarily in relation to the economy. Especially among the ASEAN nations, as a federation of small states positioned at the center of a regional formation, the choice of strategies for ensuring security and independence has expanded dramatically and flexibility of conduct has been ascertained.

Here, rather than proceeding on the basis of a definition of small states that relies on objective criteria, I want to focus on the relative scale and dialectical conduct within bilateral and multilateral relationships. On the basis of the assertion that thought is "existentially connected" with the social position of a political actor (what Karl Mannheim called *Seinsverbundenheit*)[8] that aims for autonomy, I will consider these in terms of two aspects: namely, (i) Laos's postwar relationships with China and Vietnam, respectively, and (ii) Laos and regional formation in the context of ASEAN regionalism.

While my target period begins with the outbreak of the Asian currency crisis that provided the impetus for Asian regional cooperation and the accession of Laos to ASEAN in July 1997, my consideration also includes the transformation of Laos's bilateral relationships in the mid-1980s when government policies shifted away from the policy of international isolation that had prevailed since the time of the nation's independence. During this period, as well as expanding its geographical range while maintaining political neutrality, ASEAN was also working to deepen functional cooperative relationships. Laos, aiming in the context of this ASEAN development process to convert the twin vectors of "state integration" and "regional integration through state relativization" into a dynamic of growth, became an active participant in a variety of regional cooperation initiatives as a strategy for self-restructuring in consideration of the equilibrium among its neighboring countries. When we clarify Laos's self-image as an international political actor from an international relations analysis, especially in relation to (i), we find that a foreign policy combining trade, investment, and aid linked to China's broader regional strategies has been a theme of the utmost importance for Laos's international relations.

Karl Mannheim's concept of *Seinsverbundenheit* focusses on the idea that the nature of the subject changes according to the conditions of the age. While Laos is one of the smallest powers among all the ASEAN nations in terms of its military force, economic power, and population size, Laos's sense of existence as an international political actor is contingent and changes over time. In Laos's foreign relations, as well, the temporal axis of its complex bilateral relationships with China and other nations is always associated with the spatial axis of the regional formations of the GMS and ASEAN. Its sense of existence as a small state also changes in the context of the interrelationships of the twin vectors of "integration" and "relativization."

Regional formation

If we define regions as "spatial entities made visible by policies based on regionalism as a political ideology" (Morikawa 2012), then the essence of regionalism will differ for each state participating in regional formation, and representations of the region should also reflect a variety of social phenomena. For this reason, I have incorporated a broad regional comparative analysis with a historicist approach.[9] In terms of the processes by which the bilateral relationships constituting the buffer system that has come to characterize Laos have been transformed since the 1990s, the cross-border regional cooperation of ASEAN and the regional development project of the GMS have also been subject to the political intentionality of state formation at which Laos has aimed.

While ASEAN's regionalism and cooperative relationships and the regional development of the GMS have been developed as multilateral cooperation frameworks, relationships guided by national interests are more powerfully apparent than the formation of any extra-national regional identity. For Laos in particular, although the continued existence of the single-party regime of the People's Revolutionary Party since the state was formed in 1975 has worked as an antagonistic force against the "relativization" of states that has accompanied regional integration and the formation of sub-regions, it remains the most important issue in domestic politics. As a result, the more deeply it becomes involved in regional development cooperation and regional integration through ASEAN's multilateralism, the more it looks to national identity as a touchstone in its struggles with foreign policy as well as in its attempts to coordinate efforts to mitigate the pitfalls of multilateralism through bilateral relationships with China and Vietnam. Herein lies the history of the regional order and Laos as a small state focused on *Seinsverbundenheit*.

In other words, regional formation is a historically complex process by which actors' perceptions are socialized into the frameworks of state and sub-region in the context of international relations (Ba 2016). As Laos repeatedly engages in foreign relations with Vietnam, China, and ASEAN, I want to ask how its own strategic self-perception is internalized by each of these other parties. That is the subject addressed in this chapter.

Bilateral relationships versus regional formation

Laos in the context of a buffer system

Since its independence, the foreign relationship Laos has emphasized most is its so-called "special relationship" with Vietnam. Following its independence in 1975, Laos positioned state formation and national integration under the People's Revolutionary Party as priority issues and officially announced its special relationship with Vietnam by proclaiming a Declaration of Concord between Vietnam and Laos in 1976. Taking advantage of this opportunity, the two nations set out to build a special relationship of solidarity between socialist countries in terms of political institutions and military security. At the same time, friendly relationships were also being formed between Vietnam and the USSR (Union of Soviet Socialist Republics), its ally. Sharing a socialist ideology, this solidarity was strengthened by the respective aspects of military security and economic policy, engendering a structural situation wherein the development of Laos as a socialist country was governed by international relations centered on the friendly relationship with Vietnam.

The special relationship with Vietnam was linked to circumstances whereby bilateral relationships involving China (namely Sino-Soviet relations and Sino-Vietnamese relations) had become a variable factor, and at this time Laos, in the context of its international relations with surrounding countries such as China, the USSR, and Vietnam, was merely one of the parts embedded in a "buffer system."[10] Considering Laos from the standpoint of China and Vietnam, situated at either end of Laos, rather than being a direct foreign policy partner for China and Vietnam, Laos can be positioned as a kind of by-product entity of relations between Vietnam and the USSR for China, and of relations with China for Vietnam.[11] At the time of the 1979 Sino-Vietnamese war, Laos, after choosing to honor its special relationship by supporting Vietnam, soon after severed its diplomatic relations with China. In other words, together with Vietnam the country deepened its isolation from international relations. In terms of a classification focusing on Laos's economic policy, the Period 1 corresponds to the period of the construction of the socialist state, a period that privileged nation-building, and in which foreign relations, because they had become isolated by withdrawing into the shell constituted by relations with Vietnam and USSR, served only to deepen economic hardships.

In Period 2, the "period of economic reform" from 1986 to 1997, as Vietnam sought ways to settle its problems with Cambodia, Laos, by adopting a "new economic mechanism" at the Fourth Congress of the Lao People's Revolutionary Party (LPRP) prior to Vietnam, expressed a shift toward a market economy to escape economic hardships. With this, Laos, once no more than a buffer state in mainland Southeast Asia, took its first steps from having been an object of international relations in the region to becoming a political actor in the regional order. Subsequent actions taken by Laos in the Mekong River Basin region can be identified in the transition of its bilateral and multilateral relations with China, Vietnam, Cambodia, Thailand, and ASEAN.

From a "buffer state" to an agent of Regional Formation I: relations with a changing China

From 1989 to 1991, amid the dismantling of the socialist regimes of the former USSR and Eastern Bloc, and as an end to the Cambodian problem came into sight with the 1991 Paris Peace Accords, Laos's integration into the ASEAN regional economy accelerated, occasioned by the restoration of relations with China and Thailand, and improved relations with ASEAN (Hara 2011; Pholsena and Banomyong 2005).

Following the official visit of the Laotian Prime Minister, Kaysone Phomvihane, to Beijing in 1989; the reopening of trade with China; and the official visit to Laos of Chinese Premier Li Peng in 1990, Laos's relations with China suddenly began to improve. For Laos, the three main points of focus for expanding relations with China were as follows. First, it signified the positioning of the model of state formation seen as the objective of the Chinese economic reforms since 1978 as an ideological pillar for a socialist regime. In other words, this was a state model that sought economically to introduce market principles while adhering politically to rule by a one-party dictatorship. Second was the acquisition of new economic support and the stabilization of international relations. The realization of these objectives reinforced the political and economic foundations of Laos in the context of the state formation process.[12] In particular, the Asian currency crisis stemming from the rapid devaluation of the Thai baht, which coincided with the accession of Laos as an ASEAN member nation in July 1997, had a major impact that became an occasion to review the dependence of Laos on the Thai economy and begin to rely on China for the procurement of long-term capital. As a result, Chinese investment, economic assistance, and trade began to increase rapidly after 1998 as China continued to expand its presence in an accelerated fashion to occupy a position as the largest partner in every economic sector.

Even for China, resource development in Laos and the development of the Mekong River Basin—in particular, development along Laos's northern border in connection with the construction of the North–South Economic Corridor— held major economic significance in conjunction with inland development in China's southwestern heartland, centering on Yunnan province.[13] China's interest in Laos was focused on economic and regional policies linked to the Chinese heartland, and in the fields of politics and security it has thus far avoided any aspects that might antagonize Vietnam in its "special relationship" with Laos (Storey 2011). However, in terms of political and economic issues, more than a little wariness remains regarding how China's regional strategy has extended into Laos to expand its influence. At the Tenth LPRP Congress held in 2016, Choummaly Sayasone, who had actively promoted economic strategies with a focus on relations with China, was replaced as General Secretary with the election of Bounnhang Vorachith. A general perception of Bounnhang is pro-Vietnamese and less pro-Chinese than Choummaly. Somsavat Lengsavad who was the first Chinese–Laotian politburo of the People's Revolutionary Party and took up the post of the vice prime minster in 2006. Since then, Somsavat had been wielding authority in the field of foreign affairs. However, he was not elected at the Tenth LPRP Congress and quit the politburo.

In addition to the traditional 5-year National Socio-Economic Development Plan for 2016–2020, the Congress for the first time adopted long-term strategies that included a "Ten-Year Socio-Economic Development Strategy (2016–2025)" and "Vision 2030," a long-term initiative aiming to quadruple the national income. Although the Laotian economy has grown steadily, this growth has been accompanied by less desirable phenomena, including the expansion of income disparity, spread of corruption, concerns over the expansion of China's influence, and an increase in the size of the Chinese immigrant population as well as dependence on direct investment from Chinese enterprises. Accordingly, the aim is now to assuage domestic dissatisfaction with these sudden social transformations. This is because the twin vectors of "integration and relativization" are now being reconsidered from a long-term perspective, while a self-corrective function is operating with respect to the excessive bias toward relations with China.

From a "buffer state" to an agent of Regional Formation II: relations with a changing Vietnam

Although Laos for Vietnam was by the mid-1980s beginning to retreat from its function as a part of a buffer state serving as a kind of breakwater with respect to China and Thailand, Vietnam for Laos had not undergone any major change in the sense of the two countries enjoying a "special relationship" relative to other bilateral relationships. The political and security influence wielded by Vietnam with respect to Laos remains powerful even today. However, as described earlier, with the improvement of bilateral relations between Laos and China, the increased dependence on China of the Mekong River area was remarkable, and it became undeniable that China's political and economic influence was expanding throughout Laos and the entire region. For this reason, the attempt to achieve a balance of forces while calibrating their respective distances from China emerged as an important issue for both Laos and Vietnam.[14]

Even after Laos introduced economic reform and an open-door policy in 1986, the special relationship it had enjoyed with Vietnam began shifting toward becoming an economically viable relationship once China had disappeared as a security threat. In October 1999, Cambodia and Laos agreed with a Vietnamese-led initiative to convene a summit meeting (the CLV Summit) in the Laotian capital of Vientiane, a summit that has been institutionalized as an official meeting since 2004.[15] The CLV Summit is held jointly with the CLVM Summit, which includes Myanmar, and the Ayeyawady-Chao Phraya-Mekong Economic Cooperation Strategy (ACMECS) Summit, which includes the CLVM countries plus Thailand (which entered a Treaty of Amity and Cooperation with Laos in 1992). The ADB's GMS Economic Cooperation Program, as well as the ASEAN regional cooperation frameworks and three CLV countries centered on Vietnam, have combined to establish a system in which East Asian regional cooperation is linked to the GMS, with Laos's neighboring country of Thailand serving as a point of contact (Vorapheth 2007). With this, relations with Laos as an agent of state integration and regional formation are becoming institutionalized as part of the regional order (Table 2.2).

To simultaneously achieve the apparently contradictory tasks of sustainable economic development and the maintenance of a socialist regime, Laos, at the time of the Eighth LPRP Congress in 2006, adopted a state strategy that secured as much as possible the common interests arising from the national collaboration of the CLV countries and systematically positioned ASEAN integration and the ADB-GMS Economic Cooperation Program within its foreign policy as being linked to economic development and state formation.

Laos's Seventh Five-Year National Socio-Economic Development Plan (2011–2015)[16] clearly advocates the policy objective of putting economic considerations above all else and sweeping away the old bureaucratic temperament. Laos's state strategy, in which active participation in sub-regional formation and state formation are mutually intertwined, as mentioned earlier, has three aims. The first is to actively review Laos's bilateral relationships in response to changes in the international political environment since the late 1980s, and particularly to adjust the pivot from a special relationship with Vietnam that has been conscious of China to its development-led multilateral relationships. The second is to strengthen its position as an ASEAN member nation through the solidarity of CLV and to develop a system for acquiring economic profit through regional integration and sub-regional formation mediated by GMS development projects. The third is to make active use of an external support system. With regard to the third of these, the existence of a strong regional economic interest, shared throughout the ASEAN region, in shrinking the regional disparity (the "ASEAN Divide") arising from the accession to ASEAN of the four mainland Southeast Asian states (the CLVM states) represents an important background

Table 2.2 Multilateralism of Mekong region

	Thailand	Vietnam	Laos	Cambodia	Myanmar	China	Other
Greater Mekong Sub-region (GMS)	○	○	○	○	○	○	ADB
Mekong River Commission (MRC)	○	○	○	○	○	△	
ASEAN Mekong Basin Development Cooperation (AMBDC)	○	○	○	○	○	○	ASEAN
Initiative for ASEAN Integration (IAI)	○	○	○	○	○	○	ASEAN
Asian Highway (AH)	○	○	○	○	○	○	ESCAP
Hi-Fi Plan for Private Sector Development (HI-FI Plan)							ESCAP
Forum for Comprehensive Development in Indochina (FCDI)	○	○	○	○			Japan
ASEAN-METI Economic and Industrial Cooperation Committee (AMEICC)	○	○	○	○			ASEAN, Japan

Source: Keisuke Nomoto, "International Cooperation for Development in the Mekong Subregion," *Hokusei Review, the School of Economics*, Vol. 42, No. 2, 2003, p. 76.

Note: △ stands for local governments.

consideration. Amid their exposure to the 1997 Asian currency crisis whose epicenter was in Thailand, the number of ASEAN member countries expanded to 10 thanks to the accession of Laos, Vietnam, Cambodia, and Myanmar. To neglect the internal disparities that became apparent in relation to the initial member countries would have had a negative impact on the cohesive unity of ASEAN and mainland Southeast Asia. For this reason, at the same time as seeking to reach consensus toward development and expansion inside ASEAN, Japan and other advanced countries, notably China, through the active participation of their central governments, provincial governments, and private enterprise, as a part of a regional strategy all at once accelerated their readiness to support infrastructural development in mainland Southeast Asia with a focus on development in the GMS (Menon 2012).[17]

Accordingly, the twin vectors of state "integration and relativization" born out of a process of regional formation in which Laos is an active participant, by making composite use of Laos's bilateral relationships in response to the post-Cold War international environment, CLV solidarity, and the ASEAN framework, rather than creating a conflicting dynamic, can currently be said to have brought about a positive effect on state formation.

Conclusion

In conclusion, I would like to summarize the challenges facing Laos in maintaining its own national security as well as sustainable development alongside regional formation.

With the amelioration of relations with China after 1989, while facing a qualitative transformation in its relations with Vietnam, Laos was able to leverage its active participation in ASEAN integration and cooperative frameworks of multilateral solidarity such as the CLV (under the leadership of Vietnam) and as an agent of sub-regional formation to realize sustainable economic growth and improve its own state autonomy.

Through infrastructure development projects in mainland Southeast Asia, as typified by the ADM-GMS program, Laos has in recent years been expected to play a role as an important hub of regional distribution channels for landlocked countries where routes of land and sea transport had been almost cut off for a long time due to fierce natural environments. As the Mekong region has been proceeding economic integration with infrastructure development, Laos has been regarded as a logistics platform for the transit of goods in the region. In order to facilitate the transit of goods, the member states and Yunnan province signed the Cross-Border Transport Agreement in 2006. Although it takes 2 weeks transportation time from Hanoi to Bangkok by sea route, the transportation time via Laos is now just 3 or 4 days.

However, from a geopolitical perspective, as far as the material conditions of Laos's power, economic influence, and population size are concerned, there appears to have been relatively little fluctuation. Even so, we may point to the following three points as factors underlying the emergence of the "small state as an agent of regional formation."

The first is a change in the international environment. In the context of the changes to the international environment surrounding this region that have taken place since 1989, the importance of military security has receded. Underlying the amelioration of relations between China and Laos, amid the ongoing restoration of relations between China and Vietnam, was the fact that China, in particular, had the political intention of participating peacefully in the regional order, primarily in the economic sectors of trade and investment. The second is the factor of ASEAN regional integration. The deepening and expansion of ASEAN has encouraged a shared understanding of the elimination of intra-regional disparities across the entire region. Third is that, resolution of the Cambodian conflict after the Cold War obtained the important factor in the change in the Mekong region, the period of confrontation in the region was over. In order to keep pace with the deepening of relations with China, the countries of Cambodia, Laos, and Vietnam have deepened their solidarity through the shared state goals of attempting to realize domestic cohesion—i.e., national integration—through economic growth. This was the essential key to establish common objects of regional stability and development.

Against the background of these three factors, in order to achieve coherence in terms of both sub-regional formation and the construction of a state foundation as an international relations actor, Laos has expanded its foreign policy vis-à-vis China and other large states whose influence is rising. Now, how is the coherence of international relations being secured in the disparate dimensions of the national integration of Laos as a small state and regional integration being accomplished through ASEAN regionalism and the ADB-GMS program, which has been actively supported by Japan and China? To put this another way, how has Laos linked its subjectivity as a small state with the opposing forces of "integration and relativization"? Since the end of the 1990s, when the collaborative systems of Laos's economic development strategies and GMS and ASEAN regional integration were first established, Laos has expanded its bilateral cooperative relationships with China and Vietnam. As China's presence has expanded, and the perception of China as a threat has emerged, Laos has spurred its economic development strategy with a principal focus on GMS and ASEAN integration. In this sense, Laos's foreign policy, as in realist alliance theory, rather than the actions of a small state pursuing power for its own national security based on a *logic of consequentiality*, are in fact actions that seek to adjust the ASEAN-centered regional order in a reasonable direction. Through a foreign policy based on a *logic of appropriateness*,[18] by dint of its adjustments to foreign policy in these various dimensions, Laos has obtained a neutrality within international relations. Especially in the context of its bilateral relationship with China, Laos could be regarded as sharing the philosophies of ASEAN and the GMS project without being governed by the correlations of power.

While the international relations of ASEAN and the Mekong region also reflect a structural situation of competition among national interests, by interposing the imagined community of ASEAN, Laos's foreign policy has made it possible to build cooperative relationships as an equal partner with individual countries. In this sense, the existential perception of Laos and the multilateral norms of ASEAN and the CLV framework can be interpreted as being internalized in the sub-regional strategies of China and other large states.

In the areas of international politics and military security in East Asia, the presence of China is becoming even more prominent, and uncertainty is growing with regard to the future involvement of large states such as China in regional formation. Laos is one of the weakest states of all the ASEAN nations in terms of its military force, economic power, and population size. The case of suggests the importance of the role to be played as a buffering agent by the ASEAN regionalism of a federation of small states occupying a central position in an East Asian regional formation.

Notes

1 In the context of international relations theory, Taga (2005) is among the earliest discussions to systematically position sub-regions defined by non-state actors as a key concept for a new international social unit.
2 The discussion by Pholsena and Banomyong (2005), typical of studies that discuss Laos as a buffer state, envisions Laos during the French colonial period of the early nineteenth century and centers on the historical background of Laos as a buffer zone arising out of the power relations between the British colony of Burma and the French colony of Vietnam. In association with infrastructural development in the Mekong region driven by the GMS project, the study focuses on the economic function of Laos as a strategic crossroads from the geopolitical character of buffer states.
3 The Human Development Indicator of UNDP includes life expectancy at birth, expected years of schooling, mean years of schooling, gross national income (GNI) per capita, and literacy level. Every component indicator of Laos is low level among East Asian states. See the website of Human Development Report 2016 (http://hdr.undp.org/sites/all/themes/hdr_theme/country-notes/es/LAO.pdf#search=%27UNDP+Lao +Ranking%27, accessed October 18, 2017).
4 See the website of Ministry of Foreign Affairs in Japan (http://www.mofa.go.jp/region/asia-paci/laos/data.html, accessed October 18, 2017).
5 Apart from Rothstein (1977), the series of research findings collected in Momose (1988) offers another example of a systematic approach to small states from a non-realist perspective, though this discussion deals mainly with small European states.
6 Against theories that seek power correlations in alliances (e.g., Snyder 1997), a series of works by Keohane offers a representative example of liberal institutionalism.
7 For a Japanese discussion of the concept of the sociology of knowledge (*Wissenssoziologie*), see Momose (1988) and Akimoto (2002). This is a central concept for Karl Mannheim.
8 Momose (1988) argues that the actual situation of small states fluctuates over time. From his reading of philosophy and knowledge regarding small states obtained from observation of their contemporary situation, Momose conducted a historical analysis of the structure of international politics and small states. He emphasizes the significance of considering knowledge and ideas about small states that attempt to pursue a neutral position.

9 See, Matsuura (2013).
10 A buffer system has been defined as a system in which "a small political or administrative unit [is] located between and separating two larger opposing powers" (Ingalls 1986: 233). It follows that an analysis of interstate relationships as a system will reveal the attributes of buffer states.
11 That Laos was not a direct partner in China's foreign relations is shown by the timing of the border demarcation treaty eventually signed by Laos and China. During a period when the Sino-Soviet conflict was experiencing major upheavals, China signed major border demarcation treaties with several neighbors including Myanmar and states in Central Asia. Establishing the border between Laos and China, however, had to wait until 1991, once economic relations had begun in earnest (Fravel 2008).
12 Hara (2011) analyzes Laos's geopolitical position, which emphasizes its relations with China, and it is precisely for this reason that he regards the China problem as the most important issue facing Laos. Hara notes that not all problems originate with China, however, and cites' land issues and environmental problems as being among Laos's domestic issues.
13 A variety of problems have emerged simultaneously as the result of (primarily Chinese) foreign direct investment. These include exploitation of resources, urban development, environmental damage associated with rubber plantations and other agricultural developments, and the phenomenon of the "commercialization of sovereignty" through land use rights concessions, as well as social changes associated with a dramatic increase in the Chinese immigrant population.
14 In my interviews with the Laotian government's Ministry of Planning and Investment, all officials emphasized that even if Laotian relations with China were to become closer, Vietnam would continue to remain Laos's most important foreign partner. Nevertheless, foreign study destinations for younger bureaucrats were evenly split between Vietnam and China, and it may be surmised that China is closing the gap with Vietnam in terms of its relative political influence.
15 For the background of the CLV summit meetings, refer to the following website: http://myoceanic.wordpress.com/2013/03/11/the-series-of-summits-will-be-convened-in-laos/, accessed October 18, 2017.
16 *The Seventh Five-Year National Socio-Economic Development Plan*, Approved by the Inaugural Session of the Seventh National Assembly, October 7, 2011.
17 The economic disparity in the expanded ASEAN triggered by the accession to ASEAN of the countries of mainland Southeast Asia, dubbed the "ASEAN Divide," has been raised as a priority issue for the Initiative for ASEAN Integration (IAI). For a detailed discussion, see Menon (2012).
18 The "logic of consequentiality" and the "logic of appropriateness." The former is associated with realism, the latter with constructivism (March and Olsen 1989). The body of research conducted by Acharya (2001) and Ba (2016) is representative of the study of ASEAN from a constructivist perspective. Generally, the constructivist approach makes efforts of the states to for integrating into regional community. According to Acharya, ASEAN can only be a nascent community because common values and norms are not always applied to its decisions for international relations. What Ba called is "the context and process of complex engagement."

References

Acharya, Amitav (2001) *Constructing a Security Community in Southeast Asia*, London: Routledge.
Akimoto, Ritsuo (2002) *Knowledge Sociology and the Contemporary: The Studies of Karl Mannheim*, Tokyo: Waseda University Press (in Japanese).

Amakawa, Naoko, and Norihiko Yamada (eds.) (2005) *Laos: Transformation to the Market Economy under a Single-party Regime*, Chiba: Institute of Developing Economies, JETRO (in Japanese).
Ba, Alice D. (2016) "Who's Socializing Whom? Complex Engagement in Sino-ASEAN Relations," in Amitav Acharya and Richard Stubbs (eds.) *Theorizing Southeast Asian Relations: Emerging Debates*, London and New York: Routledge, pp. 31–52.
Fravel, M. Taylor (2008) *Strong Borders, Secure Nation: Cooperation and Conflict in China's Territorial Disputes*, Princeton: Princeton University Press.
Hara, Yonosue, Norihiko Yamada, and Souknilanh Keola (2011) "Seeking Relations with China," REITI Discussion Paper 11J007 (in Japanese).
Ingalls, Gerald L. (1986) "Buffer States: Outlining and Expanding Existing Theory," in John Chay and Thomas E. Ross (eds.) *Buffer States in World Politics*, Boulder: Westview Press, pp. 231–240.
Keohane, Robert O. (1984) *After Hegemony: Cooperation and Discord in the World Political Economy*, New Jersey: Princeton University Press.
March, James G., and John P. Olsen (1989) *Rediscovering Institutions: The Organizational Basis of Politics*, New York: Free Press.
Matsuura, Masataka (2013) "Introduction: The Comparative Study of Asianism in Extended Regional Perspective," in Masataka Matsuura (ed.) *What Does Asianism Speak of?:Memory, Power, and Values*, Kyoto: Minerva Shobo, pp. 1–67 (in Japanese).
Menon, Jayant (2012) *Narrowing the Development Divide in ASEAN: The Role of Policy* (ADB Working Paper Series on Regional Economic Integration, No. 100), Manila: Asian Development Bank (https://www.adb.org/sites/default/files/publication/30403/reiwp-100.pdf, accessed October 18, 2017).
Momose, Hiroshi (1988) *Small States: Historical Philosophy and Reality*, Tokyo: Iwanami (in Japanese).
Morikawa, Yuji (2012) *The New Political Dynamics of Regional Formation in East Asia: A Spatial Theoretical Analysis of Regionalism*, Tokyo: Kokusai Shoin (in Japanese).
Morikawa, Yuji (2014) "The Laotian Border State and International Relations," CEAKS (Creation of East Asian "Kyousei" Studies) Discussion Paper No. 12 (in Japanese).
Nomoto, Keisuke (2003) "International Cooperation for Development in the Mekong Sub-Region," *Hokusei Review, the School of Economics*, 42 (2): 71–88 (in Japanese).
Oba, Mie (2004) *The Road to the Formation of the Asia-Pacific: Regionalism and the Search for Identity in the "Marginal" States of Japan and Australia*, Kyoto: Minerva Shobo (in Japanese).
Pholsena, Vattahana, and Ruth Banomyong (2005) *Laos: From Buffer State to Crossroads?*, Chiang Mai: Mekong Press.
Rothstein, Robert L. (1977) *The Weak in the World of the Strong: The Developing Countries in the International System*, New York: Columbia University Press.
Snyder, Glenn H. (1997) *Alliance Politics*. Ithaca, New York: Cornell University Press.
Storey, Ian (2011) *Southeast Asia and the Rise of China: The Search for Security*, London: Routledge.
Stuart-Fox, Martin (2005) *Politics and Reform in the Lao People's Democratic Republic*, London: Asia Research Center.

Taga, Hidetoshi (2006) "Regional Grand Designs and Regionalism: The Old and New Layers of the Westphalian System—From a Comparative View of Asia and Europe," in Shingo Nakamura, Hidetoshi Taga, and Hideo Kojimoto (eds.) *Deciphering the European and East Asian Communities from a Sub-Regional Perspective: A Grand Design Comparison of the European North Sea Region and the East Asian Trans-border Region*, Hirosaki: Hirosaki University Press, pp. 81–88 (in Japanese).

Vorapheth, Kham (2007) *Laos: la redéfinition des stratégies politiques et économiques, 1975–2006*, Paris: Indes Savants.

Yamamoto, Takehiko (2007) "Japan's 'East Asian Community Diplomacy' and Community Vision: Between Bilateralism and Multilateralism," in Takehiko Yamamoto and Satoshi Amako (eds.) *New Regional Formations,* Tokyo: Iwanami Shoten, pp. 145–162 (in Japanese).

3 Alternative Mekong regionalism from the perspective of regional hegemony and civil society

Seiichi Igarashi

Introduction

The Mekong River stretches 4,900 kilometers across five countries—namely, Cambodia, Laos, Myanmar, Thailand, and Vietnam—as well as part of China. Rich in a diverse range of resources and home to approximately 250 million people, this international river basin is often referred to as the Mekong region. In addition to the five countries mentioned above, the geographical scope of the region often includes China's Yunnan province and sometimes the Guangxi Zhuang Autonomous Region.

In October 1988, the Prime Minister of Thailand, Chatichai Choonhavan, used his inaugural speech to advocate the transformation of Indochina (the Mekong region) "from battlefields to marketplaces."[1] His call was realized in short bursts following the signing of the Paris Peace Accords in October 1991, which finally ended the Cambodian Civil War that had embroiled Vietnam and China since 1970. In October 1992, the Greater Mekong Sub-region (GMS) Economic Cooperation Program—an initiative of the Asian Development Bank (ADB)—was launched in order to develop the Mekong region. One of its flagship projects, namely, the construction of three economic corridors (the East-West, North-South, and Southern Economic Corridors), appears well on its way toward completion. Since the 1990s, at least ten other international cooperative programs or organizations related to the Mekong region have been established. Some experts have dubbed this upsurge of regional regimes the "Mekong Congestion."[2] The Mekong region is currently referred to as the "New Asian Frontier," and attracts many corporations from around the world seeking investment opportunities. To provide their own corporations with logistics assistance and encourage regional economic development, the governments of developed countries have invested enormous amounts of money into both "hard" and "soft" aid in this region.[3]

The actors propelling the Mekong region forward are not limited to the government and corporations; the emergent civil society taking on the identity of Mekong should be recognized as the "third entity" involved in the region's construction. Indeed, civil society actors have formed close-knit networks that transcend borders and participated in policymaking related to the Mekong

Congestion as a mouthpiece for local residents. They have also engaged in various advocacy activities to express concerns, particularly in regard to the negative impact of rapid development. As such, they have become a new political force for an "alternative" Mekong regionalism that expedites the correction of "state-centric" or "market-oriented" Mekong regionalism.

Pioneering a new theoretical perspective that incorporates civil society and empirically examining the activities of civil society actors, this chapter reveals the unexplored realities and functions of the civil society initiating an "alternative" Mekong regionalism from below and uncovers a new political phase in the region that has been overlooked in previous studies.

The first section examines the theoretical framework, which includes the bottom-up regionalism by civil society. This section introduces the perspective of regional hegemony that various actors—including civil society—struggle over the content of regionalism by integrating and revising two theoretical approaches that belong to relfectivism in international relations: the New Regionalism Approach (NRA), which attempts to overcome the existing Euro- and state-centric approaches; and the neo-Gramscian approach (NGA), which analyzes the world order and civil society from the view of the intellectual leadership exercised by dominant forces in global capitalism. The second section traces the origin of top-down Mekong regionalism to the 1950s and demonstrates its characteristics. Providing an overview of the Mekong Congestion since the 1990s, the third section explains how it is predominantly oriented toward "neoliberal regionalism" and "state-centric regionalism." The fourth section explores the activities of civil society networks attempting to correct regionalism from above that gives priority to economic development. The final section analyzes the reality of regional hegemony in the Mekong region. More specifically, it explores the participation of civil society actors in regional policymaking and examines the effectiveness and limits of regional civil society.

Theoretical approaches to regionalism and civil society

From rationalism to reflectivism

Earlier theoretical approaches in regionalism research include David Mitrany's functionalism, Ernst Haas's neofunctionalism, and Béla Balassa's stages of economic integration (Mitrany 1966; Haas 1958; Balassa 1962). Belonging to the rationalism school of thought, these mainstream theories fell into decline as regional integration in Europe began stagnating after the 1970s. Although some of these studies have been inherited by theories on interdependence and international regimes, interest in regionalism dissipated over time.

Research on regionalism began flourishing again in the 1990s, when Europe revived its integration process (Keohane and Hoffmann 1991; Bulmer and Scott 1994). This revival in regionalism studies saw the emergence of new approaches, including: supranational institutionalism, which partly inherited neofunctionalism; liberal institutionalism, which focuses on the state's role in building a single market; and multi-level governance (MLG), which emphasizes institutions and actors (Garrett and Tsebelis 1996; Moravcsik 1993; Marks 1993). These mainstream theoretical approaches used Europe as the subject of analysis and were mainly interested in examining the formal institutions and integration of markets.

A "second wave" of regionalism began to spread across the globe in the 1980s. In contrast with earlier regionalism theories, this "second wave" exposed the limitations of the mainstream theoretical approaches that predominantly focused on analyzing Europe and gave birth to a new theoretical approach—the NRA, which broke the mold of the teleological thinking that set the status of Europe as the desirable endpoint. A novel reflectivist approach stemming from critical international relations theory, NRA empathetically differentiates the "new regionalism" developed after the Cold War from the "old regionalism" formed under the structure of the Cold War (Hettne 2003: 23–24). According to the NRA, a region is not an *a priori* object but rather a social construction in which both the state and various non-governmental actors are involved (De Lombaerde, Söderbaum, Langenhove, and Baert 2010: 738). The NRA identifies five characteristics of the new regionalism: first, it was formed within the context of globalization and multipolar world order; second, its development process is from the bottom up—that is, it is voluntarily initiated within the region; third, it is open, reflecting deepening interdependence; fourth, it is an inclusive and multidimensional process; finally, it involves various non-governmental actors (Hettne 2003: 23–24).

From the perspective of counteracting the state-centered rationalist approach, the NRA places emphasis on regionalism from below as initiated by civil society actors. Focusing on the actual process of regionalization, the NRA acknowledges that economic, social, and cultural networks are expanding much more rapidly than formal political cooperation. Moreover, it not only regards the state (government) as an actor promoting regionalism from above, but also the market (corporations) and civil society as actors promoting regionalism from below (Schulz, Söderbaum, and Öjendal 2001: 250–255). Although the market and civil society are both considered part of regionalism from below, the NRA does not necessarily consider them complimentary; rather, it acknowledges that they often tend to oppose each other.

For instance, adopting Karl Polanyi's "double movement" as the framework for analysis, Björn Hettne classifies the current market-oriented globalization as the "first movement," and the diverse political forces attempting to re-embed this into the society as the "second movement." Hettne argues that the new regionalism forms part of this "second movement," as does the accompanying formation of a regional transnational civil society associated with the post-Westphalian international order (Hettne 2003: 30–38). However, the new regionalism as the "second movement" does not necessarily fulfil the role of an opposing force against economic globalization. James Mittelman notes that most new regionalisms are of the neoliberal type and serve as a sort of "negative regionalism" that propels economic globalization (Mittelman 2000: 112–116). Opposition to this type of neoliberal regionalism often comes from the lower levels of the region's transnational civil society, which Mittelman refers to as forces of "transformative regionalism" (Mittelman 1999: 47–48).[4] Actors related to transformative regionalism generally share awareness with movements on the global level, such as the "anti-globalization movement," "anti-corporate globalization movement," and "alter-globalization movement" (George 2004; Juris 2008). In a normative sense, the NRA considers neoliberal regionalism as "evil" and the opposing transnational civil society's resistance as "good" (Marchand 2001: 210).

Although vividly aware of the role of civil society, the NRA is still in its infancy with respect to its theoretical and empirical analyses of civil society.[5] In particular, civil society's directionality cannot simply be described as an opposition to market-driven neoliberal regionalism. The actual policymaking process requires that we pay close attention to both the various identities of civil society that cannot be reduced to anti-neoliberalism and civil society's relationship with the states, as well as the regional agencies, organizations, and institutions in which the states and their sovereignty continue to play a crucial role ("state-centric regionalism").[6]

Regional hegemony

Viewed through the lens of neo-Gramscian perspective such as the concept of hegemony, another figure of regionalism and civil society emerges that differs from that of the NRA. Although realism also analyzes international relations using the concept of hegemony, this work defines hegemony from the perspective of the relative power that a state possesses. This approach uses hegemony to express the materialistic (military and economic) predominance of one powerful state over others (Keohane 1984: 31; Miller 1996: 324). Regional frameworks can be regarded as a tool to gain hegemonic power over a particular state (Hurrell 1995: 50–53). Essentially, realism focuses on interstate relations and neglects civil society and its relation to the state. As such, the hegemony in realism has nothing to do with civil society. Neo-Gramscians approach hegemony from a different perspective. For instance, Robert Cox defined hegemony as "a structure of values and understandings about the nature of order that permeates a whole system of states of non-state entities" (Cox 1996: 151). Stephen Gill defined it as "a condition where a high degree of compatibility exists in the world order between more dominant states and forms of civil society" (Gill 1996: 15).[7]

In the context of globalization of the market economy that has progressed since the end of the Cold War, the dominant hegemony imposed by the global "historical bloc" comprising the state and the market (powerful corporate forces and their allies in government, as well as other various networks promoting globalization), has become pervasive worldwide to seek to maintain the status quo of the global economy. At the same time, however, a counter-hegemony from below is emerging in the realm of transnational or global civil society (Cox 1999: 10–12; Gill 2000: 133–139). With the development of new regionalism, this hegemonic order can be observed in regional agencies, organizations, and institutions in which the state and capital form the dominant hegemony of neoliberalism.

Among the major characteristics of neo-Gramscian thought is its understanding that (global/transnational) civil society uniquely and ambiguously corresponds to the state or economy. For instance, Robert Cox and Stephen Gill assert that counter-hegemony is formed in transnational and global civil society in opposition to the hegemonic power of world capital and the ideology of neoliberalism toward eradicating inequality, environmental harm, and proliferation of weapons. At the same time, it can act to encourage the stability of the status quo where the influence of the state and corporations—which comprise a powerful hegemonic force—has permeated (Cox 1999: 10–11,13; Gill 2000: 139; Butko 2006: 91–93). Neo-Gramscians thus reveal the existence of the ambivalent aspects of the relationship between civil society and the state/economy often overlooked by existing studies of global/transnational civil society and the NRA.

This ambiguity of civil society indicated by neo-Gramscians leads us to another perspective. In addition to work on the opposing dynamics of civil society, which the NRA focuses on as transformative regionalism, there is also increasing research on the cooperative phase—which has drawn the interest of rationalist approaches such as MLG. The latter can be called "participatory regionalism" (Acharya 2003). This form of regionalism can be seen accompanying the deepening of regionalism in all regions to varying degrees. This movement is probably most advanced in Europe, where many civil society actors are involved in policymaking at the supranational level (European Union) and supplement a so-called "democracy deficit." Likewise, participation by civil society actors in policymaking is gaining momentum in Southeast Asia (Igarashi 2018: 91–125). However, with regional agencies exerting strong control from above, participatory regionalism can turn into "regional corporatism" or "corporatist regionalism" (Rüland 2012), in which civil society can be placated by the dominant hegemony and the act of participation loses its significance.

Nonetheless, it should be noted that neo-Gramscians tend to overlook the hegemonic struggles over various issues and identities—such as human rights, gender equality, protection of migrant workers, peace, and environmental protection—that empirical civil society attempts to realize. This is largely because neo-Gramscians, mindful of the process of capital accumulation, focus on the relationship between the form of the state (such as welfare, liberal, and neoliberal types) and civil society. Indeed, studies that have analyzed the integration of Europe using the NGA are predominantly interested in topics like employment, labor relations, and the social relations of production (Bieler and Morton 2001; Overbeek 2003).[8]

Taking these points into consideration, this chapter understands the region-forming process as a transnational hegemony project in which a variety of ideas, discourses, and norms related to the regionalism created by both state and non-state actors compete, conflict, and cooperate. Neoliberalism currently dominates, and the forces of capital hegemony alter the shape of states while eroding civil society at the regional and global levels. As such, despite being restricted by

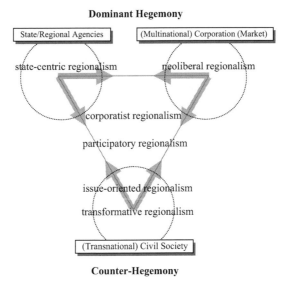

Figure 3.1 Hegemonic phases in regionalism
Source: Created by the author.

Note: Issue-oriented regionalism may be placed in a different position depending on the field and actors. Its placement is therefore provisional.

the economic structure and captured by the dominant hegemony, civil society can create a counter-hegemony and become a site for the radicalization of various issues often distorted or overlooked in neoliberal and state-centric regionalism. This is due to its nature as a transformative and issue-oriented entity ("issue-oriented regionalism"). It should be noted that this hegemonic struggle can often emerge through civil society's relationships with the neoliberal-oriented regional agencies and institutions upon which the state exerts its authority (see Figure 3.1). Thus, a focus on transformative and issue-oriented regionalism initiated by civil society will reveal a new political phase of the transnational hegemonic struggle over a variety of issues at the regional level—a phase likely to be overlooked by the NRA and NGA.

The origin of Mekong regionalism and its development

Mekong regionalism originated in the 1950s. In 1951, a plan was considered by the Economic Commission for Asia and the Far East (ECAFE) for the economic development of the lower Mekong basin. In May 1952, the first report on the development of Mekong River, titled *The Development of the International River Mekong: Technical Problems Related to Flood Control and Water Resources Development*, was published (Molle, Foran, and Floch 2009: 4). Based on the ECAFE's recommendations, the Committee for Coordination on the Lower

Mekong Basin (also known as the Mekong Committee or MC) was established in September 1957. MC members included Cambodia, Laos, Thailand, and Vietnam. While the MC's statute declared that its mission was to "promote, coordinate, supervise, and control the planning and investigation of water resources development projects in the Lower Mekong basin," it did not specify what role the MC would play (MC 1957). Nonetheless, under the influence of the United States Bureau of Reclamation in the Department of the Interior, the ECAFE prepared a development plan intended to transform the Mekong region into the "Tennessee Valley Authority of Asia" (Goh 2007: 25; Matthews and Geheb 2015: 3) and pushed forward with the construction of large-scale dams that would generate hydroelectric power, which was believed to contribute to the region's economic development (Cosslett and Cosslett 2014: 126–129). In addition to its ability to implement plans, the ECAFE had interests in various areas—such as agriculture, industry, electricity, transportation, flood control, salt damage, and human-made structures (MC 1970). At any rate, Mekong regionalism took on development orientation from the outset.

In establishing the MC, a unique agreement was reached as the development of the Mekong Basin moved forward. Article 5 of the statute required the participation of all member states at meetings and unanimity among members (MC 1957). By giving each member a *de facto* veto right, Article 5 clarified the MC's intention to promote the development of Mekong while respecting the sovereignty of member countries and their respective national interests. The stipulation on unanimity would later be inherited by the present Mekong River Commission (MRC), which took over the functions of the MC.

It was also during this period that the phrase "Mekong spirit" began to be used. In 1964, for instance, U Nyun, the executive secretary of the ECAFE, first described Mekong spirit as follows:

> . . . the four riparian countries assisted by the United Nations and the co-operating countries are working together as true partners in progress in the true Mekong spirit of collective responsibility, friendly co-operation and understanding firmly determined to achieve a fuller and richer life for all people who dwell in the Mekong basin.
> (Mirumachi 2015: 119)

The following is an excerpt from an MC annual report, which is often referred to as the nexus of the Mekong spirit:

> The Mekong Development Project "seeks the comprehensive development of water resources of Lower Mekong Basin, including mainstream and tributaries, in respect of hydroelectric power, irrigation, flood control, drainage, navigation improvement, watershed management, water supply and related developments, for the benefit of all people in the Basin, without distinction as to nationality, religion or politics."
> (Cosslett and Cosslett 2014: 104)

Le-Huu and Nguyen-Duc point out that the phrase "Mekong spirit" began acquiring many different meanings over time, including that of a shared vision and mutual understanding (Le-Huu and Nguyen-Duc 2003: 50–51). Although many interpretations exist, the simplest definition of Mekong spirit is "mutual respect between riparian states and a willingness to engage in dialogue toward cooperative river basin management" (Hirsch and Jensen 2006: 19).

However, the MC ceased its operation and activities in April 1975, when the capitals of Cambodia and South Vietnam fell toward the end of the Vietnam War. In January 1978, Thailand, Laos, and Vietnam established the Interim Mekong Committee (IMC) to replace the MC.

The IMC's mission was described as "promoting the development of water resources of Lower Mekong Basin to increase agricultural and power production to meet effectively the needs for reconstruction and growing development of the countries of Indochina and the growing economic development needs of Thailand" (IMC 1978). Similar to the MC, the IMC initiated a small number of dam construction projects and built facilities for freshwater fishery and irrigation (JICA Research Institute 1996: 27–28). However, during a discussion of the conditions for Cambodia to regain its membership to the committee, a dispute between Thailand and Vietnam erupted over the issue of the use of Mekong River water, eventually forcing the IMC to suspend its operation in April 1992 (Makim 2002: 11).

The deepening of Mekong regionalism from above: "Mekong Congestion"

Although the IMC suspended its activities, numerous regional cooperative frameworks have been formed in rapid succession since the end of Cambodian Civil War. This multi-layered formation is sometimes called the Mekong Congestion (Table 3.1).

Following the signing of the Paris Accords in October 1991, the ADB invited representatives from China, Myanmar, Laos, Thailand, Cambodia, and Vietnam to the Office of the Secretary in Manila in March 1992. During this meeting, the ADB proposed a research project on cross-border economic cooperation. In October 1992, the first Ministerial Conference was held to discuss the possibility of economic cooperation among the six countries, during which the GMS Economic Cooperation Program was launched (ADB 1993: xiv–xvi). Its policy area initially included Cambodia, Laos, Myanmar, Thailand, Vietnam, and China's Yunnan province; the Guangxi Zhuang Autonomous Region was added in 2005.

Among the unique features of the GMS Economic Cooperation Program is its "two plus principle," which replaces the stipulation on unanimity characteristic to Mekong regionalism and demonstrates its commitment to utilitarian pragmatism. Two conditions are required to implement the program: first, each project must involve at least two countries (a purely sub-regional project); second, the project has to be a national one that will benefit the whole region (a national project with sub-regional dimension) (Ishida 2008: 119). The consent of the

Table 3.1 Summary of Mekong Congestion

Name	Year	Participating countries	Leadership	Main interests	Main source of funds
		Thailand / Laos / Vietnam / Cambodia / Myanmar / China / Japan / United States		Agriculture / Irrigation / Food (Security) / Environment / Water resource (Security) / Investment/Trade / HRD/Education / Infrastructure/Transportation / Energy / Telecommunication / ICT/Knowledge/Science / Industry/business support / SME / Tourism / Public health / Disaster / Poverty reduction / Fishery / Navigation / Local community / Migration / Exchange	
MC	1956–1975	○ ○ ○ ○	ECAFE	○ ○ ○ ○	ADB, AUS, CAN, EC countries, JPN, UN, US
IMC	1978–1992	○ ○ ○	Laos, Vietnam, Thailand	○ ○ ○ ○	ADB, AUS, CAN, EC countries, JPN, UN, US
GMS	1992	○ ○ ○ ○ ○ ○	ADB, Japan	○ ○ ○ ○ ○	ADB, GMS countries, JPN, US
MRC	1995	○ ○ ○ ○ △	Cambodia, Laos, Vietnam, Thailand	○ ○ ○ ○ ○ ○	ADB, EU countries, JPN, UNDP, US, WB
AMBDC	1995	○ ○ ○ ○ ○ ○	Singapore, Malaysia	○ ○	ASEAN countries
MI	1996	○ ○ ○ ○ ○ ○	Cambodia, Laos, Vietnam, Thailand, Myanmar, China	○ ○ ○ ○ ○ ○ ○ ○ ○	ADB, CHN, JPN, MRC, NLD, NZ, KOR, THA
AMEICC	1998	○ ○ ○ ○ ○ ○ ○	ASEAN, Japan	○ ○ ○ ○ ○	ASEAN, JPN
ET	2000	○ ○ ○ ○	Cambodia, Thailand	○ ○ ○ ○ ○	THA
ACMECS	2003	○ ◇ ○ ○	Thailand	○ ○ ○ ○ ○ ○ ○ ○ ○	THA
CLV-DTA	2004	○ ○ ○	Cambodia, Vietnam	○ ○ ○ ○ ○ ○ ○ ○ ○	ADB, JPN, UNDP
MJS	2009	○ ○ ○ ○ ○ ○	Japan, Cambodia, Laos, Vietnam, Thailand, Myanmar	○ ○ ○ ○ ○ ○ ○ ○ ○ ○	JPN
LMI	2009	○ ○ ○ ○ ○ ○	US	○ ○ ○ ○ ○ ○ ○ ○ ○ ○ ○	ADB, AUS, EU, JPN, KOR, NZ, US, WB
LMRDC	2015	○ ○ ○ ○ ○ ○	China	○ ○ ○ ○ ○ ○ ○ ○	CHN

Source: Created by the author from various sources.

Note: ○=Participated ◇=Participated later △=Observer. The abbreviations that don't appear in the text represent followings: AUS=Australia; CAN=Canada; CHN=China; EC=European Community; EU=European Union; HRD=Human resource development; ICT=Information and communication technology; JPN=Japan; KOR=South Korea; NLD=the Netherlands; NZ=New Zealand; SME=Small and medium-sized enterprises; THA=Thailand; UN=United Nations; UNDP=United Nations Development Programme; US=the United States; WB=World Bank.

other four countries is not required if and when these two conditions are met and the two countries involved agree. The program started with a focus on six categories: namely, transportation, communication, energy, human resources, environment, as well as trade and investment (ADB 1993: xiv–xvi). The ADB aims to make the GMS "the new frontier in the East Asian miracle" and raise the average individual income of member countries by three to four times by 2020 (Parnwell 2001: 236).

The MRC was established as a successor organization of the MC and IMC in April 1995. Its members included Thailand, Cambodia, Laos, and Vietnam, while China and Myanmar served as observers. According to the Agreement on the Cooperation for the Sustainable Development of the Mekong River Basin reached in April 1995, the MRC's areas of cooperation were irrigation, hydroelectric power generation, navigation, flood control, fishery, timber floating, recreation, and tourism. Unlike the GMS Economic Cooperation Program, the MRC's decision was unanimous (MRC 1995).

With the urging of the Singaporean Prime Minister, Goh Chok Tong, and support of the Malaysian Prime Minister, Mahathir Mohamad, the ASEAN Mekong Basin Development Cooperation (AMBDC) was established in December 1995. The AMBDC's main objective is to narrow the economic development gap between ASEAN members and promote economic cooperation with a focus on transport, trade, and human resource development. One of the AMBDC's major projects is the Singapore–Kunming Rail Link (SKRL) (Morizono 2002: 19–20). The ASEAN has a unique decision-making process—aptly named the "ASEAN way"—based on the principle of consensus and non-interference in domestic affairs. The AMBDC abides by this method. Although China joined the AMBDC, Japan and South Korea have yet to agree to the invitation. The AMBDC is important as a forum for policy dialogue and allows the "ASEAN and China to foster sub-regional economic development and cooperate on poverty reduction."[9]

The Mekong Institute (MI) is an intergovernmental organization whose main objective is to develop human resources. The New Zealand government established the MI in northern Thailand's Kohn Kaen University in February 1996, as a development aid project aimed for the GMS countries. The MI has been managed by the governments of six GMS countries since 2003. Granted the status of an intergovernmental organization by the Thai government in August 2007, the MI offers diverse programs with a focus on supporting the development of small- to medium-sized corporations.[10]

The ASEAN Economic Ministers (AEM) and Ministry of Economy, Trade, and Industry (METI) of Japan (AEM-METI) established the AEM-METI Economic and Industrial Cooperation Committee (AMEICC) in November 1998. A sub-organization of AEM-METI, the AMEICC discusses topics such as economic cooperation and collaboration between Japan and ASEAN countries. It also implements economic and industrial cooperation projects within the ASEAN based on direction provided by the AEM-METI.[11]

A development cooperation program first proposed by Cambodia, the Emerald Triangle (ET) was officially established in June 2000. ET member regions include the Ubon Ratchathani and Sisaket Provinces of Thailand; Champasak and Salavan Provinces of Laos; as well as the Preah Vihear, Stung Treng, and Oddar Meanchey Provinces of Cambodia. The main objective of this program is facilitating cooperation between countries with regard to agriculture and tourism (Hatsukano 2012: 32–34).

The Ayeyawady-Cho Phraya-Mekong Economic Cooperation Strategy (ACMECS) is a cooperative framework first proposed by the Thai Prime Minister, Thaksin Shinawatra, at the ASEAN Special Meeting in 2003. This group is comprised of Laos, Myanmar, Thailand, Vietnam, and Cambodia. Its objective is to realize balanced development in the Mekong sub-region.[12] The ACMECS focuses its effort on developing the frontier regions of its member countries, encouraging the creation of cross-border micro-regions.

The Cambodia-Laos-Vietnam Development Triangle (CLV-DTA) began with a proposal made by Cambodia's Prime Minister, Hun Sen, in 1999. An unofficial first three country summit was hosted based on this proposal, and an agreement to cooperate in developing the Development Triangle was reached. Vietnam has since taken a *de facto* leadership role in the CLV-DTA. At the 10th ASEAN Summit in 2004, leaders of the three countries approved and officially launched the Socio-Economic Development Master Plan for the CLV-DTA, which includes 13 regional/local governments (Shiraishi 2013: 2–7). The CLV-DTA's objective is to encourage cooperation in areas such as transportation, infrastructure, energy, and trade/investment. Similar to the AMBDC, the CLV-DTA is a proponent of the ASEAN way. For instance, Chapter IV of the Master Plan states that "[t]he implementation of cooperation projects in the Development Triangle follows the 'consensus' principle." It further states that "Cambodia and Vietnam as well as Laos and Vietnam have had agreements on bilateral cooperation mechanisms and policies in various areas," and "these mechanisms and policies have been increasingly improved based on sovereignty respect by concerned parties, advancing towards regional integration" (CLV-DTA 2004).

The Mekong-Japan Summit (MJS) began in November 2009, during the Hatoyama administration. The "Tokyo Declaration" and 63 articles of the "Action Plan" were unveiled at the first Summit. The five countries participating in the Summit—Thailand, Vietnam, Laos, Cambodia, and Myanmar—shared their intention to reinforce the three pillars: first, the comprehensive development of the Mekong region, including overcoming issues in the environment, climate change, and vulnerabilities (the beginning of the initiative was called "A Decade toward the Green Mekong."); second, the promotion of cooperation and exchange; and third, the establishment of a "partnership toward a common prosperous future." This summit is held annually and has served to strengthen the relationships between Japan and the Mekong countries.[13]

In July 2009, the United States (US) established the Lower Mekong Initiative (LMI) as a multinational partnership for cooperation within the sub-region. This initiative—which includes Cambodia, Laos, Myanmar, Thailand, and Vietnam—serves as a platform to address cross-border and interdisciplinary issues together.[14] It focuses on agriculture, food security, connectivity, education, energy security, environment, water, gender, as well as health and hygiene. It has been regarded as a symbol of the United States' return to Asia.[15]

Finally, the Lancang-Mekong River Dialogue and Cooperation (LMRDC) is a newly launched cooperation framework under the leadership of China. The participating countries are the same as those in the ADB's GMS. Its objectives include maintaining peace and stability in the region and promoting development and prosperity.[16] Its first foreign ministers' meeting was held in April 2015, followed by the first conference in November 2015. Although details are unclear, Zhang Jinfeng—a former Chinese ambassador to Cambodia—stated that their focus would be on infrastructure development, economy, trade, investment, water resources, environmental protection, poverty reduction, and agricultural development.[17]

From the perspective of international relations, the Mekong Congestion can be described as "overlapping regimes" or a "regime complex." Some experts posit that overlapping regimes can promote international order while providing fertile ground for conflicts and disputes (Adachi 2011). With regard to the Mekong Congestion, there is a view that the creation of the sub-region and accompanying establishment of various frameworks have been helpful in building trust within the region (Nomoto 2002: 99). For instance, the Chair's Statement from the Second Mekong-Japan Foreign Ministers' Meeting in 2009, included the following:

> The Ministers noted with satisfaction the existing multi-sectorial cooperation mechanisms, which have been complemented each other in promoting development and prosperity in the Mekong region, such as the Mekong River Commission (MRC), the ASEAN-Mekong Basin Development Cooperation (AMBDC), the Greater Mekong Subregion Cooperation (GMS), the Ayeyawady-Chao Phraya-Mekong Economic Cooperation Strategy (ACMECS), the Mekong-Ganga Cooperation with India (MGC) and the recently conducted U.S.–Lower Mekong Ministerial Meeting. The Ministers reaffirmed their commitments to enhancing the role of each framework and the importance of further promoting high-level dialogues as well as other consultations between all stakeholders in order to achieve better cooperation in the region.[18]

In terms of conflicts and disputes, concerns over a struggle for leadership among the sovereign states including those from outside the region may exist.[19] Indeed, the requests of GMS countries that the ADB adjust various sub-regional economic frameworks from as early as 1996, are a testament of this sentiment (ADB Institute and IOM 2005: 10). Japan is attempting to gain economic benefit from the Mekong region through the GMS (especially the development of the East-West Economic Corridor), AMEICC, and MJS. The US is seeking to penetrate the Mekong region through the LMI. Meanwhile, China may be aspiring to incorporate the Mekong region through the GMS (especially the South-North Economic Corridor), AMBDC, and the newly established LMRDC. This leadership struggle is also seen among the ASEAN countries. Indeed, Thailand is trying to expand its influence in the Mekong region through the ACMECS. In response to Thailand's actions, Singapore and Malaysia—which are not in the basin—are taking the lead in establishing the AMBDC. Moreover, as if competing with Thailand's increasing clout in the Mekong region, Vietnam urged the development of the West-East Corridor at the ASEAN Summit and led the CLV-DTA (Ogasawara 2005: 54–56). As realists insist, ambitious states within and outside the Mekong region seem to use regional frameworks as a tool to gain hegemonic power in regional order. The struggle over economic gain in the Mekong region might be explained by using the perspectives of postclassical realism, as Swe and Chambers did (Swe and Chambers 2011). From these perspectives, it can be said that placing long-term economic benefit over short-term security, the states are seeking to maximize their economic power though regional frameworks in the Mekong region.

While it remains to be seen whether the Mekong Congestion will provide order and stability, there is a strong possibility that some kind of coordination can be achieved. For example, although most frameworks generally work independently, each donor in the MJS has sought to exchange information informally in order to gain as much knowledge about the activities as possible.[20] Moreover, the arrangements of various frameworks have already been up for discussion at a LMI meeting.[21]

Table 3.1 also reveals that areas of interest vary from one framework to another. Many frameworks are focusing on economic issues. The most significant tendency of the Mekong Congestion is "development-oriented regionalism" and neoliberal regionalism centered on market-driven development and investment driven against the backdrop of economic globalization. It is also evident that respecting the sovereignty of member countries has been prioritized by some regimes, as indicated in the ASEAN way, and that some countries—including those from outside the region—exercise their leadership and engage in hegemonic struggle with other countries (state-centric regionalism).

The expansion of Mekong regionalism from below by civil society: transformative and issue-oriented regionalism

In response to the neoliberal and development-oriented regionalism in the Mekong region, an increasingly conspicuous movement in the sphere of civil society has emerged seeking to correct Mekong regionalism from above. Forming cross-border networks in various areas, a wide variety of civil society actors have strategically built cooperative or oppositional relationships with the state and other international agencies (Table 3.2). An alternative Mekong regionalism from below is gradually being realized with the activities of these actors, and a Mekong (civil) public sphere is emerging. This section discusses several organizations as examples of this emergent public sphere and examines their characteristics and activities in detail.

Table 3.2 Civil society networks interested in the Mekong Region

Name	Year	Head Office	Main Interests
NGO Forum Cambodia (NFC)	1980	Phnom Penh	Development, environment, land
Toward Ecological Recovery and Regional Alliance (TERRA)	1986	Bangkok	Environment, development
Women's Education for Advancement and Empowerment (WEAVE)	1990	Chiang Mai	Gender, human rights, education
Mekong Regional Law Center (MRLC)	1995	Bangkok	Legal support, human trafficking, Environment
World Wildlife Fund (WWF) Greater Mekong	1995	Bangkok	Environment
Living River Siam (LRS)	1999	Chiang Mai	Development, minority ethnic groups
Mekong Basin Agricultural Research Network (MEKARN)	2001	Ho Chi Minh City	Agriculture
Mekong Migration Network (MMN)	2003	Chiang Mai	Immigration
Mekong Program on Water Environment and Resilience (M-POWER)	2004	Laos*	Environment
Sustainable Mekong Research Network (SUMERNET)	2005	Bangkok	Development
Mekong Plus	2007	Ho Chi Minh City	Community development, gender
River Coalition of Cambodia (RCC)	2007	Phnom Penh	Environment
Mekong Energy and Ecology Network (MEE Net)	2008	Bangkok	Energy, environment
Save the Mekong Coalition (SMC)	2009	Bangkok	Development, food, fishery
Mekong Legal Advocacy Institute (MLAI)	2009	Chiang Mai	Legal support
Japan International Volunteer Center (JVC)	1980	Tokyo	Agriculture, environment, HR development
FoE Japan	1980	Tokyo	Development, environment
Shanti Volunteer Association (SVA)	1981	Tokyo	Education, refugees
International Rivers	1985	State of California	Environment, food, human rights
World Vision	1987	Tokyo	Human trafficking
NGO Forum on ADB	1991	Manila	Development, environment
Mekong Watch (MW)	1993	Tokyo	Development, environment
EarthRights International (ERI)	1995	Washington DC	Environment, human rights, labor, women
Mekong Club	2013	Hong Kong	Human trafficking

Source: Created by the author.

Note: The head office of Mekong Program on Water Environment and Resilience (M-POWER) indicates the location of the coordinator.

Toward Ecological Recovery and Regional Alliance/ Foundation for Ecological Recovery

The Foundation for Ecological Recovery (FER) is one of the organizations playing a key role in strengthening cross-border solidarity in the region's civil society. Taking a stance against "top-down" Mekong regionalism, the FER has submitted various policy recommendations.

A nonprofit organization established in Bangkok, Thailand, in 1986, the FER's institutional mandate is "to conduct research and produce research based documents regarding ecological issues with the perspective of sustainable development and greater participation of local communities within the Mekong Region."[22]

In 1991, the FER established Towards Ecological Recovery and Regional Alliance (TERRA), with the objective of creating a new development paradigm through the promotion the networks between non-governmental organizations (NGOs) and people's organizations (POs) in the Mekong region, as well as by criticizing the neoliberal discourse advanced by organizations like the ADB (Dore 2003: 9). TERRA has evidenced numerous interests, including: coal-fired power plants in Myanmar, the Dawei deep seaport/industrial park development project, Mekong River mainstream/tributary dams in the Lower Basin, the Salween river, the Nam Theun 2 Dam, the MRC, tree planting, Mekong rapids blasting, nuclear power, the Samut Prakarn wastewater management plan, agrofuel, and biofuel.[23]

TERRA's magazine, *Watershed*, explains its opposing stance to neoliberal regionalism as follows:

> The Asian Development Bank (ADB) continues to promote and finance dam construction, river basin hydropower plants, and electricity transmission development under its Greater Mekong Subregion initiative. Dam projects supported by the Bank are proceeding on the basis of feasibility studies and environmental impact assessments that ignore or dismiss all major impacts of these dams on national economies, rivers, forests, and the livelihoods of local communities, as well as the disastrous experience of hydroelectric dams within the Mekong region-including those dams financed by the ADB itself.
> (TERRA 1997: 38)

Nette, a TERRA staff member, has also stated,

> For over two decades Japanese Official Development Assistance [ODA] to Thailand has promoted large-scale infrastructure development and free market growth. The result, hydroelectric dams, highways and industrial development, has meant big profits for Japanese corporations at the expense of rural communities and the environment. Now Japan's ODA is repeating the same formula in the Mekong region.
> (Nette 1997: 45)

Since its inception, TERRA has targeted regional development agencies. Their reason for this is threefold. First, the resolution of the Cold War revived developmental plans conceived during the 1960s, and the bulk of the responsibility to carry out those plans fell on the IMC and ADB. Second, given that many regional advocacy NGOs had partnered with Western international groups in the past, it was more appropriate and feasible to target agencies supported by Western countries. Finally, the steps to influence governments within the Mekong region were extremely limited. As such, their early advocacy activities concentrated on opposing the IMC, which promoted dam construction. Moreover, since the ADB began their programs in earnest in the 1990s, TERRA's advocacy activities also came to include large-scale infrastructure development projects (Hirsch 2007: 194–195).

The general stance of TERRA against the MRC is observable in numerous documents. For instance, the statement submitted to the Thai government by 30 NGOs, including TERRA, in April 1995, emphasized the following points: (1) They support the principle of equal cooperation among the riparian countries of the Mekong River Basin through the equal participation of Mekong citizens; (2) they oppose the influence of the dam-building industry in the discussion, planning, and determination of the objectives of the 1995 Agreement; (3) they oppose the Mekong water diversion plans of the Government of Thailand; and (4) sustainability that benefits all members of society and does not damage the natural environment must be realized.[24] Furthermore, in her criticism, TERRA director, Premrudee Daoroung, stated that, "the MRC has failed to facilitate an open discussion to ensure a more equitable and sustainable use of the Mekong River" (TERRA 2007a). These discourses indicate that TERRA emphasizes sustainable and participatory regionalism in Mekong regionalism.

Thus far, TERRA have criticized the MRC's lack of appropriate involvement, frequently referring to the Agreement on the Cooperation for the Sustainable Development of the Mekong River Basin reached in April 1995, which established the MRC.[25] Article 7 of the Agreement declares that the MRC would "make every effort to avoid, minimize, and mitigate harmful effects that might occur to the environment, especially the water quantity and quality, the aquatic (ecosystem) conditions, and ecological balance of the river system, from the development and use of the Mekong River Basin water resources or discharge of wastes and return flows." TERRA have demanded that the MRC respect Article 7 and promote the sustainable management and development of the Mekong River. Dams with which TERRA is concerned in terms of their environmental effect include: Pak Beng, Luang Prabang, Xayabouri, Pak Lay, Xanakham, Pak Chom, Ban Koum, Lat Sua, Thakho, Don Sahong, Stung Treng, and Sambor (TERRA 2011).

The ADB is another international agency in the region targeted by TERRA. An example of this is the case of the Samut Prakarn wastewater management project, which involves a wastewater treatment facility located at the Chao Phraya River estuary in South Bangkok that began operating in 1986. Funded by the ADB and Japan's ODA, the project has attracted a broad range of criticism from local residents. As TERRA notes, the project has contradicted many of the ADB's stated policies: an insufficient environmental assessment, involuntary resettlement, lack of social assessment, lack of investigation of the effect on fisheries, effects that exacerbate poverty, an insufficient economic cost analysis, and a superficial project evaluation process (TERRA 2001).

TERRA has also expressed concern regarding Nam Theun Dam 2 from the outset. Located in the province of Khammouane in Central Laos, Nam Theun Dam 2 is a hydroelectric power project supported by the ADB and World Bank. While its main objective was to acquire foreign currency through the sale of electricity to Thailand, it was criticized as a "poverty reduction dam." Early on, TERRA pointed out that the construction of this dam would completely alter the flow of the Xe Bang Fai River, thereby severely affecting the abundant fishing resources that support the food security of several hundred local communities and 50,000–120,000 residents (TERRA 2004a).[26] In fact, Tomomi Higashi, a member of Mekong Watch, a Japanese NGO, noted that there was no long-term plan in place to recover the livelihoods of the local residents forced to relocate as a result of the construction of the reservoir. She further noted that there has already been massive damage to the fishing resource, as well as a loss of agricultural land in the Lower Basin where the dam discharges water (Higashi 2013).

Mekong Energy and Ecology Network

TERRA's sister organization, the Mekong Energy and Ecology Network (MEE Net), was established in 2008 and focuses on energy issues. The MEE Net's objective is to "monitor the energy sector and address the region-wide energy problem by developing an 'energy network' and to develop analyses and strategies that are effective in challenging mega-infrastructure within the sector"[27] because the "rush for cheap electricity and profits has led to a situation where the negative impacts of large-scale energy projects are disproportionately and indiscriminately passed onto local communities" in the Mekong region.[28] Its vision is to create energy development that is "democratic, sustainable, transparent, economically rational, appropriate to the environment, and socially just."[29]

The MEE Net is unique in that it serves as a cross-border network. Founded in 2009 and based in Bangkok, its coordinating team began working toward supporting its partners in other states, formulating policy recommendations, and facilitating communication and collaboration between partners (Sunchindah and Theeratham 2014: 4). Its affiliated organizations currently include five NGOs in Myanmar, two in Cambodia, three in Thailand, three in Vietnam, as well as several Western international NGOs active in the Mekong region (see Table 3.3). Moreover, the MEE Net is currently trying to form a network with individual activists in China (Sunchindah and Theeratham 2014: 5).

The MEE Net focuses on three themes.[30] The first theme is "Know Your Power," which signifies that increasing the knowledge of its partners regarding the power sector would improve their abilities and foster a more democratic and participatory process for all stakeholders (MEE Net 2012). The second focus

88 Seiichi Igarashi

Table 3.3 MEE Net affiliated organizations

Myanmar	ACTIVITIES
	Renewable Energy Association Myanmar (REAM) (1999)
	Burma River Network (BRN) (1992)
	Promotion of Indigenous and Nature Together (POINT) (2012)
	Karen Environmental and Social Action Network (KESAN) (1997)
Cambodia	The NGO Forum on Cambodia (1980)
	3S Rivers Protection Network (3SPN) (2001)
Thailand	Towards Ecological Recovery and Regional Alliance (TERRA) (1986)
	Mekong Commons (1986)
	Palang Thai (2003)
Vietnam	Center for Sustainable Development of Water Resources and Adaptation to Climate Change (CEWAREC) (2008)
	Green Innovation and Development Centre (GreenID) (2011)
	People and Nature Reconciliation (PanNature) (2004)
Mekong Region	Service Centre for Development Cooperation (KEPA) (1985)
	EarthRights International (1995)
	The Heinrich Böll Stiftung (1997)
	International Rivers (1985)
Foundation	Siemenpuu Foundation (1998)

Source: Created by the author based on information from http:// www.meenet.org/our-partners/, accessed October 13, 2017. Numbers in parentheses indicate the year of establishment.

pertains to "Transboundary Issues." Propelled by the development of the GMS, the growth of the power sector is having a transboundary impact. The MEE Net is attempting to study this impact on neighboring countries. Finally, the "Flow of Capital" signifies the MEE Net's ambition to monitor the connection between capital and profits with respect to the power sector (MEE Net 2013).

In comparison to the advocacy-oriented TERRA, the MEE Net concentrates its efforts on capacity building within its partner organizations. To this end, it provided a training workshop on energy in 2009, and another on electric power systems, energy planning, renewable energy practices, and consumer-side distribution control system (DMS) in 2010. It also hosted two international conferences: "Know Your Power" in 2012, and "Transboundary Issues" in 2013. Through these activities, the MEE Net effectively offers a wider range of support to its partners and other civil society organizations (Sunchindah and Theeratham 2014: 14, 23).

Save the Mekong Coalition

As a result of increasing public concern on the effect of dams on the lives of several million people, food security, and migratory fishing resources, 25 civil society actors—including TERRA—formed a loosely connected coalition called the Save the Mekong Coalition (SMC) in March 2009. Its objective is twofold: (1) to direct public attention to the risks associated with dam construction in important international rivers and (2) persuade policymakers to adopt sustainable and peaceful methods for satisfying the demand for energy and

Table 3.4 Non-governmental organizations participating in the Save the Mekong Coalition

Cambodia	Rivers Coalition in Cambodia (RCC)
Thailand	Towards Ecological Recovery and Regional Alliance (TERRA)
	Living River Siam, formerly Southeast Asia Rivers Network (SEARIN)
	Thai People's Network for Mekong
	Palang Thai
	Focus on the Global South
	Salween Watch
Vietnam	Center for Water Resources Conservation and Development (WARECOD)
	PanNature
Myanmar	Burma Rivers Network (BRN)
China	China Development Brief
	Green Earth Volunteers
Outside the Mekong Region	
Australia	TEAR Australia
	Oxfam Australia
	Manna Gum, Australia
	Mekong Monitor Tasmania
United States	International Rivers
	The Mangrove Action Project (MAP)
	Bank Information Center (BIC)
	EarthRights International
Canada	Probe International
Holland	Both ENDS
Norway	The Association for International Water Studies (FIVAS)
United Kingdom	The Corner House, UK
Uruguay	World Rainforest Movement
Japan	Mekong Watch

Source: Created by the author based on information from http://www.savethemekong.org/link.php?page=1&initP=1&finP=3, accessed June 10, 2015.

water.[31] By September 2014, the number of organizations involved in the SMC had risen to at least 45 (see Table 3.4).[32] The SMC differs from other anti-dam construction movements in that it has successfully garnered the understanding and support of the fast-growing middle class in Thailand, enabling it to hold a photo exhibition in downtown Bangkok and carry out a petition campaign using postcards (Doi 2013).

Immediately following its inception, the SMC began advocacy activities related to dam development in the Mekong River—including a petition campaign on the risks associated with 11 of the dam projects in the Mekong mainstream (SMC 2009). In October 2009, it delivered 23,110 signatures to the prime ministers of Cambodia, Laos, Thailand, and Vietnam.[33] The SMC also demanded the suspension of the Xayabouri dam project in Laos in October 2010, asserting that the MRC's coordination had been insufficient and ill-prepared, as well as decrying the lack of transparency and consultation with the residents (SMC 2010). In November 2013, the SMC also demanded the suspension of the Don Sahong dam project in Laos based on its significant impact on the environment (SMC 2013). Through these activities, the SMC has successfully gained the attention of a wide range of audiences, highlighting the risks associated with neoliberal regionalism.

Mekong Migrant Network

The upsurge of economic development programs obviously allows for easier cross-border travel. Indeed, the flow of workers from neighboring countries into Thailand is experiencing remarkable growth (MMN and AMC 2008: v).

In the Mekong region, there is no binding international treaty related to labor migration or the protection of migrant workers. Instead, less binding memorandums of understanding (MOUs) have been signed between the receiving country, Thailand, and the sending countries—Laos (October 2002), Cambodia (May 2003), and Myanmar (June 2003). The main objectives of these MOUs are to establish the proper procedures for migrant workers, deport migrant workers who overstay their work period to their home countries, provide appropriate protection for migrant workers, as well as prevent illegal work and human trafficking.

While these MOUs have resulted in progress on the registration of unskilled workers, the process seems geared toward the control/management of workers and is not sufficiently utilized for protecting the rights of migrant workers. Indeed, unskilled workers have been exposed to harsh conditions in the receiving country. One of the leaders of the NGO community, William Gois, has noted several important issues—including the harsh treatment of migrant workers, non-recognition of domestic work, human trafficking, workers being deprived of the freedom of movement and association, non-recognition toward family reunification, and lack of support for workers returning to their home countries (Gois 2007: 126–128). Generally, migrant workers in Southeast Asia are viewed solely as temporary/transient workers, and there is a lack of awareness toward their social integration or inclusion. Consequently, a variety of civil society networks have emerged to protect the rights of these migrant workers.

The Mekong Migrant Network (MMN) is representative of the civil society networks concerned with labor migration in the Mekong region. It originated as a result of a joint project launched in September 2001 by the Asian Migrant Center (AMC), a Hong Kong-based NGO, that involved more than 20 research partners present in the Mekong region. The birth of MMN in October 2003 was a direct result of this project. The MMN comprises two NGOs from Myanmar, six from Cambodia, five from China, two from Laos, 19 from Thailand, and five from Vietnam (see Table 3.5). The MMN's objectives are to monitor government policies regarding migrants in the Mekong region, study government migrant policies, conduct policy recommendation activities for the recognition of the basic human rights of migrant workers and their families, as well as offer training workshops to develop skills.

Table 3.5 Mekong Migrant Network members (as of March 2015)

Myanmar	Labour Rights Defenders and Promoters (LRDP)
	88 Generation Peace and Open Society (Labour Department)
Cambodia	Cambodian Women for Peace and Development (CWPD)
	Cambodia Human Rights and Development Association (ADHOC)
	Cambodian Women's Crisis Center (CWCC)
	Coordination of Action Research on AIDS and Mobility Cambodia (CARAM Cambodia)
	Legal Support for Children & Women (LSCW)
	Banteay Srei
China	Migrant Workers' Education and Action Research Centre (MWEAC)
	Ruili Women and Children Development Centre
	Association for Women's Capacity Building and Community Development in Yunnan
	Women Migrant Education Research Professional Association
	Yunnan Health and Development Research Association
Laos	Faculty of Social Sciences, National University of Laos
	Lao Women Union
Thailand	MAP Foundation
	Thai Action Committee for Democracy in Burma (TACDB)
	National Catholic Commission on Migration
	EMPOWER Foundation
	Federation of Trade UnionsBurma (FTUB)
	Foundation for AIDS Rights (FAR)
	Foundation for Women
	Friends of Women Foundation
	Foundation for Education and Development (formerly Grassroots HRE)
	The Human Rights and Development Foundation (HRDF)
	Institute for Population and Social Research (IPSR), Mahidol University
	Maryknoll ThailandOffice for Migrants at Immigration Detention Center in Bangkok
	Mekong Ecumenical Partnership Program-Christian Conference of Asia (MEPPCCA)
	Pattanarak Foundation
	Peace Way Foundation
	Raks Thai Foundation
	Shan Women's Action Network (SWAN)
	Yaung Chii Oo Workers Association (YCOWA)
	STUDIO XANG
Vietnam	Center of Research and Consultancy for Development (CRCD)
	Southern Institute of Sustainable Development (SISD)
	Education & Psychology Association, Ho Chi Minh City
	The Applied Social Work Center
	Resource Center for Management and Sustainable Development (MSD)
Hong Kong	Asian Migrant Centre (AMC)

Source: Created by the author with information from http://www.mekongmigration.org/?page_id=14, accessed October 13, 2017.

Although the aforementioned MOUs have laid out an official immigration process in the Mekong region, the reality is that the majority of migrant workers use unofficial means. Illegal migrants are often a target of "Arrest, Detention, and Deportation (ADD)." This prompted the MMN to initiate a study of the ADD policy in September 2004. Consequently, the MMN began an ADD campaign, engaging in the systematic monitoring of ADD-related incidents, policy dialogue with policymakers, and cooperation with other organizations for more effective advocacy activities. The MMN also set up a website focusing on ADD in December 2012.[34] Moreover, in October 2013, the MMN submitted a report on ADD policies and their implementation in Thailand as part of their broader recommendations to the government of Thailand and the other countries involved (MMN 2013).

Regional hegemony in the Mekong region

Increased participation in the "Mekong Congestion"

The multitiered development of cooperative frameworks and the increasing empowerment of civil society in the region have consequently expanded opportunities for civil society actors to participate in the formal policymaking process. In the following section, the ADB's GMS Economic Cooperation Program, the MRC, and the MI are examined.

(a) Asian Development Bank's Greater Mekong Sub-region Economic Cooperation Programs

The ABD recognized the importance of NGOs early on, approving their role in the 1987 policy document entitled "The Bank's Cooperation with Non-Governmental Organizations." In this document, the ADB acknowledged that cooperation with NGOs is a means to supplement its various activities.[35] The ABD's experience in cooperating with NGOs would later be reflected in its GMS Economic Cooperation Programs.

In February 2001, for instance, the ADB established its NGO and Civil Society Center with an aim of strengthening cooperative relationships between civil society actors.[36] Furthermore, the ADB has sought to share its vision on poverty reduction and sustainable development by signing an MOU with the international environmental NGO, World Wildlife Fund (WWF).[37] Since 2005, the WWF has been responsible for a project called the Biodiversity Conservation Corridor Initiative under the core environmental program of the GMS (ADB 2006: 29; ADB 2007: 20). In 2010, the ADB piloted a regional NGO anchor in the GMS intended to strengthen relations with civil society (ADB 2012: 32).

The organizational structure of the GMS is presented in Figure 3.2. The forums and working groups at the bottom of this figure are those in which civil society actors are especially involved in the GMS. This currently includes the Sub-regional Transport Forum, Working Group on Agriculture (WGA), Sub-regional Trade Facilitation Working Group, Tourism Working Group, Regional Power Trade Coordination Committee, Working Group on Environment, Working Group on Human Resource Development, Sub-regional Investment Working Group, and Sub-regional Telecommunications Forum (ADB 2010: 40).

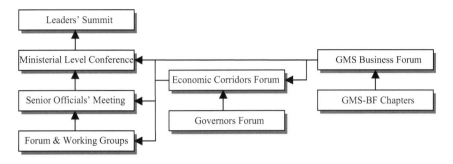

Figure 3.2 GMS organizational framework.
Source: Created by the author based on data from the Asian Development Bank (ADB), *Strategy and Action Plan for the Greater Mekong Subregion East-West Economic Corridor*, Mandaluyong City: Asian Development Bank, 2010, p. 43.

Among these, the WGA and WGE have enjoyed the active participation of civil society actors including the WWF at their annual meetings. Among the flagship projects of the GMS Economic Cooperation Program that began in 1998, the framework involved in the East-West Economic Corridor has also offered more participation opportunities for non-governmental actors, including civil society actors. Its consultation process involves governmental officials from the member states as well as representatives from the private sector, NGOs, and development partners (ADB 2010: 14).

NGOs have also been participating in individual projects more actively. For instance, in the GMS railroad repair project in Cambodia between 2011 and 2012, civil society actors supported local residents affected by the project during the consultation process. Civil society actors also played an important role in supporting the resettlement plan and other projects during the GMS Corridor City Development Project in Indonesia. Civil society actors were also the main entity to implement the GMS Southern Coastal Corridor Project intended to prevent the spread of HIV/AIDS and human trafficking. Finally, in 2013, civil society actors managed and maintained the local irrigation infrastructure for the GMS East-West Economic Corridor Agriculture Infrastructure Sector Project in Laos (ADB 2014: 50, 62, 69).

(b) Mekong River Commission

In 1998, the MRC published a booklet, "Public Participation in the Lower Mekong Basin," advocating the "bottom-up" process (MRC 1998). Awareness of resident participation within the MRC increased to such an extent that the strategic plan for 2006–2010, for example, promoted "stakeholder participation, through close communication and collaboration with civil society, NGOs, and emerging River Basin Organizations" (MRC 2006: ix) (see Table 3.6). In reality, however, the level of participation by civil society actors remained

Table 3.6 Changes in the MRC's Strategic Plan

1999–2003	2001–2005	2006–2010
Project approach: Direction was organized around sector programs and projects. MRC interventions were focused at the project level.	Program approach: A shift in strategic direction with focus moving toward a basinwide and program approach. MRC interventions were through the provision of policy and technical advice from a basinwide perspective. Each NMC had its own Strategic Plan 2001–2005. A high priority was given to knowledge generation. Cooperation between MRC and China on data sharing during flood seasons began in 2002.	Strategic goals were reoriented toward support to propoor development. Updated program structure in a crosscutting program and sector program matrix, underpinned by the Basin Development Plan process. <u>Engagement with civil society and the private sector</u>

Source: Mekong River Commission (MRC), Strategic Plan 2011–2015, 2010, p. 3.

Note: Underline added by the author.

low (Dore and Lazarus 2010: 365–366). For instance, an independent study on the MRC stated the following:

> The Strategic Plan describes the importance of public involvement, public opinion, civil society and NGOs in ensuring the success of integrated water resources management of the Mekong River Basin. However, it is the impression of the RT [Review Team] that the present attitudes and practices in the MRC regard the member governments as the primary, if not the only, stakeholders that should be involved with the MRC. A clear commitment and strategy for involving civil society is lacking.
> (Hawkesworth et. al. 2007)

The awareness of the need for cooperation with diverse stakeholders started growing when Jeremy Bird became the chief executive officer of the MRC in April 2008 (Hirsch 2008: 41). This is especially evident in the new initiatives launched under the Lower Basin Development Plan in 2008, in which civil society organizations were considered "a vehicle to reach the interests of the wider population, particularly more marginalized groups" (MRC 2010a: 4). Indeed, all current MRC programs (Agriculture and Irrigation Program, Basin Development Plan Program, Climate Change and Adaptation Initiative, Drought Management Program, Environment Program, Fisheries Program, Flood Management

Alternative Mekong regionalism 95

and Mitigation Program, Information and Knowledge Management Program, Initiative on Sustainable Hydropower, Integrated Capacity Building Program, and Mekong Integrated Water Resources Management Project) include civil society actors as stakeholders.[38]

In 2008, the Regional Stakeholder Forum was launched to renew the involvement and commitment of stakeholders and the public in the MRC and Basin Development Strategy (BDP) process. The first Regional Stakeholder Forum was held in Vientiane in March 2008, followed by the second in Chiang Rai in October 2009, the third in Vientiane in July 2010, and the fourth in Siem Reap in November 2014 (MRC 2008; MRC 2009; MRC 2010b; MRC 2014). The Regional Stakeholder Forum has enabled civil society actors to participate in regional-level policymaking.

(c) Mekong Institute

The participation of civil society actors has been increasing within the MI as well. For example, the Mekong Forum has been held every two years since 2011. It aims to create an open, informal, and supportive environment to bring together delegates from a variety of organizations—including private and non-profit, governmental and intergovernmental, civil society, research and academic institutions, as well as development partner agencies (MI 2011b: i). In fact, it has welcomed the participation of diverse stakeholders, including representatives of civil society actors. A more recent example is the Regional Multi-Stakeholder Policy Consultation Workshop on Cross-Border Contract Farming held in September 2015, in which related government ministries, provincial authorities, contracting companies, farmer/producer associations, and NGOs participated.[39]

Formed in collaboration with the US Agency for International Development (USAID) in June 2015, the Lower Mekong Food Security Database is another good example of NGO participation. It seeks to enhance collaboration among donors, national governments, and other development organizations in food security, as well as agriculture projects in Cambodia, Laos, Myanmar, Vietnam, and Thailand.[40] Many of its 567 partner organizations are NGOs.[41]

The aforementioned MMN has built a collaborative relationship with the MI. For instance, it participated in the policy dialogue that the MI hosted on labor migration and made recommendations on issues regarding migrant policies and the unfair treatment of migrants (MI 2007). Furthermore, in November 2008 and December 2009, the MMN and MI conducted training on the managing of migrant workers for policymakers and those who implement them in the countries of the Mekong River Basin (MI 2009). Nonetheless, the management ability of staff and the departments involved in immigration still leaves much to be desired. The civil society actors participating in this segment have thus played an advocacy role to raise the awareness of staff regarding the rights of migrants.[42]

Since 2001, the MMN has also participated in the experts' meetings hosted by the Labor Migration and Care Program, a three-year project the MI began with support from the New Zealand government. During one such meeting, it was pointed out that the current policies on labor migration are outdated and bear little in common with the Cebu Declaration signed by ASEAN Leaders in January 2007. This Declaration calls on the countries of origin and destination to ensure the dignity of migrant workers (MI 2011a: 20). Given the fact that the Mekong Congestion discounts the issue of labor migration while the MOUs initiated by the states tend to emphasize migrant management, the participation of parties from civil society has resulted in a program that takes the importance of the protection of migrants' rights into account.

Participatory or corporatist regionalism?

While the aforementioned examples of civil society's increasing participation in regional-level policymaking give the impression of developing participatory regionalism, they actually indicate the presence of hegemonic control and conciliation over civil society. For instance, Achara Banjongprasert, who has observed water-related governance in the Mekong region, criticizes that the process for NGO participation in the formal intergovernmental forum only occurs after the project has already been proposed or the decisions made. In other words, civil society actors participating within the "top-down" and state-centric water resource governance merely play the role of "giving the green light" or "rubber stamping" when it comes to projects (Banjongprasert 2013: 10–11).

With regard to the GMS, Oxfam's Australian study has also highlighted that despite actors other than the ADB and government officials having participated in the consultation process of certain projects, many of these consultations were superficial, and the participating international organizations and civil society groups were limited to those approved by the ADB. In fact, radical organizations such as TERRA and the SMC—which promote transformative regionalism— have continuously requested an amendment to the ADB's policies from the outside, while cooperative organizations like the WWF and MMN are partners of the ADB (ADB 2013: 32). Moreover, the residents most affected by the diverse GMS projects were found to be virtually unaware of those projects (Ransley, Cornford, and Rosien 2008: 73). According to AsiaDHRRA, Binadesa, and PhilDHRRA, which studied the ADB's policy process, "there are no concrete mechanisms or steps where [civil society organizations] can provide feedback, though the ADB stresses that all the processes have participatory components." As such, they asserted that the involvement of civil society actors should not be limited to post-project review, but occur in the planning process (AsiaDHRRA, Binadesa, and PhilDHRRA 2010: 49).

The MRC has been criticized for its state-centric regionalism. For instance, during its Environment Program in 2001–2005, the MRC's senior environmental specialist, Ian Campbell, stated that the MRC is controlled by the governments and does not have the power to tell the governments what or what not to do (Woods 2005: 18). As Hirsch points out, the MRC "has a relatively weak role in governing water-related decisions within the Mekong River Basin" and "national interests as articulated by member governments take precedence over basin-wide considerations" (Hirsch 2012: 158). This can thus be said to reveal the stark reality that the MRC is restrained by the hegemony of the sovereign states (Ransley, Cornford, and Rosien 2008: 73). This weakness of MRC as a regional organization also makes it difficult to control the region's large hydropower dam project, which is essentially a joint endeavor between the private sector and state agencies. Consequently, the construction of the dam is progressing in a context of deepening regional economic integration and is largely shaped by a measured degree of neoliberal water resource development and energy security government policies (Middleton, Grundy-Warr, and Li 2013: 230).

As in the case of the GMS Economic Cooperation Program, critics have argued that participation in the MRC has similarly lost its meaning. Although diverse stakeholders have participated in the Regional Stakeholder Forum since 2008, as described earlier, the MRC "maintains its control over who is deemed a significant stakeholder, who is invited to attend, who is invited to speak, and whose commentary is published in final proceedings." Indeed, at the third forum, the presentation by WorldFish, an NGO invited to present on fisheries in relation to the BDP program, was cancelled as soon as the group presented an analysis that was extremely critical of the MRC's Strategic Environmental Assessment (SEA) of the effect of mainstream hydroelectric dams (Hirsch 2012: 160).

This phenomenon has also been observed in environmental assessments. For example, the MRC entrusted the International Centre for Environmental Management (ICEM) with the SEA, which was conducted in four phases (scoping, baseline assessment, impact assessment, and avoiding and mitigating) over a period of 16 months from May 2009. During the course of this assessment, the ICEM consulted more than 60 line agencies, 40 NGOs, and approximately 20 international development organizations. Its final SEA report pointed out a variety of negative effects of the dam project (International Centre for Environmental Management 2010: 7). Nevertheless, the dam construction went ahead without further review. Hamazaki has called attention to the fact that the SEA of the mainstream dam construction project does not include the feedback that should be gathered following the evaluation of environmental effects. In other words, the SEA simply served to predict the effects of the dam construction and present options for avoiding or alleviating them (Hamasaki 2014: 105). As such, reviewing or making changes to the plan was never intended—the dam construction was a foregone conclusion from the outset. NGOs are thus demanding a more open and transparent dialogue with the MRC (RCC 2007; SMC 2012).

Although the participation of a wide variety of stakeholders has increased, it is an undeniable fact that the current governance of the Mekong region demonstrates certain characteristics of corporatist regionalism by top-down dominant hegemony. Analyzing the governance of the GMS Economic Cooperation Programs and MRC mainly from the viewpoint of multi-stakeholder platforms (MSPs), Dore claims that "no claim is made that all 'earn the label' of MSP" (Dore 2007: 206). Thus, an effective framework for including civil society actors has yet to be developed.

Conclusion

Taking the perspective of reflectivism in international relations and unearthing the activities of civil society, this chapter has explored a new political dimension of Mekong regionalism: hegemonic struggles among various actors, including civil society, over projects related to Mekong regionalism.

Called the Mekong Congestion, various collaborative frameworks in the Mekong region are being implemented from above by a diverse range of states and international organizations. Meanwhile, Mekong regionalism from below is currently being realized as the growing civil society networks show increasing interest in diverse issues related to the Mekong Congestion and Mekong regionalism, such as the environment, development, and labor migration. As a result, state-centric and neoliberal regionalism initiated from above by the state and capital, as well as an alternative regionalism proposed from below by civil society, are competing over how the Mekong region should be formed and developed. Civil society's counter-hegemony has attempted to correct the form of regionalism advanced by the dominant hegemony. Meanwhile, the dominant hegemony has expanded its corporatist regionalism under the guise of participatory regionalism and sought to absorb civil society.

Similar to other regions, the Mekong region is reinforcing neoliberal regionalism in the context of economic globalization. Multinational companies have advanced into the region, especially in the four developing Mekong countries, at an accelerating rate to fight over the 200 million consumers. The flow of people, products, and money in the Mekong region has thus occurred at an increasingly rapid pace, making the issue of economic growth even more critical. Consequently, the region is becoming more entrenched in the system of new international division of labor.

Such economic growth will also place strain on the demand for energy. Estimating that the energy demand in Southeast Asia will increase some 80% by 2035, a 2013 International Energy Agency (IEA) report forecasts the promising expansion of hydroelectric power in Cambodia, Laos, Myanmar, Thailand, and Vietnam (IEA 2013: 1, 39). The destruction of the ecosystem and involuntary resettlement of local residents remains a significant concern if dam construction projects for meeting the energy demand continue.

Furthermore, the infrastructure projects and penetration of corporations brought about by the Mekong Congestion will further encourage the cross-border movement of people and labor. However, there is currently no effective cooperative framework to ensure the fair treatment and protection of migrant workers, and no end to the many ADDs to which the MMN calls attention. There are also significant human right issues facilitating the spread of human trafficking.

The voices of civil society must be heard and their participation ensured in order to eliminate these negative aspects of state-centric and neoliberal regionalism and realize a Mekong regionalism backed by sustainability, people-oriented growth, and social justice.

Acknowledgements

This study is supported by the Japan Society for the Promotion of Science (JSPS) Grant-in-Aid for Scientific Research (C) (Grant No. 15K03311, FY2015-FY2018, The New Phase of Mekong Regionalism: Regime Congestion and Transnational Public Sphere from "below") and the Ministry of Education, Culture, Sports, Science, and Technology (MEXT) Grant-in-Aid for Scientific Research on Innovative Areas (Research in a proposed research area) (Grant No. 16H06551, FY2016-FY2020, Civilizations and Global Networks: From the Ecosphere to the Globalization of Thought, Economy, and Movement).

Notes

1 https://apnews.com/3cd9a748b284afa8c300c665551cb935, accessed October 13, 2017.
2 The Asian Development Bank (ADB) is attributed as the first to use this term.
3 For example, a meeting with the leaders from the Mekong region (Cambodia, Laos, Thailand, Myanmar, and Vietnam) was held in Tokyo in July 2015. Prime Minister Shinzo Abe proposed the "New Tokyo Strategy 2015" through the Ministry of Foreign Affairs and announced his intention to invest JPY 750 billion in Official Development Assistance (ODA) (https://www.mofa.go.jp/mofaj/s_sa/sea1/page1_000117.html, accessed October 13, 2017).
4 Von Bülow is one of the few researchers studying transformative regionalism. She meticulously examined transformative regionalism led by civil society actors opposing neoliberal regionalism promoted by the North American Free Trade Agreement (NAFTA) and El Mercado Común del Sur (MERCOSUR) (von Bülow 2010).
5 As Hettne, one of the editors of a five-volume tome on the NRA, eloquently notes, "…our project, in spite of good intentions to the contrary, has been too state-centric and too focused on formal organizations rather than pinpointing the processes of more informal organization that take place on the ground" (Hettne, Inotai, Sunkel 2001: xxxii).
6 However, there is an awareness as regards the relationship with the state. For instance, Hettne points out that "to overcome the Westphalian, state-centered 'old' regionalism, a strong civil society at the regional level is needed" (Hettne 2003: 37).
7 The quoted portion is in an introduction in the Japanese translation.
8 Taking this topic further, Nakamura discerns the superiority of the dominant hegemony while recognizing that European integration is a form of multidimensional network governance. He indicates the formation of transnational hegemony blocs composed of diverse forces, which attempt to rearrange the European capitalism to accommodate global competitive conditions while partially involving certain actors in civil society (Nakamura 2005: 41).
9 http://asean.org/asean-economic-community/asean-mekong-basin-development-cooperation-ambdc/overview/, accessed October13, 2017.
10 Interview with Ms. Phornphan Srikhatthanaprom, a labor migration project coordinator at MI. on September 11, 2012 in Khon Kaen, Thailand.
11 http://www.ameicc.org/site/about, accessed October 13, 2017.
12 http://www.tica.thaigov.net/main/en/aid/40616-Ayeyawady-Chao-Phraya-Mekong-Economic-Cooperation.html, accessed October 13, 2017.
13 https://www.mofa.go.jp/mofaj/area/j_mekong_k/s_kaigi/j_mekong09_sg.html, accessed October 13, 2017.
14 https://www.lowermekong.org/about/lower-mekong-initiative-lmi, accessed October 13, 2017.

15 On this topic, in 2009, then US Secretary of State, Hilary Clinton, stated, "I want to send a very clear message that the United States is back, that we are fully engaged and committed to our relationships in Southeast Asia" (https://2009-2017.state.gov/secretary/20092013clinton/rm/2009a/july/126271.htm, accessed October 13, 2017).
16 http://news.xinhuanet.com/english/2015-04/06/c_134127704.htm, accessed October 13, 2017.
17 http://www.globaltimes.cn/content/949016.shtml, accessed October 13, 2017.
18 https://www.mofa.go.jp/region/asia-paci/mekong/fm0910/statement.html, accessed October 13, 2017.
19 Research studies on this topic include those of Noda (2012) and Shiraishi (2012).
20 Interview with an anonymous officer, Ministry of Foreign Affairs of Japan, on October 2, 2017, in Tokyo, Japan.
21 Interview with an anonymous officer, Ministry of Foreign Affairs of Japan, on January 20, 2015, in Chiba, Japan.
22 http://www.terraper.org/web/en, accessed October 13, 2017.
23 http://www.terraper.org/web/en, accessed October 13, 2017.
24 Statement on Cooperation for the Sustainable Development of the Mekong River Basin, 4 April 1995, Chiang Rai, Thailand.
25 For example, refer to the following: TERRA 2007b.
26 The negative effect on the Asian elephants, which are already endangered, is also a cause for concern (TERRA 2004b).
27 http://www.meenet.org/about-us/who-we-are/, accessed October 13, 2017.
28 http://www.meenet.org/425-2/background-to-energy/, accessed October 13, 2017.
29 http://www.meenet.org/about-us/our-vision-and-mission/, accessed October 13, 2017.
30 http://www.meenet.org/425-2/regional-themes/, accessed October 13, 2017.
31 http://www.savethemekong.org/issue_detail.php?sid=13, accessed June 10, 2015.
32 The number is based on the signatures in the open letter addressed to prime ministers of various countries (SMC 2014).
33 http://www.savethemekong.org/news_detail.php?nid=65&langss=en, accessed June 10, 2015.
34 http://mekongmigration.org/add/, accessed October 13, 2017.
35 https://www.adb.org/documents/cooperation-between-asian-development-bank-and-nongovernment-organizations, accessed October 13, 2017.
36 https://www.adb.org/site/ngos/ngo-civil-society-center, accessed October 13, 2017.
37 Memorandum of Understanding on Working Arrangements between Asian Development Bank and World Wide Fund for Nature, 26 September 2001.
38 http://www.mrcmekong.org/about-mrc/completion-of-strategic-cycle-2011-2015/, accessed October 13, 2017.
39 http://www.mekonginstitute.org/news-activities/detail/2015/09/14/regional-multi-stake/, accessed October 13, 2017.
40 http://foodsecurity.mekonginstitute.org/, accessed October 13, 2017.
41 http://foodsecurity.mekonginstitute.org/partners, accessed October 13, 2017.
42 Interview with Ms. Noriko Morita, then Information Officer of the MMN, on February 21, 2011 in Chiang Mai, Thailand.

References

Acharya, Amitav (2003) "Democratization and the Prospects for Participatory Regionalism in Southeast Asia," *Third World Quarterly*, 24 (2): 375–390.

Adachi, Kenki (2011) "An Analysis of Coordination between Overlapping International Regimes," *The Ritsumeikan Journal of International Studies*, 23 (3): 423–438.

ADB Institute and IOM (2005) *Managing Regional Public Goods: Cross-border Trade and Investment, Labor Migration, and Public Health*, Tokyo: Asian Development Bank Institute.

AsiaDHRRA, Binadesa, and PhilDHRRA (2010) Strengthening Social Accountability Mechanisms for Food Security and Agricultural Development: A Look at the Asian Development Bank (ADB).

Asian Development Bank (ADB) (1993) *Subregional Economic Cooperation: Initial Possibilities for Cambodia, Lao PDR, Myanmar, Thailand, Viet Nam and Yunnan Province of the People's Republic of China*, Manila: Asian Development Bank.

Asian Development Bank (ADB) (2006) ADB Cooperation with Civil Society: Annual Report 2005.

Asian Development Bank (ADB) (2007) ADB Cooperation with Civil Society: Annual Report 2006.

Asian Development Bank (ADB) (2010) *Strategy and Action Plan for the Greater Mekong Subregion East–West Economic Corridor*, Mandaluyong City: Asian Development Bank.

Asian Development Bank (ADB) (2012) ADB Cooperation with Civil Society: Annual Report 2010.

Asian Development Bank (ADB) (2013) *Facilitating Safe Labor Migration in the Greater Mekong Subregion: Issues, Challenges, and Forward-Looking Interventions*, Mandaluyong City: Asian Development Bank.

Asian Development Bank (ADB) (2014) *ADB Cooperation with Civil Society Biennial Report 2011 and 2012*, Mandaluyong City: Asian Development Bank.

Balassa, Bela (1962) *The Theory of Economic Integration*, London: Allen & Unwin.

Banjongprasert, Achara (2013) "The Framing of Mekong as an Economic Region and the Challenges of NGOs Advocacy and Civil Society Activists," a paper presented at the ICIRD Conference, Chulalongkorn University, Thailand.

Bieler, Andreas, and Adam David Morton (eds.) (2001) *Social Forces in the Making of the New Europe: The Restructuring of European Social Relations in the Global Political Economy*, Basingstoke: Palgrave.

Bulmer, Simon, and Andrew Scott (1994) *Economic and Political Integration in Europe: Internal Dynamics and Global Context*, Oxford: Blackwell Publishers.

Butko, Thomas J. (2006) "Gramsci and the "Anti-Globalization" Movement: Think before You Act," *Socialism and Democracy*, 20 (2): 37–41.

Cambodia Laos Vietnam Development Triangle (CLV-DTA) (2004) Socio-Economic Development Master Plan for Cambodia-Laos-Vietnam Development Triangle.

Committee for the Coordination of Investigations of the Lower Mekong Basin (MC) (1957) Statute of the Committee for Co-ordination of Investigations of Lower Mekong Basin Established by the Governments of Cambodia, Laos, Thailand and the Other Republics of Vietnam in Response to the Decision Taken by the United Nations Economic Commission for Asia and the Far East, Phnom Penh (Cambodia), on 31 October 1957.

Committee for the Coordination of Investigations of the Lower Mekong Basin (MC) (1970) Report on Indicative Basin Plan: A Proposal Framework for the Development of Water and Related Resources of the Lower Mekong Basin 1970.

Cosslett, Tuyet L., and Patrick D. Cosslett (2014) *Water Resources and Food Security in the Vietnam Mekong Delta*, Cham: Springer.

Cox, Robert W. (1996) *Approaches to World Order*, Cambridge: Cambridge University Press.

Cox, Robert W. (1999) "Civil Society at the Turn of the Millennium: Prospects for an Alternative World Order," *Review of International Studies*, 25 (1): 3–28.

De Lombaerde, Philippe, Fredrik Söderbaum, Luk Van Langenhove, and Francis Baert (2010) "The Problem of Comparison in Comparative Regionalism," *Review of International Studies*, 36 (3): 3–22.

Doi, Toshiyuki (2013) "Mainstream Dam Development and Regional Civil Society Cooperation," in Mekong Watch, *Nature and Our Future: The Mekong Basin and Japan*, Tokyo: Mekong Watch (in Japanese).

Dore, John (2003) "The Governance of Increasing Mekong Regionalism," a Paper Presented at Regional Centre for Social and Sustainable Development (RCSD) Conference, Chiang Mai University, Thailand.

Dore, John (2007) "Mekong Region Water-Related MSPs: Unfulfilled Potential," in Jeroen Warner (ed.) *Multi-Stakeholder Platforms for Integrated Water Management*, Aldershot: Ashgate, pp. 205–234.

Dore, John, and Kate Lazarus (2010) "De-Marginalizing the Mekong River Commission," in François Molle, Tira Foran, and Mira Käkönen (eds.) *Contested Waterscapes in the Mekong Region: Hydropower, Livelihoods and Governance*, Singapore: Institute of Southeast Asian Studies, pp. 357–382.

Garrett, Geoffrey, and George Tsebelis (1996) "An Institutional Critique of Intergovernmentalism," *International Organization*, 50 (2): 269–299.

George, Susan (2004) *Another World is Possible if...*, London: Verso.

Gill, Stephen (1996) *American Hegemony and the Trilateral Commission*, Cambridge: Cambridge University Press, 1991/Translated by Seiji Endo, *Chikyu Seijino Saikochiku: Nichi-Bei-Oh Kankei to Sekai Chitsujo*, Asahi Shimbun (in Japanese).

Gill, Stephen (2000) "Toward a Postmodern Price? Battle in Seattle as a Moment in the New Politics of Globalisation," *Millennium: Journal of International Studies*, 29 (1): 131–140.

Goh, Evelyn (2007) *Developing the Mekong: Regionalism and Regional Security in China: Southeast Asian Relations*, Abington: Routledge for the International Institute for Strategic Studies.

Gois, William (2007) "Migration in the ASEAN Region," in Alexander C Chandra and Jenina Joy Chavez (eds.) *Civil Society Reflections on South East Asian Regionalism*, Quezon City: The South East Asian Committee for Advocacy, pp. 119–132.

Haas, Ernst B. (1958) *The Uniting of Europe: Political, Social, and Economic Forces, 1950–1957*, Stanford: Stanford University Press.

Hamasaki, Hironori (2014) "Water Governance of the Mekong River Basin from the Perspective of Dam Development," *Policy Science*, 21 (3): 99–116.

Hatsukano, Naomi (2012) "Will the Emerald Triangle Development Cooperation be Re-Activated?: The Silent Cooperation Scheme between Cambodia, Lao PDR, and Thailand," in Masami Ishida (ed.) *Five Triangle Areas in the Greater Mekong Subregion*, Bangkok: Bangkok Research Center, pp. 32–55.

Hawkesworth, Nigel, John Broderick, Thi Cu Hoang, John Fox, Vanessa O'Keefe, Pech Sokhem, Savengkith Phommahack, and Vitoon Viriyasakultorn (2007) Independent Organisational, Financial and Institutional Review of the MRC Secretariat and the National Mekong Committees.

Hettne, Björn, Andras Inotai, and Osvaldo Sunkel (2001) "Editors' Introduction," in Björn Hettne, Andras Inotai, and Osvaldo Sunkel (eds.) *Comparing Regionalisms: Implications for Global Development*, New York: Palgrave, pp. xxvii–xxxii.

Hettne, Björn (2003) "The New Regionalism Revisited," in Fredrik Söderbaum and Timothy M. Shaw (eds.) *Theories of New Regionalism: A Palgrave Reader*, Hampshire: Palgrave Macmillan, pp. 22–42.

Higashi, Satomi (2013) "Development Project that Creates 'Poverty': Nam Theun 2 Hydroelectric Project," in Satoru Matsumoto and Ryo Oshiba (eds.) *World Bank from the Viewpoint of an NGO: Between the Civil Society and International Organizations*, Kyoto, Minerva Shobo, 2013, pp. 187–214.

Hirsch, Philip (2007) "Advocacy, Civil Society, and the State in the Mekong Region," in Barbara Rugendyke (ed.) *NGOs as Advocates for Development in a Globalising World*, London: Routledge, pp. 185–199.

Hirsch, Philip (2008) "13 Years of Bad Luck?: A Reflection on MRC and Civil Society in the Mekong," *Watershed*, 12 (3): 38–43.

Hirsch, Philip (2012) "IWRM as a Participatory Governance Framework for the Mekong River Basin?" in Joakim Öjendal, Stina Hansson, and Sofie Hellberg (eds.) *Politics and Development in a Transboundary Watershed: The Case of the Lower Mekong Basin*, Dordrecht, pp. 155–170.

Hirsch, Philip, and Kurt Mørck Jensen (2006) *National Interests and Transboundary Water Governance in the Mekong*, Sydney: Australian Mekong Research Centre, University of Sydney.

Hurrell, Andrew (1995) "Regionalism in Theoretical Perspective," in Louise Fawcett and Andrew Hurrell (eds.) *Regionalism in World Politics: Regional Organization and International Order*, New York: Oxford University Press, pp. 37–73.

Igarashi, Seiichi (forthcoming) *New Regionalism and Civil Society in East Asia: Hegemony, Norm, and Critical Regionalism Approach*, Tokyo: Keiso Shobo (in Japanese).

Interim Mekong Committee (IMC) (1978) Declaration Concerning the Interim Committee for Coordination of Investigations of the Lower Mekong Basin, Signed by the Representatives of the Governments of Laos, Thailand, and Vietnam to the Committee for Coordination of Investigations of the Lower Mekong Basin, Singed at Vientiane on 5 January 1978.

International Centre for Environmental Management (2010) MRC Strategic Environmental Assessment (SEA) of Hydropower on the Mekong Mainstream: Summary of the Final Report, Hanoi, Vietnam.

International Energy Agency (IEA) (2013) *Southeast Asia Energy Outlook*, Paris: International Energy Agency.

Ishida, Masami (2008) "GMS Economic Cooperation and Its Impact on CLMV Development," in Chap Sotharith (ed.) *Development Strategy for CLMV in the Age of Economic Integration*, Chiba: Institute of Developing Economies (IDE)-JETRO, pp. 115–140.

JICA Research Institute (1996) *Report on The Mekong River Commission: Current State and Its Future*, Tokyo: JICA Research Institute (in Japanese).

Juris, Jeffrey S. (2008) *Networking Futures: The Movements against Corporate Globalization*, Durham: Duke University Press.

Keohane, Robert O. (1984) *After Hegemony: Cooperation and Discord in the World Political Economy*, Princeton: Princeton University Press.

Keohane, Robert O., and Stanley Hoffmann (eds.) (1991) *The New European Community: Decision-making and Institutional Change*, Boulder: Westview Press.

Le-Huu, Ti, and Lien Nguyen-Duc (2003) *Mekong Case Study*, Paris: UNESCO and IHP.

Makim, Abigail (2002) The Changing Face of Mekong Resource Politics in the Post-Cold War Era: Re-Negotiating Arrangements for Water Resource Management in the Lower Mekong River Basin (1991–1995), Working Paper No. 6, Australian Mekong Resource Centre University of Sydney.

Marchand, Marianne H. (2001) "North American Regionalisms and Regionalisation in the 1990s," in Michael Schulz, Fredrik Söderbaum, and Joakim Öjendal (eds.) *Regionalization in a Globalizing World: A Comparative Perspective on Forms, Actors and Processes*, London: Zed Books, pp. 198–210.

Marks, Gary (1993) "Structural Policy and Multilevel Governance in the EC," in Alan Cafruny, and Glenda Rosenthal (eds.) *The State of the European Community*, New York: Lynne Rienner, pp. 391–410.

Matthews, Nathanial, and Kim Geheb (2015) "On Dams, Demons and Development: The Political Intrigues of Hydropower Development in the Mekong," in Nathanial Matthews, and Kim Geheb (eds.) *Hydropower Development in the Mekong Region: Political, Socio-Economic and Environmental Perspectives*, London: Routledge, pp. 1–16.

Mekong Energy and Ecology Network (MEE Net) (2012) "Know Your Power: Towards a Participatory Approach for Sustainable Power Development in the Mekong Region," Mekong Energy and Ecology Network Conference Report.

Mekong Energy and Ecology Network (MEE Net) (2013) Following the Money Trail of Mekong Energy Industry.

Mekong Institute (MI) (2007) Policy Dialogue Proceedings: Transborder Migration Policy Implementation and Monitoring: Its Effectiveness and Current Policy Gaps in the Greater Mekong Sub-Region Regional Policy Formulation Program.

Mekong Institute (MI) (2009) End of Course Summary Report, Regional Training Course: Labour Migration Management in the Greater Mekong Sub-Region.

Mekong Institute (MI) (2011a) Proceedings: Experts' Meeting, Mekong Institute's Labor Migration and Care Program (2011–2013), Mekong Institute, Khon Kaen, Thailand.

Mekong Institute (MI) (2011b) Mekong Forum 2011: Proceedings, July 12–13, 2011, Khon Kaen, Thailand.

Mekong Migration Network (MMN) and Asian Migrant Center (AMC) (2008) *Migration in the Greater Mekong Subregion: Resource Book: In-Depth Study: Arrest, Detention and Deportation*, Hong Kong: Mekong Migration Network and Asian Migrant Center.

Mekong Migration Network (MMN) (2013) *No Choice in the Matter: Migrants' Experiences of Arrest, Detention, and Deportation*, Hong Kong: Mekong Migration Network.

Mekong River Commission (MRC) (1995) The Agreement on the Cooperation for the Sustainable Development of the Mekong River Basin, April 5, 1995.

Mekong River Commission (MRC) (1998) *Public Participation in the Lower Mekong Basin*, Vientiane: Mekong River Commission.

Mekong River Commission (MRC) (2006) *Strategic Plan 2006–2010: Meeting the Needs, Keeping the Balance*, Vientiane: Mekong River Commission.

Mekong River Commission (MRC) (2008) Stakeholder Consultation on MRC's Basin Development Plan Phase 2 (BDP2) and its Inception Report, March 12–13, 2008`, Vientiane, Lao PDR.

Mekong River Commission (MRC) (2009) 2nd Regional Stakeholder Forum on the Basin Development Plan: Consultation Proceeding, Chiang Rai, Thailand.

Mekong River Commission (MRC) (2010a) Stakeholder Analysis for the MRC Basin Development Plan Programme Phase 2 (BDP2): Complementary Document to the Stakeholder Participation and Communication Plan for the Basin Development Planning in the Lower Mekong Basin, Final Report, Updated Version.

Mekong River Commission (MRC) (2010b) 3rd Regional Stakeholder Forum on the Basin Development Plan Forum Proceedings, Vientiane, Lao PDR.

Mekong River Commission (MRC) (2014) 4th Regional Stakeholder Forum on the Basin Development Strategy, Siem Reap, Cambodia.

Middleton, Carl, Carl Grundy-Warr, and Yong Ming Li (2013) "Neoliberalizing Hydropower in the Mekong Basin: The Political Economy of Partial Enclosure," *Social Science Journal*, 43: 299–334.

Miller, Benjamin (1996) "Competing Realist Perspectives on Great Power Crisis Behavior," in Benjamin Frankel (ed.) *Realism: Restatements and Renewal*, London: Frank Cass, pp. 309–357.

Mirumachi, Naho (2015) *Transboundary Water Politics in the Developing World*, New York: Routledge.

Mitrany, David (1966) *A Working Peace System*, Chicago: Quadrangle Books.

Mittelman, James H. (1999) "Rethinking the 'New Regionalism' in the Context Globalization," in Andras Inotai, and Osvaldo Sunkel (eds.) *Globalism and the New Regionalism*, New York: St. Martin's Press, pp. 25–53.

Mittelman, James H. (2000) *The Globalization Syndrome: Transformation and Resistance*, Princeton: Princeton University Press.

Molle, François, Tira Foran, and Philippe Floch (2009) "Introduction: Changing Waterscapes in the Mekong Region," in François Molle, Tira Foran, and Mira Käkönen (eds.) *Contested Waterscapes in the Mekong Region: Hydropower, Livelihoods, and Governance*, London: Earthscan, pp. 1–19.

Moravcsik, Andrew (1993) "Preferences and Power in the European Community: A Liberal Intergovernmental Approach," *Journal of Common Market Studies*, 31 (4): 473–524.

Morizono, Koichi (2002) *Current State and Issues of Regional Cooperation in Indochina (Greater Mekong Region): From the Point of View of Our Nation's Regional Development Cooperation*, Tokyo: JICA (in Japanese).

Nakamura, Kengo (2005) *European Integration and Transformation of Modern State: EU's Multi-Dimensional Network Governance*, Kyoto: Showado (in Japanese).

Nette, Andrew (1997) "Japanese ODA: Moving into the Mekong," *Watershed*, 3 (1): 45–48.

Noda, Yasuhiro (2012) "The Asian Development Bank and Regional Aid Coordination: Japan, China, and the Development of the Greater Mekong Subregion," in Hyo-Sook Kim, and David M. Potter (eds.) *Foreign Aid Competition in Northeast Asia*, Sterling, VA: Kumarian Press, pp. 107–127.

Nomoto, Keisuke (2002) "International Cooperation for Development in the Mekong Subregion," *Journal of JBIC Institute*, 12: 73–100 (in Japanese).

Ogasawara, Takayuki (2005) "Development Cooperation and International Relations in the Mekong Region," in Masami Ishida (ed.) *Mekong Regional Development: Last Frontier of East Asia*, Tokyo: Institute of Developing Economies, pp. 41–62 (in Japanese).

Overbeek, Henk (ed.) (2003) *The Political Economy of European Employment: European Integration and the Transnationalization of the (Un)employment Question*, London: Routledge.

Parnwell, Michael J. G. (2001) "Sinews of Interconnectivity: Tourism and Environment in the Greater Mekong Subregion," in Peggy Teo, T. C. Chang, and K. C. Ho (eds.) *Interconnected World: Tourism in Southeast Asia*, Amsterdam: Pergamon, pp. 231–247.

Ransley, Carol, Jonathan Cornford, and Jessica Rosien (2008) *A Citizen's Guide to the Greater Mekong Subregion: Understanding the GMS Program and the Role of the Asian Development Bank*, Melbourne: Oxfam Australia.

River Coalition in Cambodia (RCC) (2007) Public Statement: With Six Proposed Dams Threatening the Sustainability of the Lower Mekong River, November 16, 2007.

Rüland, Jürgen (2012) "The Limits of Democratizing Interest Representation: ASEAN's Regional Corporatism and Normative Challenges," *European Journal of International Relations*, 20 (1): 237–261.

Save the Mekong Coalition (SMC) (2009) Call for Help from Save the Mekong Coalition.

Save the Mekong Coalition (SMC) (2010) Call for Halt to the PNPCA Process and Cancellation of Xayaboury Dam.

Save the Mekong Coalition (SMC) (2012) Press Release: For Immediate Release as Mekong Leaders Gather, Public Awaits Answers on Xayaburi Dam.

Save the Mekong Coalition (SMC) (2013) Mekong under Treat: Urgent Moratorium by Heads of Government on Don Sahong Dam is Required.

Save the Mekong Coalition (SMC) (2014) Concerns on Don Sahong Dam Prior Consultation Process.

Schulz, Michael, Fredrik Söderbaum, and Joakim Öjendal (2001) "Key Issues in the New Regionalism: Comparisons from Asia, Africa and the Middle East," in Björn Hettne, Andras Inotai, and Osvaldo Sunkel (eds.) *Comparing Regionalisms: Implications for Global Development*, New York: Palgrave, pp. 234–276.

Shiraishi, Masaya (2012) "Mekong Regional Cooperation: China, Japan, and the United States," *Waseda Asia Review*, 12: 10–16 (in Japanese).

Shiraishi, Masaya (2013) "The 'Development Triangle' Plan by Cambodia, Laos, and Vietnam: An Overview," *Journal of Asia-Pacific Studies*, 19: 1–44 (in Japanese).

Sunchindah, Apichai, and Patharaporn Theeratham (2014) Evaluation of Mekong Energy and Ecology Network: Under the Mekong Cooperation Programme of Siemenpuu Foundation, Bangkok.

Swe, Thein, and Paul Chambers (2011) *Cashing in Across the Golden Triangle: Thailand's Northern Border Trade with China, Laos, and Myanmar*, Chiang Mai: Mekong Press.

Towards Ecological Recovery and Regional Alliance (TERRA) (1997) "Asian Development Bank: Money and Power in the Mekong Region," *Watershed*, 2 (2): 38–44.

Towards Ecological Recovery and Regional Alliance (TERRA) (2001) ADB's Inspection Panel and Concerns Raised by Local Communities, Briefing Paper No. 2.

Towards Ecological Recovery and Regional Alliance (TERRA) (2004a) The Environmental and Economic Impacts of the Nam Theun 2 Hydroelectric Project on Communities Living in the Xe Bang Fai River Basin, TERRA Briefing.

Towards Ecological Recovery and Regional Alliance (TERRA) (2004b) Endangered Elephants of the Nakai Plateau: Nam Theun 2 Dam Threatens Large Population of Asian Elephants in Lao PDR, Press Briefing.

Towards Ecological Recovery and Regional Alliance (TERRA) (2007a) Mekong River Commission Facing Crisis of Legitimacy, Press Release.

Towards Ecological Recovery and Regional Alliance (TERRA) (2007b) International Alarm Raised on Dams Across Mekong Mainstream, MRC Must Wake up to its Responsibilities, Press Release.

Towards Ecological Recovery and Regional Alliance (TERRA) (2011) The Mekong: River of Life under Treat.

von Bülow, Marisa (2010) *Building Transnational Networks: Civil Society and the Politics of Trade in the Americas*, Cambridge: Cambridge University Press.

Woods, Kevin (2005) "Transboundary Environmental Governance in the Greater Mekong Subregion: The Politics of Participation," *Watershed*, 10 (2): 10–23.

4 Civil society vs. GMS states in terms of infrastructure and hydropower development projects

Kosum Saichan and Hiroshi Komatsu

Introduction

In recent times, transboundary investment by Thailand in the Greater Mekong Sub-region (GMS) has been increasing through both national and private sectors. Example projects include the Dawei Special Economic Zone Project and the Salween hydropower dams in Myanmar; the Koh Kong and Oddar Meanchey sugar plantations in Cambodia, implemented under the economic land-concession policy; and the Hongsa Mine and Power Station, Xayaburi Dam, and the Don Sahong Dam in Laos (My Mekong 2017).

In the background of these developments is the deepening of the economic regional integration within ASEAN; furthermore, investment in these projects has been spurred by Myanmar's democratization. Myanmar is a country with good appeal as a potential investment destination. Its location means it is possible to ship exports directly to Africa, the Middle East, and further west, and it also shares borders with China and India. Further, it is the richest country in ASEAN with regard to natural resources such as oil, gas, and coal and, compared with Thailand and others, its labor force is less expensive and more efficient. However, before its transformation into a democratic regime, it had been dominated by a military dictatorship, which resulted in sanctions from the West and a lack of financial assistance from international financial institutions (Mahitthirook 2017); consequently, its investment potential suffered.

However, once Myanmar adopted a democratic regime, a major change occurred. In October 2016, in preparation for the country's "opening up," and in an attempt to fully develop the investment environment in Myanmar, the new regime implemented Myanmar Investment Law, which concerns an integration of the existing Foreign Investment Law and the Myanmar Citizens Law. This new law is designed to unify rules on investment and to clarify Myanmar's investment regulations, which had been complicated up to this point. As a result, investors from all over the world began to view Myanmar as an attractive new investment destination, and it is predicted that this new law will spur increased foreign direct investment (FDI) in the country. Further, in addition to the aforementioned revision, Myanmar concurrently entered into a number of bilateral agreements concerning the development of infrastructure and the large-scale industrial development of certain areas of the country. In particular, with the rise of Myanmar as a country attracting overseas investment, as well as its population of efficient workers who are willing to provide labor for low wages, the private sector in Thailand has shown an increased interest in establishing industrial parks and special economic zones (SEZs).

At present, Myanmar is advancing in terms of economic development and is preparing for admittance into the ASEAN Economic Community (AEC), which is a new regional economic-promotion community. However, overseas investors are worried about Myanmar's inexperienced infrastructure, especially the country's unstable power-generation capacity and the transport-communication difficulties in some areas. Consequently, official development assistance (ODA), along with other forms of assistance from the government, non-governmental organizations (NGOs), and international organizations, is now playing an important role in developing infrastructure in Myanmar. However, due to the current acceleration of infrastructure development, the people of Myanmar are now facing various socioeconomic problems: for example, a shortage of competent labor, inefficient education, and economic disparity between the rich and the poor, which may cause further social problems in the future.

Considering the entire Mekong River Basin, it is worth noting that 11 dams are planned for construction in the downstream area. Problems associated with the use of the water resources of the Mekong River are extremely difficult to solve, mainly due to the diverse and complicated uses and plans the upstream and downstream riverbank states have for the water. In response to these differences of opinions, in 1995 Cambodia, Laos, Thailand, and Vietnam founded the Mekong River Commission (MRC) to coordinate the shared use of water resources. The first trial of the MRC's powers occurred in 2010, when Laos proposed the construction of the Xayaburi Dam. Negotiations between the four countries did not go well and, in 2012, Laos and Thailand decided to proceed with the construction of the dam despite opposition from Cambodia and Vietnam. This discord has persisted to the present day, as Laos is now in the early construction stages of its second Mekong hydroelectric power plant, called the Don Sahong Dam, despite objections from neighboring countries. The developmental histories of these two projects clearly show that the MRC consultation mechanism is not functioning, and the future of cooperation in the Mekong region remains uncertain (Lobrigo 2017).

In this backdrop, large-scale development, including dams, is taking place in GMS; however, we cannot overlook the impact this is having on local residents. With such large-scale development, when local residents feel dissatisfaction and/or deception, the investment risk for enterprises increases. Further, it is difficult to implement successful projects by providing inappropriate compensation or by plundering or exploiting land, labor, water resources, and/or forestry. Regarding dam construction in the region, hydroelectric power is a huge revenue source for stakeholders but, concurrently, it is a threat to the food security of millions of people. Thus, most people do not benefit from the dams. In fact, such large-scale projects in Thailand's neighboring countries are resulting in explicit or implicit human rights abuses, and it cannot be said that sufficient consideration is being given to human rights and the environment during the planning and implementation of these projects.

Civil society is playing an important role in this matter, helping to implement measures to combat the human rights violations and environmental destruction caused by such large-scale projects and dam constructions. In the Mekong basin, civil society aims to solve these problems by supporting local people, lobbying governments and companies, and by widely publicizing the problems in society through transnational activities. Thus, this chapter focuses on the civil societies that are engaged in activities to protect the lives of the local residents and the natural environment of the Mekong River basin from the planned development in the region; this is examined by focusing on two cases: Myanmar's SEZs and Laos's Hydropower Plan. First section provides an outline of Myanmar's Dawei SEZ and examines its impact on the community. Second section analyzes civil society's response to the project in terms of the actions of local and international NGOs. Third section identifies the background of Laos's hydroelectric power-generation plan. In forth section the responses of NGOs in the Mekong region to the dam projects and the significance of corporate accountability are considered. Finally, we present agendas for the realization of human rights protection and sustainable ASEAN, which are clarified through an analysis of the responses of governments and civil society to huge projects.

Dawei Special Economic Zone Project in Myanmar

Development of the Dawei Special Economic Zone Project

Dawei is the central city of the Tenasserim Division, southern Myanmar, and Dawei SEZ consists of seven large projects: the Dawei Deepwater Port Project; a road connection between Dawei and Ban Nam Pu Ron, which is located in Kanchanaburi province; and the development of an industrial power system, a plumbing system, telecommunications, real estate, and a shopping mall. The Dawei Deep Seaport Development and Industrial Estate, which was commenced in 2008, is a large joint project undertaken by the Thai and Myanmar governments and private sectors. The agreement between the two countries was concluded through several means, such as ODA, a joint venture between the two countries through a special purpose vehicle (SPV), and FDI; to establish an appropriate SPV, Thailand's Neighboring Countries Economic Development Cooperation Agency (NEDA) engaged in cooperation with Myanmar's Foreign Economic Relations Department. The resulting SPV specifically focuses on securing investment in Dawei SEZ, mainly through selecting potentially interested investors; in particular, for the Myanmar government, overseas investment forms a core development strategy for transforming Myanmar from an agricultural country into an industrialized country.

On June 19, 2008, the Italian-Thai Development Public Company Limited (ITD), which is one of Thailand's largest contractors, signed an agreement with

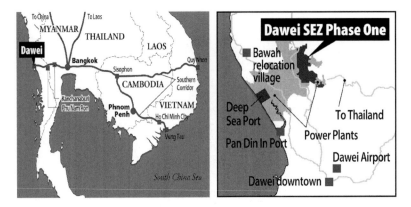

Figure 4.1 Dawei Special Economic Zone Phase One
Source: Created by the authors based on multiple sources.

the Myanmar government to conduct a feasibility study of the project. Then, on November 2, ITD also signed a contract with the Port Authority of Myanmar to acquire the rights to develop the Dawei Deep Seaport, including the industrial park and the transportation route between the two countries. Beginning in 2012, 240 billion baht (approximately 6.72 billion US dollars) was invested over the course of four and a half years; this includes funding for the development of an industrial park road, small-scale harbor, water-supply facility, electric power, and the land acquisition fee for a road from the Thai border to Dawei SEZ (Figure 4.1). These construction projects are positioned as the first phase of a 75-year plan to ultimately develop an area of 250 km^2 into a giant industrial park. ITD has already secured the rights to build such a park.

Focusing on the aforementioned road from Dawei to the Thai border, in 2015 the Thai government agreed to provide a loan of 4.5 billion baht (approximately 128 million US dollars) for the construction of a 132-km road that connects Dawei Deep Seaport to Ban Phu Nam Ron in Thailand's Kanchanaburi province. However, although the Thai Cabinet approved this loan plan, construction has been delayed because the new Myanmar government requested a review of the loan plan. ITD is prepared to resume the construction but is waiting for a decision from Thailand and Myanmar to continue the project (Theparat 2017a).

Electricity and oil plans for the area are also progressing. In August 2016, ITD signed an agreement to begin the development of these plans, receiving an investment of 1.7 million US dollars for the initial stage of a mega plan. Approximately 500 million dollars will be spent on 450 MW gas-fired power plants, and another 500 million dollars will be spent on petrochemical plants and a petroleum refiner to meet the demand within Dawei. ITD also plans to invest in additional coal-fired power plants after the development of the Dawei industrial zone has been completed (Theparat 2017b).

With regard to actions taken concerning Dawei SEZ thus far, the assistance from Thailand to Myanmar has mainly been in the form of social support, with a particular focus on education. However, infrastructure development is emerging as a new development aid, and this includes the construction of transportation (roads, railways, transmission systems, and oil and gas pipelines) connecting the deep-water port and Kanchanaburi to Dawei. The goal of the Myanmar government is to make Dawei a new "gateway" to attract new investors; opportunities to invest in infrastructure development and future growth in this country are available to investors all over the world. In fact, as this project was delayed due to a lack of funds and intra-regional disputes, Myanmar, Thailand, and ITD were forced to invite foreign investors and to revise the plan and share investment (Saichan and Saisin 2014).

It should also be noted that the interest of the Thai government is not limited to just Dawei. If it can secure Thai investors, the Thai government is prepared to negotiate with Myanmar with regard to upgrading industrial parks to SEZs. On the other hand, the Thai government is also committed to advancing the plan to develop the SEZs of one of its cities, Mae Sot, which is adjacent to the town of Myawaddy in Myanmar (Theparat 2017c).

Impact of the Dawei Special Economic Zone Project

Despite the potential benefits involved, the construction of Dawei SEZ may have a serious impact on the lives of thousands of people living in Dawei. For example, it will be difficult for people who have lost land and raw materials as a result of the development to continue their indigenous economic activities; the socioeconomic influence of the development extends to individuals, families, and economic communities. Along with these socioeconomic impacts, environmental and social problems, such as land deprivation, inappropriate and unfair migration and compensation, and losses of productive farmland and forestry without compensation may also arise (Saichan and Saisin 2014). Further, due to migration policies in the project area, communities that have a rich history of centuries of occupation in the district have been moved to new areas. In fact, the number of villages affected by this project is estimated to be between 20 and 36, meaning approximately 4,384–7,807 households or 22,000–43,000 people (Dawei Development Association 2014a).

In principle, in order to incorporate the local people's will, it is indispensable that measures such as information provision; residents' participation; public hearings; and transparent assessments of the impact the project will have on the environment, society, and residents' health be considered. However, this project does not accommodate these measures. Consequently, civil society is acting to respond to such situations; these activities are being undertaken not only in local

Dawei but also outside the region. The civil societies' response is examined in the next section.

Local Dawei civil society and international civil society

Dawei civil society

The most interesting aspect of the Dawei civil society is that it is composed of various groups; for example, women's organizations, religious organizations, ethnic groups, and expert groups, and these are cooperating to address the negative effects of the Dawei SEZ development. In particular, the Dawei Development Association (DDA) is playing a central role in this cooperation. DDA was founded in 2011 by youths in Dawei, and it focuses on building respect for the environment and land rights as well as for the management of natural resources, with the ultimate goal of ensuring sustainable development in the region. When the Dawei development project was first implemented, DDA held a conference with other local groups and people; it then cooperated with outside NGOs in Yangon and Thailand to address the issues raised. It also established a local media group to widely disseminate information on the current situation of Dawei to the world through the Internet. However, there are many obstacles to its activities, and it cannot be said that it has enjoyed unfettered progress. For example, it is expensive for DDA to secure Internet access, and connection speeds in the area are much slower than those in other areas; in addition, regional conflict also poses a great risk.

In 2014, DDA released a statement requesting the Thai and Myanmar governments to take responsibility for and make efforts to secure a resolution to the problems caused by Dawei SEZ. In the statement, it requested the upholding of international environmental protection standards, the ensuring of respect for the human rights of local people, that residents be permitted to participate in decision-making, abstinence from the use of threats and compulsion on local communities and from forced resettlement, and the disclosure of information. The following remark from DDA's coordinator gives a good description of their stance: "We are not opposing the project, but we are demanding responsibility and accountability of damages occurred in Dawei SEZ project the last three years. ITD replied that this is not their responsibility. But ITD announced that they have won their bid for the initial phase of Dawei SEZ. How did this happen?" (Dawei Development Association 2014b).

Furthermore, a network for monitoring the work that involves a group of Karen women who live near Dawei airport has been established. This monitoring network functions with the help of training and guidance from Thai and Yangon NGOs. Additionally, a lawyers' group in Dawei also participates in the network. The lawyers' group was initially established to support people who require legal aid; however, in recent years it has frequently addressed legal disputes related to the Dawei development project. Moreover, monks, village leaders, and doctors, all of whom hold leading positions in their local areas, are also engaging in the movement. Meanwhile, activists and scholars in Thailand and activists and local residents in Dawei are exchanging and sharing a lot of information on this matter. Strengthening this overall cooperation among local actors is important for securing transparency, fairness, and respect for human rights regarding the Dawei project, and it will lead to the realization of democratic development in Myanmar (Saichan and Saisin 2014).

International non-governmental organizations and the transnational civil society network in Dawei Special Economic Zone

Domestic NGOs in Myanmar and Thailand are not the only parties concerned about the development of Dawei, authoritative worldwide NGOs have also highlighted the harmful effects of this project. For example, the International Commission of Justice (ICJ), based in Geneva, has stated that companies involved in the planning and construction of Dawei SEZ have neglected to disclose impact assessments and other relevant information concerning the project. In fact, despite ICJ investigators requesting stakeholders such as investors and developers to provide information on the environmental impacts of the project and that they submit it to accounting inspections, these stakeholders have not provided any substantive answers; ICJ considers the disclosure of information and the ensuring of transparency in regard to the Dawei project to be critically essential in order to avoid adversely affecting local people. Consequently, the ICJ asked the new government of Myanmar to mandate companies to comply with the transparency requirements of the current legislation and to establish a new law on environmental impact assessments; according to the ICJ's international legal adviser, under international law, the Myanmar government must defend the local people's right to participate in environmental decisions and to have access to reliable information (Sathisan and Tigar 2015; Lewis 2016).

NGOs' requests to the Myanmar government relating to international norms such as international law are realized through transnational collaboration across the border between Thailand and Myanmar. Investment activities by Thai companies in neighboring countries such as Laos, Myanmar, and Cambodia have raised concerns in regard to whether these companies are implementing appropriate measures to ensure the upholding of human rights and the reduction of environmental impact; in fact, there have been several reports of the unfair environmental destruction activities of Thai companies in these countries, and, consequently, Thai and Myanmar NGOs have insisted on protecting human rights and the environment. In February 2017, a statement to the Thai and Myanmar governments and Thai enterprises requesting compliance with the United Nations Guiding Principles on Business and Human Rights (UNGPs) and other international treaties was published by 27 Thai NGOs and the DDA. The organizations also asked the government of Thailand to comply with the cabinet decision of May 2016, which recommended the establishment of a system that would compel the private sector to respect the fundamental rights of local communities. Further, it also asked the Myanmar government to ensure that foreign companies comply with Myanmar environmental law and allow residents to participate in decision-making processes (Rujivanarom 2017a).

The background of the civil society's activities is that these development projects have not led to regional economic development; on the contrary, they have resulted in the exploitation of local people's land and have caused adverse effects on residents and the environment. In fact, Thai government agencies are also beginning to address the issues caused by Thai companies in Dawei; for example, the Thai National Human Rights Commission conducted a survey of the environmental problems, land disputes, and human rights violations caused by fraudulent operations in Heinda's tin coal mine. In this regard, the commissioner explained that the Thai government complies with the UNGPs, which impose the mandatory observation of human rights and the prevention of environmental destruction in areas where companies operate, with solutions for these issues, where they exist, being drawn from relevant organizations and enterprises (Rujivanarom 2017a).

Dam projects in Laos

Background of the Dam projects

The Mekong River flows south through six countries, reaching the South China Sea after travelling over 4,350 kilometers, and large-scale electricity development projects have been conducted on this vast river for over 20 years. Dam developers and related governments have publicized the clear benefits that result from such development, mainly in terms of energy security and economic development; in fact, it has been claimed that economic development through dam development will lead to poverty reduction. Dam development, however, constantly deteriorates the environment, resulting in clear negative impacts on the ecosystem, including biodiversity, fish stocks, and the lives of local residents. Thus, despite the consequent energy security and poverty reduction, the merits of the hydropower industry are doubtful.

The demand and supply of electricity in each Mekong River country differs greatly. Thailand, Vietnam, and China are countries that have relatively higher power consumption and can only supply a fraction of the electricity required to meet domestic demand; meanwhile, Cambodia, Myanmar, and Laos export electricity to these countries. In less-developed Mekong countries, the distribution of electricity to many rural areas is quite poor, meaning that the electricity produced rarely stays in these nations. Further, in the countries exporting electricity, the market is small. Thus, in these states, most of the hydroelectric power produced is exported to vast urban areas in more developed neighboring countries, such as Thailand and Vietnam. In fact, the overall pattern is that electricity generated in the Mekong River basin area is transmitted from rural areas to cities, from undeveloped countries to developed and developing countries. This unbalanced power allocation is a feature of the energy infrastructure in the Mekong region. Additionally, hydropower is the leading actor in regional electric-power competition, and it is an incentive for foreign investment and development aid (Samuelsson 2016).

There is a claim that economic growth and revenue from large-scale hydroelectric power development has become a means of implementing "poverty reduction" measures, and that such development can lead to sustainable development. For example, in Laos, a country with ambitions to become the "battery of Southeast Asia," 25 dams are in the planning stage and 11 are under construction, and this number is even larger if dams in the feasibility-study stage are included. However, political and social factors in the country are actually hindering social development. Laos has a high degree of corruption, and freedom of press and civil society is limited; hence, it cannot be said that it is a mature democratic society. Consequently, it is difficult to guarantee accountability, transparency, and participation opportunities in regard to the country's hydropower projects, which have a serious impact on local residents and the environment. Further, it is also difficult to achieve sustainable development in the nation, not only for economic reasons, but also for political reasons (Samuelsson 2016).

Additionally, even if Laos underwent a democratic process, its proposed dam development is not necessarily economically sustainable. In project plans, negative influences on the local community and the environment due to dam construction are taken into consideration, but not always to a sufficient degree. If compensating local communities and implementing environmental measures are taken seriously, it will raise costs and the creation of these dams would not make business sense. Furthermore, even if profits from hydroelectric power generation occur in the short term, there are associated long-term problems and dangers, such as extensive regional flooding and irreparable damage to watersheds and ecosystems. In fact, even before taking into account the negative impact on the environment and the local community, it has been highlighted that the construction cost of a huge dam is actually too high to generate profits. For example, cost estimation during the planning stage is often based on optimistic and simplistic predictions, while the planning period is not only noticeably time-consuming, but delays also frequently occur at regular intervals. Thus, from the viewpoint of efficiently solving energy problems, the agility and flexibility of energy policies are impaired; thus, hydropower generation by huge dams is still questionable (Samuelsson 2016).

The impact of Dam projects

China has already built six dams on the Mekong River, Laos and Cambodia have 11 more, and dozens of dams are planned for the main tributary (Rujivanarom 2017b). However, over the past two decades, over 80 dam projects in the area have caused social and environmental damage. Since the 1980s, China has not announced its dam construction projects to the mainstream or downstream countries, or held consultations with them in this regard. The cross-border impacts of these dams are felt throughout the Mekong region, and the construction of downstream dams is now being given due consideration. However, the Pak Mun Dam in Thailand, the Nam Theun 2 Dam in Laos, and the Yali Falls Dam in Vietnam have evidenced the serious social and environmental costs of dam construction. If transparency, participation opportunities, and a responsible power plan are not implemented and given top priority when such dams are being constructed, the discourse on sustainable hydroelectricity remains a falsehood (Trandem 2014).

With regard to the social and environmental problems caused by dam construction in the Mekong basin, the role of regional organizations cannot be overlooked. In 2010, Strategic Environmental Assessment (SEA), which is responsible for the sustainable management of the Mekong River, was established by the MRC. SEA stated that 11 planned mainstream cascaded dams proposed by Laos and Cambodia will have a serious impact on the Mekong River ecosystem and pose a threat to the lives and food supply of millions of people in the region (Trandem 2014). Many risks related to dams cannot be mitigated, which can result in significant losses to economic and social environmental resources. Considering this, regulating the rapid construction of hydropower in the Mekong downstream region is currently the most important task facing MRC, as these projects are threatening the sustainable management of the Mekong River and its resources (Trandem 2015).

Meanwhile, the SEA report also acknowledged that Mekong countries have an information gap that poses a serious obstacle to implementing proper evaluation and decision-making concerning project proposals and, after considering the aforementioned issues, the report concluded with a recommendation of a 10-year postponement of all decisions concerning Mekong dams. However, the government of Laos disregarded this recommendation, continued its plans for the first mainstream Mekong dam, and built the foundation for this dam.

Nevertheless, despite this disregarding of its role, a possible touchstone for MRC is the Don Sahong Dam plan (Figure 4.2). The future of this dam, planned in southern Laos but located less than two kilometers from the border with Cambodia, depends on the intentions and leadership of the member states, Thailand, Laos, Cambodia, and Vietnam, and it may constitute an opportunity for MRC to evolve hydroelectric diplomacy (Trandem 2015).

The Xayaburi Dam, located in northern Laos, is also an important project that can be used to forecast the future of national cooperation in the Mekong watershed. The Xayaburi Dam is the first case to undergo the MRC's prior consultation process (PCP), which began in 2010. The PCP was established under the Mekong Agreement in 1995 as a means for neighboring governments to evaluate others' projects. With regard to the dam construction planned for the mainstream of the Mekong River, it aims to obtain consent from all member countries, regardless of whether they are participating in the project. However, for the Xayaburi Dam, this process encountered difficulties from the beginning. Dam construction began at the same time that the PCP was implemented, which circumvented the purpose of the procedure. There was no proper consideration of this project, basic data on construction were not gathered, and cross-border

Civil society vs. GMS states 117

Figure 4.2 Map showing the sites of the Xayaburi and Don Sahong Dams
Source: Created by the authors based on multiple sources.

impact assessments were not given due attention. Instead, the government of Laos began preliminary construction of the Xayaburi Dam and agreement negotiations. MRC attempted to reopen discussions on the Xayaburi Dam at the Special Joint Committee and the MRC Council, but the countries could not reach an agreement. Thus, in this project, regional cooperation could not overcome the benefits of sovereignty (Trandem 2015).

Reactions from civil society and corporate accountability in ASEAN

Demanding a halt to the Don Sahong Dam

The Lao government is currently advancing construction of its second mainstream dam, Don Sahong, and the preparatory work is already in progress. However, although public consultations with Cambodia, Thailand, and Vietnam are being held, there is no doubt that these countries oppose this project.

Since the signing of a memorandum for the Don Sahong Dam in 2006, scientists, Mekong experts, riverbank communities, civil society, and some Mekong states have expressed opposition. The reason for this is that the project's impact on food security will extend across the border and across the region. Consequently, the Cambodian, Thai, and Vietnamese governments are seeking an assessment of the further cross-border impacts of the project. Cambodia and Thailand are also urging the freezing of all decisions on the dam until the completion of the two impact assessments that are currently underway: an MRC

Council Study (CS) and a Mekong Delta study. Over the past decade, the opposition of the Mekong community to the Don Sahong Dam program has been expressed through public protests, international petitions, and workshops. For example, in October 2014, a domestic and foreign NGO federation submitted a complaint to the Malaysian Human Rights Commission (SUHAKAM) on behalf of the Cambodian and Thai communities that would be affected by the Don Sahong Dam. This complaint asked SUHAKAM to investigate the socioeconomic impacts the dam would have in these countries, and to guarantee that Mega First Corporation Berhad, a Malaysian/Chinese company that has been awarded the dam construction project, complies with international human rights standards, including the obligation to provide information to affected communities (Community Resource Centre et al. 2014; International Rivers 2015).

Despite the obvious opposition of the people of Mekong and the disagreement between the four governments, the Don Sahong Dam project is continuing at a rapid pace. The government of Laos avoided conducting the MRC's consultation procedure concerning dam construction management in the Mekong mainstream, arguing that such negotiation is unnecessary because the Don Sahong Dam is a "tributary" dam; this is despite the fact that the Khone Phapheng Falls, which are adjacent to the Don Sahong Dam, are globally important riverbank hotspots. Furthermore, it has also disregarded concerns relating to the fact that Mega First Corporation Berhad has no previous dam-construction experience.

With regard to construction work, Sinohydro, owned by the Chinese government, received 720 million US dollars for design and construction work implementation contracts. In March 2015, Sinohydro announced that several companies, including the national utility company Électricité du Laos (EDL), would establish a joint venture, the Don Sahong Power Company Limited (DSPC), to perform this project; EDL has a 20% stake in DSPC. Then, in September 2015, DSPC signed a 25-year deal with the Lao government and agreed that EDL would purchase electricity from the dam. At face value, it seems that dam construction is being conducted by overseas private enterprises, but in reality, it follows the intentions of Lao government enterprises, and we can see a pattern of a small number of stakeholders using their positions to obtain interests (Kemp 2017).

International non-governmental organizations and corporate accountability in the Mekong Region

NGOs in each Mekong country have conducted various activities to uphold human rights and protect the environment, not only in regard to the Don Sahong Dam but also concerning other huge dam projects. Regarding the aforementioned Xayaburi Dam, local and international civil society expressed concern at an early stage in regard to the impacts it would have on local fish stocks and the nearby environment, and showed the necessity of postponing decisions on the dam for 10 years, repeating the recommendation of the MRC's SEA report. Civil society also requested opportunities to participate in the consultation process and the disclosure of specific documents relating to the project (Trandem 2015).

On March 14, 2017, members and supporters of the Save the Mekong Coalition (SMC) gathered from Thailand, Cambodia, Vietnam, and other regions to mark an international action day for the river. The Save the Mekong Coalition has expressed its concerns to the MRC, the Mekong governments, and international donors in regard to the transboundary and cumulative effects the dam project and the expedited dam construction is having at a time when regional decision-making is dysfunctional. The coalition is requesting that no further decisions be made unless the participation of communities affected by the project is guaranteed and information based on appropriate investigations is secured. In particular, community members from Thailand and Cambodia have expressed concern with regard to the limited information available on Mekong River projects, and especially with regard to the fact that the impact on people has not been appropriately considered. The participation of local communities in the evaluation and decision-making processes of the Mekong mainstream project is extremely limited; this clearly suggests that the concerns of local residents and neighboring governments have not been considered. In short, such statements have been precipitated by the present circumstances concerning the lack of cross-border influence on dam developers (Ross 2017).

The NGO forum in Cambodia is concerned about the potential impact of Don Sahong Dam because approximately 60 million people live in the Mekong downstream basin and approximately 300 million people live in its surrounding area. For example, the Khone Phapheng Falls are important routes for fish in the river because migratory fish can pass through them, even in the dry season. Thus, many fishery experts have concluded that the dam construction, which will block the falls, will have a serious impact on fish habitats. It has long been known that the construction of huge dams can pose a threat to food security. In 2012, the Cambodian government reported that if the Sambor and Stung Treng dams were built on the Mekong, the numbers of fish caught would reduce by 50% by 2030; Cambodia relies on fish for approximately 70% of its protein intake, a much higher percentage than that of other countries. Also, in a Mekong Delta study led by the Vietnam National Mekong Committee, the 11 mainstream dam plans were estimated to halve the influx of sediment into the delta and to reduce the number of fish caught by more than half; for Vietnam, the decline of fish catch would cause damage to catfish exports amounting to tens of billions of dollars (Anonymous author 2015).

In February 2017, at the Mekong River Commission's Regional Stakeholder Forum on the Procedures for Notification, Prior Consultation, and Agreement (PNPCA) concerning the Pak Beng hydropower project and the MRC CS, Vietnamese NGOs submitted a public statement entitled "Consultation on the Management and Use of Water in the Mainstream Mekong River" to the MRC and national Mekong River committees. This statement requested the following: the provision of guidelines by the CS for the planning and use of sustainable water resources of the Mekong River; the application of the PNPCA process to each hydropower dam; the reassessment of the PNPCA process by MRC; the reconstruction and establishment of communication channels for media and citizens;

and the guaranteeing of access to information, expression of opinion, and participation opportunities for affected communities. These Vietnamese NGOs wish to provide necessary support in collaboration with the Vietnam National Mekong Committee and related organizations within PNPCA by obtaining timely information in regard to the Pak Beng hydroelectric project during the consultation process (Vietnamese NGOs and individuals 2017).

Thai NGO organizations are concerned about the influence of Thai investment in neighboring countries on human rights and the environment. Following the UNGPs, as well as international human rights treaties, they have urged the Thai government to establish a powerful mechanism to ensure that all organizations, including companies involved in overseas investments, ensure transparency and compliance with human rights and environmental standards. In fact, local communities have attempted to make such organizations accept responsibility for violations of human rights and environmental standards by bringing their cases to Thai courts. In response, the National Human Rights Commission of Thailand (NHRCT), in cooperation with regional and local human rights institutions, scrutinized violations and investigated numerous complaints concerning Thai cross-border investment. Consequently, in May 2016, NHRCT recommended that the Thai government prevent and correct human rights violations, ensure that Thai enterprises consider human rights, and improve the formal objection system for victims in Thailand with regard to extraterritorial obligations (ETOs)/business and human rights (BHR) and Thailand's cross-border development investment in Southeast Asia; the government agreed to implement these suggestions (The Network of Thai People in Eight Mekong Province et al. 2017).

In December 2015, the establishment of AEC marked a major milestone for ASEAN economic cooperation. Economic growth through regionalization has advantages and disadvantages. With regard to benefits, it may result in employment, increased income, and an increase in national revenues for beneficial public services such as welfare and education. However, with regard to harmful effects, infringement of workers' rights, deprivation of land and natural resources from the local community, corruption and bribery, and deterioration of the environment may result. Unless governments and companies accept responsibility for predicting and avoiding such social environmental losses and human rights violations, deepening the ASEAN economic integration will not be a success (Middleton 2016).

Over the past few decades, the focus on corporate social responsibility (CSR) has increased globally, and within ASEAN it is no exception; for example, in 2010 the ASEAN CSR network was established; this aims to promote responsible businesses and enable them to achieve sustainable, equitable, and inclusive social, environmental, and economic development. According to a report on CSR and human rights by the ASEAN Intergovernmental Commission on Human Rights (AICHR), which was created in October 2009, there are two main reasons for CSR being useful for human rights protection. One is that many companies are integrating CSR into their core business, and the other is that investors and consumers are becoming increasingly interested in the human rights violations of corporations. Furthermore, cooperation in regard to defending human rights is becoming common among major multinational corporations. However, there are many problems. For example, CSR is still considered voluntary and is being implemented in Asia on a philanthropic basis. In addition, CSR activities should be performed "bottom up," beginning with the worksite and staff but, in reality, they are implemented "top-down," beginning with top executive management (AICHR 2014: 4–7).

In 2011, the UNGPs, which has the framework of "protect, respect, remedy," was approved by the UN Human Rights Committee. This advocates that governments protect human rights, that companies respect human rights, and that both parties work to correct human rights violations. Furthermore, it also recommends that states consider how corporate activities in other countries affect human rights; this is known as "extraterritorial obligation." Moreover, the AICHR has the potential to impose further ETOs.

With regard to economic development, pursuing only economic profits and pursuing human-centered sustainable development are mutually exclusive. In order to achieve human-centered economic growth, corporate accountability based on the upholding of human rights is essential. It is also suggested that governments increase the enforcement of regulations and establish an appropriate redress system. Furthermore, the development of extraterritorial obligations will greatly contribute to the protection of human rights and the realization of fair and sustainable regional formation (Middleton 2016).

Conclusion

In the two cases described earlier, the Dawei SEZ Project in Myanmar and the dam projects in Laos, the governments concerned and local agencies in the area are requested to seriously address the consequences, such as by conducting impact assessments, surveilling pollution and accidents, and implementing disaster preparation. Foreign investors are also encouraged to establish mechanisms and mobilize personnel to protect against the associated risks. Meanwhile, local communities are expected to play a key role in making suggestions and to act to protect their rights, monitoring the works of these projects and providing information to ensure that development is sustainable and fair. Further, transnational collaboration across borders and with international NGOs is also a necessary tool for the success of such projects. Finally, ensuring the corporate accountability of businesses is absolutely necessary for ASEAN sustainability.

In addition, as clarified in this chapter, civil society is also developing cross-border activities in response to the negative effects of developmentalism along the Mekong River. At present, the ideal foundation for this is international norms such as respect for human rights and environmental protection. By relying on these norms structured by international law, civil society has greatly contributed to the formation of an alternative Mekong public sphere that is not based on economic development. This normative sub-region formation by civil society networks as well as by national and international organizations can be positioned as a pioneering case for other sub-regions in Asia where transnational civil society activities are not yet as developed.

References

Anonymous Author (2015) Don't Risk What You Can't Afford to Lose (http://www.internationalrivers.org/blogs/263/guest-blog-dams-don-t-risk-what-you-can-t-afford-to-lose, accessed October 3, 2017).

ASEAN Intergovernmental Commission on Human Rights (AICHR) (2014) AICHR's Thematic Study on CSR and Human Rights in ASEAN (http://aichr.org/?dl_name=AICHRs_Thematic_Study_on_CSR_and_Human_Rights_in_ASEAN.pdf, accessed October 3, 2017).

Community Resource Centre, EarthRights International, International Rivers, NGO Forum on Cambodia, Northeastern Rural Development, and Cambodian Rural Development Team (2014) Complaint to the Human Rights Commission of Malaysia Against Mega First Corporation Berhad, Project Developer of the Don Sahong Dam, Lao PDR (http://www.internationalrivers.org/sites/default/files/attached-files/complaint_against_mega_first_corp_berhad.pdf, accessed October 3, 2017).

Dawei Development Association (2014a) Network Calls for Significant Problems to be Addressed before Dawei SEZ Project Revived (http://www.burmapartnership.org/wp-content/uploads/2014/10/PR_-Thai-MPs-visit_9.10.14-Eng.pdf, accessed October 3, 2017).

Dawei Development Association (2014b) Network Calls for Myanmar and Thailand Governments to Acknowledge Responsibility and Address Significant Problems in Dawei SEZ before New Concessions Granted (http://www.burmapartnership.org/wp-content/uploads/2014/11/11.11.14_DDA_ASEAN-Summit-Press-Release-.pdf, accessed October 3, 2017).

International Rivers (2015) The Don Sahong Dam (http://www.internationalrivers.org/sites/default/files/attached-files/dsh_factsheet_2015_-_english.pdf, accessed October 3, 2017).

Kemp, Melody (2017) The Dammed Don: Lao Hydropower Project Pushes ahead despite Alarm from Scientists (https://news.mongabay.com/2017/01/the-dammed-don-lao-hydropower-project-pushes-ahead-despite-alarm-from-scientists, accessed October 3, 2017).

Lewis, Simon (2016) "Government Told to Demand Transparency from SEZ Firms," *The Irrawaddy*, June 18, 2016.

Lobrigo, Frank E (2017) "Dams Threaten to Cut Mekong Rice Supply," *The Nation*, April 14, 2017.

Mahitthirook, Amornrat (2017) "Myanmar gives Road Link Boost," *Bangkok Post*, February 4, 2017.

Middleton, Carl (2016) ASEAN: How About Accountability Beyond Borders? (http://www.aseannews.net/asean-accountability-beyond-borders, accessed October 3, 2017).

My Mekong (2017) Position Statement: Thailand's Extraterritorial Obligations in Transboundary Investments (http://www.mymekong.org/mymekong/?p=1185, accessed October 3, 2017).

The Network of Thai People in Eight Mekong Province et al. (2017) Position Statement: Thailand's Extraterritorial Obligations in Transboundary Investments (http://www.mymekong.org/mymekong/?p=1185, accessed October 3, 2017).

Ross, Kate (2017) A Shared Commitment to the Future of the Mekong River (http://www.internationalrivers.org/blogs/259/a-shared-commitment-to-the-future-of-the-mekong-river, accessed October 3, 2017).

Rujivanarom, Pratch (2017a) "Law Needed to Regulate Thai Investors' Abuses Abroad: Thai, Myanmar Groups," *The Nation*, February 27, 2017.

Rujivanarom, Pratch (2017b) "Mekong Diplomacy: A Bridge that has Failed," *The Nation*, January 24, 2017.

Saichan, Kosum, and Achareeya Saisin (2014) Transborder Civil Society and International Mega Development Project in Myanmar: A Case Study of Dawei Deep Sea Port and Industrial Estate Project, Chiang Mai: ASEAN Studies Center, Chiang Mai University (in Thai).

Samuelsson, Marika (2016) Facing the Reality of Hydropower (http://www.mekongcommons.org/facing-reality-hydropower, accessed October 3, 2017).

Sathisan, Vani, and James Tager (2015) Investments in Myanmar: Silence Cannot be the Answer (http://www.icj.org/investments-in-myanmar-silence-cannot-be-the-answer, accessed October 3, 2017).

Theparat, Chatrudee (2017a) "B4.5bn Dawei Development Loan Okayed," *Bangkok Post*, February 15, 2017.

Theparat, Chatrudee (2017b) "ITD Seeks Update on Dawei Plan," *Bangkok Post*, February 7, 2017.

Theparat, Chatrudee (2017c) "Firms Urged to Invest in Myanmar," *Bangkok Post*, 4 February.

Trandem, Ame (2014) Is the Mekong at a Tipping Point? (http://www.internationalrivers.org/blogs/263-0, accessed October 3, 2017).

Trandem, Ame (2015) Changing Tides for a Common Future: The MRC and Hydro-Diplomacy (http://www.internationalrivers.org/blogs/263/changing-tides-for-a-common-future-the-mrc-and-hydro-diplomacy, accessed October 3, 2017).

Vietnamese NGOs and individuals (2017) Statement from Vietnamese Non-Governmental Organization to the Mekong River Commission (http://www.mekongeye.com/2017/02/22/statement-from-vietnamese-non-governmental-organization-to-the-mekong-river-commission, accessed October 3, 2017).

5 Changing borderland local communities with development of the GMS program

Ekamol Saichan

Introduction

The capital and big cities of most countries play a dominant role in the development as well as economy of their states. These cities not only harbor administrative authorities but also launch economic activities. Moreover, these places are attractive to prospective residents and investors who spend money for running different types of businesses due to their abundant facilities, human resources, and convenient communication and transportation for both domestic and international purposes. The large number of jobs and high salary also draw people hoping to have a better future. There is no doubt about the richness of entertainment in different forms or activities. These attractive conditions and atmosphere are easily observed in most countries' capitals and big cities. However, especially in centralized states of developing countries in Southeast Asia or the Association of Southeast Asian Nations (ASEAN), the big gap between growth and development among capital cities and rural areas is a serious problem. We have observed the situation of "urban bias development" for about half of century.

Specifically, in mainland Southeast Asia, until the 1980s, the situation in areas called borderlands was worse than in the rest of the country. These places were at the edge of each state and surrounded the country in different forms. In many cases, these areas comprised jungles, mountain ranges, rivers, etc. Not only the distance from the capital and big cities but also shortage of or difficulty obtaining basic infrastructure facilities in everyday life created inconvenient conditions for people to settle here in communities. The borderlands still had dispersed communities with very small populations, except for towns or communities located near or opposite the big cities of neighboring countries, such as in the cases of Nongkhai province in Thailand and Vientiane, the capital of Laos. The latter community is large enough in terms of urban size, population, and economic scale to generate the growth of the opposite town.

Some examples of difficulties in accessing border communities are found in the cases of Lao Bao on the border between Vietnam and Laos and Boten on the border between Laos and China. Just 33 years ago, these were small remote villages in the jungles of Vietnam and Laos. Particularly, the Lao Bao village of Vietnam was dominated by ethnic minorities: the Pako, Van Kieu, and Kado with very few Vietnamese (or Kinh people). Although, towns nearest to Lao Bao (Khe Sanh) and Boten (Luang Namtha) were at a distance less than 50 kilometers, it took an entire day to travel to either place. At that time, there were no regular roads, and villagers could only travel by walking. Additionally, basic services such as electricity, running water, healthcare, and education were unavailable. People's daily lives totally depended on natural resources such as forest and river products. There were few visitors for trade or other purposes. The villagers themselves seldom traveled outside their communities, except for collecting forest products and hunting for food.

Although bigger border communities such as towns and provinces were equipped with basic infrastructure such as electricity, running water, asphalt roads, sanitary system, hospitals, schools, groceries, restaurants, and cinema theaters, their atmosphere was rather quiet, particularly after 8.00 pm at night. All government offices closed at 4.30 pm, and most private services closed at 5.00 or 6.00 pm. Consequently, the communities, especially their public roads, remained silent from 8.00 pm until 6.00 am the following morning, except on annual festival nights. Unsurprisingly, government officials of countries such as Thailand did not want to work in border towns. At that time, transfer of government officials from inner towns or cities to border towns or provinces was regarded as a punishment. From the economic perspective, these communities had very modest economies with small volume of trade, mainly domestic trade with local people. There was very little border or international trade and foreign tourism. Because of these reasons, border communities or towns were not attractive areas for national and international economies.

Until recently, some signs of changes have appeared in several parts of the world. From 1986, socialist governments of Vietnam and Laos implemented the reform policies of *Doi Moi* (Economic Reform) and *Jintanakarn Mai* (New Economic Mechanism), respectively. Moreover, the Berlin Wall separating East Berlin (socialist regime) and West Berlin (liberal system) was torn down in 1989; the Socialist Soviet Union disintegrated into several countries with more liberal economies in 1991; and (socialist) Cambodia was forced to organize liberal general elections under the supervision of the United Nations (UN) in 1993. These events led the world in a neoliberal direction under the hegemony of the United States. Although China and Southeast Asian countries such as Vietnam and Laos kept their communist (or socialist) one-party systems, their economies (and some social aspects) became liberal and they shared markets with other capitalist countries of the world, especially those in the West, East Asia, and Southeast Asia.

Several economic cooperation and development projects of regional groups, sub-regional groups, and individual countries have been developed and launched in different parts of the world, such as the North American Free Trade Agreement (NAFTA), ASEAN Free Trade Area (AFTA), ASEAN Plus Three (China, Japan, and Korea), ASEAN–EU, Greater Mekong Sub-region (GMS), and North-South and East-West Economic Corridor of GMS. The terms globalization,

126 *Ekamol Saichan*

regionalization, single market, and single currency, as well as other terms with similar implications, have been widely discussed and mentioned as trends of world development. Consequently, this trend of neoliberal development has led to several rapid changes, such as in the flow of capital, labor, goods and services, patterns of connectivity, tourism growth, and increase in cooperation projects in different areas of the world.

For mainland Southeast Asia, rapid political and socioeconomic changes have occurred since the mid-1980s. Such changes, both positive and negative, have transpired after a long period of political instability, civil war, economic stagnation, and atmosphere of antagonism or enmity, particularly between Thailand and Indochina (Cambodia, Laos, and Vietnam). Some examples of these changes are cargo boat connectivity through the Mekong River, new highways, increased international checkpoints, border trade on overland routes, and the growth of local and international tourists. These changes have had a significant impact on the communities and everyday life of people in this area. Cities, towns, and other communities in these countries have to adapt themselves to deal with the changes.

This chapter mainly focuses on changes in border communities, which were once perceived as marginal areas where life was difficult. Normally, international trade and foreign travel abroad is conducted through capital or big cities; however, recently, border communities or towns in the Mekong Basin have become the main route of communication and trade.

A good example of this phenomenon is the case of Thailand. In the past five years, the value of Thailand's border trade with its neighboring countries was over 60% of its international trade. This is attributable to changes in several aspects, ranging from political and socioeconomic conditions, and communication factors to the process of international cooperation. This change has had a drastic effect on existing border towns of Thailand and its neighboring countries. Consequently, border communities have been forced to change their shapes and characteristics in several aspects such as building new roads, founding special economic zones, more hotels, guest houses and restaurants, and a variety of residents for serving investment and visitors (Table 5.1).

This study's analysis is based on the intensive field survey conducted in six twin border towns of GMS countries: Mae Sot (Thailand) and Myawaddy

Table 5.1 The proportion of Thailand's border trade with neighboring countries in GMS

Thailand with (%)	2011	2012	2013	2014	2015	2016
Cambodia	73.87	65.89	67.24	69.85	66.30	61.59
Laos	86.14	88.31	85.12	86.30	91.60	98.19
Myanmar	85.44	85.39	82.64	81.85	83.20	81.7
Vietnam	2.87	3.98	5.22	12.37	11.54	11.32
China	1.60	1.69	1.91	2.38	2.76	2.83

Source: Adapted from Department of Foreign Trade, Ministry of Commerce (Thailand), Statistics of Border Trade and Transboundary Trade of Thailand Report (2011–2013), 2014 and Statistics of Border Trade and Transboundary Trade of Thailand Report (2014–2016), 2017.

(Myanmar), Chiang Khong (Thailand) and Houay Xai (Laos), Boten (Laos) and Mohan (China), Mukdahan (Thailand) and Savannakhet (Laos), Dansavan (Laos) and Lao Bao (Vietnam), and Aranyaprathet (Thailand) and Poipet (Cambodia)

This field survey was conducted in March 2017, except for Mohan, which the author could not visit due to the problem of visa on arrival. Moreover, some information was accumulated from long experience in dealing with GMS countries as the Chair of GMS Studies Center, Faculty of Political Science, and Member of Sustainable Development of Social Science Faculty, Chiang Mai University, Thailand.

The emergence of the territorial state and the significance of the border

For 10 centuries (5th to the 10th century CE), most parts of the world were dominated by the feudal system. The feudal state had no specific territory with boundaries under the single sovereignty. The state's size was always changing, sometimes overnight, depending on the strength of their leaders and armies. Its people could also move in and out at any time. The perception of nationality was not identified as a commitment. The idea of sovereignty or supreme power of the state over its population and land was not recognized as a political machine for managing an organization. Thus, fluctuation (appearance and disappearance) of different states was common. This political pattern led to a large number of states during this period. It was estimated that, before the colonial period (19th century), Southeast Asia had around 42 feudal states (Osborne 2000).

As the Christian religious state (the Vatican) and its peripheries in Europe declined since the late 15th century, secular kings or emperors attempted to increase their power and separated from the domination of the Pope. Additionally, they fought with aristocrats and lords for centralizing their power. These secular leaders were fascinated by the political term "sovereignty," which referred to the theory of absolute and undivided power and was coined by French political philosopher Jean Bodin (1530–1596) in his book *Six Livres de la République* (Friedeburg 2010).

At that time, the idea of sovereignty fit with the kings' need to have their own power separate from that of religious states in order to dominate over all aristocrats and lords in their feudal states. This notion of power legitimized their rule and state. Thus, the new modern state developed gradually in Europe since the late 16th century. There are four major characteristics of the new modern state—(fixed) territory, population, single government (at the capital city), and sovereignty. This new type of state is called the "(modern) nation-state." As mentioned previously, the concept originated in Europe, but it was applied to former European colonies in Latin America, Asia, and Africa after their independence. Therefore, the late 16th century is a political turning point for state development.

In the early nation-state period, the area where the territories of two or three states met was called the "frontier." The term "border" was not recognized due to the unclear territories of most states. Hence, "frontier" came to mean the front part of an army. Later, interaction among different states such as in maintaining authority over the territory and citizens, collecting tax, and providing rights of individual members gradually forced them to display clear boundaries. Thus, the notion of a (fixed) territorial state with sovereignty (normally through government) over its people, land, air space, and sea became widely accepted in international relations. The term "border" also gradually replaced "frontier" because it provided a clearer meaning for practicing domestic and international laws (Donnan and Haller 2000; Bigo 2005). Borders can take the form of natural objects (e.g., rivers, canals, ranges of mountain, or forests) or human-made objects (e.g., walls, fences, or barriers). The border's function and role can be both positive and negative, which we will discuss in detail later. Most countries have experienced border issues (Baramova 2010).

In Southeast Asia, the emergence of nation-states, with the exception of Thailand, started after the end of World War II in 1945 as they gained independence from the colonial West, mainly Britain and France. The Thai nation-state was formed gradually with the name "Siam" since the late 19th century. Understandably, the colonial West played a crucial role in drawing demarcations of Southeast Asian countries. Each country's territory depended on its colonial history and treaties between colonial powers. Thailand is an exception due to its political status as a buffer state between Britain and France. The formation of nation-states in Southeast Asia after World War II was different from that in Europe in the late 16th and early 17th centuries. European nation-states formed by gradually integrating the same or similar ethnic groups based on their historical development, whereas Southeast Asian nation-states were separated by the demarcation of the colonial West. Consequently, ethnic and border conflicts became, and still are, serious problems in Southeast Asia.

After formation of nation-states with fixed territories, all populated areas along the demarcation or border became border communities or towns of different sizes. Theoretically, all people, whether they live in the inner or border areas of a state, must identify their "nationality." For crossing borders, people, goods, and other objects require documents and permission. Moreover, they need to follow the respective laws and regulations for entering neighboring or other countries. Hence, apart from international checkpoints at the airports and seaports of each country, overland or border checkpoints of present territorial nation-states are very important units. This condition has led to increasing the importance of border towns in several aspects. However, people's perception of the modern nation-state, particularly that of local people in border communities, is vague. For example, several local people cross borders through natural or traditional routes (across rivers or mountain ranges) despite the close presence of official checkpoints. Government staff members have also observed this pattern of crossing. In addition, the importance of border towns is dependent on several factors such as uncertainty of the political situation, economic atmosphere, government policies, and development projects. Most GMS border towns and communities have rapidly and drastically increased in size and importance since the 1990s.

Borders in different Southeast Asian contexts: fluctuation of border communities

Borders under ideological conflicts in Indochina and the end of the Vietnam War and the Cold War

To understand the present situation of border towns or communities in GMS, we need to look back at the developments and changes in this area. As mentioned previously, this was the so-called "Southeast Asia" area dominated by the feudal system of the local elite. The main characteristic of this system was dispersion of power among strong leaders or groups without a fixed territorial state and sovereignty. People could move to other places to find a convenient location to live. However, once settled in an area under the influence of the rulers, they were forced to serve the ruling class. In the meantime, they might find a way to escape to other leaders. At that time, this situation led to the creation of a large number of power centers.

The first invaders from the West were Portugal in 1511, followed by Spain, Netherlands, Britain, France, and the United States; this led to occupation of the present Southeast Asia, mainly in the 19th century, with the exception of Siam or present Thailand. After domination, the Western colonial powers applied the concept of the nation-state (particularly, fixed territory without sovereignty) to their colonies by combining some centers of power. An example includes the combination of Luang Prabang, Vientiane, and Champasak to create the present Laos (Evans 2002). Moreover, colonial areas of France, that is, Cambodia, Laos, and Vietnam, were administered as a political domain under the name of "Indochina." At that time, France had created several treaties for demarcating the territory between its two political units (Cambodia and Laos) with Siam. Britain also utilized the same political pattern of treaties between its colonies (Burma, now Myanmar and Malaysia) and Siam, but these treaties were signed before France's treaties. All treaties have been effective until the present day. This a main reason for territorial or border conflicts between Thailand (Siam) and its neighboring countries for several decades. This is a negative heritage of colonial powers in Southeast Asia (Osborne 2000).

After World War II, most parts of Southeast Asia gradually became independent nation-states. However, peace did not follow independence. Some new nations, such as Malaysia and Burma (Myanmar), faced ethnic conflicts. However, ideological conflicts had a more serious impact on the development of Southeast Asia. After World War II, the world was divided into two camps: the capitalist or liberal block led by the United States and the socialist block led by the Soviet Union. In Asia, victory of the Chinese Communist Party in mainland China in 1949 led to the entry of the United States, a new world leader, into Southeast Asia in 1951. The United States claimed the burden of protecting the "Free World." Since then, Indochina and Thailand were in a constant state of war for three decades (1945–1975) under the title of the "Cold War."

There was also an atmosphere of war in Indochina and Burma during the French and British colonial periods. In Burma, under the short Japanese occupation, the Japanese army forced Allied prisoners of war to build a railway linking the borders between Burma and Thailand in the Kanchanaburi province. The Japanese army's aim was to cross Thailand for further invasion into Indochina of the French colonies. At that time, the Japanese army's cruelty and spread of malaria in the jungle killed several thousands of Allied prisoners of war. This was why "the bridge on the River Kwai," which was part of this railway line, became a well-known railway bridge. Now, it is part of the land-route development project for promoting tourism in Thailand. It is also expected to be a rail route to link the east (Vietnam and Cambodia) and the west (Myanmar) parts of GMS.

In Indochina, the Thai frontier sometimes functioned as a safe house for leaders of the liberation or independent movements. A classical case was that of Ho Chi Minh, leader of the Việt Minh Movement for Vietnamese independence from France. He was also recognized as a leader in the fight for the independence of Cambodia and Laos. It is believed that he sometimes stayed in Nakorn Phanom province, a frontier community of Thailand along the Mekong River during 1928–1929. He lived in Nakorn Phanom to escape arrest from the French army in Vietnam and raised funds from Vietnamese refugees in Thailand to support the Việt Minh Movement. Recently, the local government of Nakorn Phanom province provided financial support to maintain his old residence as well as the house of Uncle Ho in remembrance. Both Thai and Vietnamese governments have recognized this activity. At present, Uncle Ho's village in Nakorn Phanom province is a tourist destination for both Thai and Vietnamese people (Quoc Toan 2013).

During the colonial period of mainland Southeast Asia, the frontier (or border) areas between Siam (Thailand) and neighboring countries such as Burma (Myanmar) and Indochina had no serious conflicts. Their local people traveled between countries easily without documentation. The major border conflicts included disputes concerning territories between Siam and the colonial powers of Britain and France. However, after World War II, the Indochinese countries could not form a real nation-state, especially as the French continued to occupy Vietnam. Additionally, since 1951, the United States supported the governments of Cambodia and Laos at their capital cities, Phnom Penh and Vientiane, respectively. However, the Việt Minh Movement's victory in July 1954 over the French army at Dien Bien Phu in the northern part of Vietnam was the end of French colonial rule in Indochina; however, the United States dominated the southern part of Vietnam. This led to the separation of Vietnam into two countries: North Vietnam (Hanoi as the capital) and South Vietnam (Saigon, later Ho Chi Minh City, as the capital) (Osborne 2000).

Although Indochinese countries became independent states with serious fighting between the right (capitalist ideology) and left (socialist ideology) wings, their concept of nation-state from the perspective of international relations in this sub-region was not strict. The lives of local people in communities bordering Thailand and Cambodia, Laos, and Burma were similar to those before independence. This is because easy border crossing was the common ideology of capitalism under the United States. However, underdeveloped conditions in terms of poor communication and transportation in these new nation-states prevented the growth of border communities in the 1950s and 1960s. Life in most border towns was quiet and slow. Their immigration and customs offices were in small buildings with very few officials. Tourists, especially foreign tourists, were uncommon except in Nong Khai province. At that time, visitors to Nong Khai took small boats to cross the Mekong River in order to visit Vientiane, Laos' capital, to buy low-priced luxury goods, such as American cigarettes, French perfumes, and clothes. Tax-free goods were imported to Laos to serve American soldiers in Laos. This was the reason for the rapid growth of Sri Chiang Mai community, a border district of Nong Khai province located on the riverbank directly opposite Vientiane. In addition, the main battlefield of the Vietnam War was in Vietnam and some inner parts of Cambodia and Laos. Thus, war did not have a strong effect on border communities except between the border of Laos and South Vietnam. Thai officials undertook strict security measures to prevent expansion of the Communist Party of Thailand along the Mekong River border.

Period of difficulties for border communities under different regimes in Mainland Southeast Asia (1975–1986)

The victory of left wing movements guided by communist or socialist ideology in Indochina led to the end of the Vietnam War in 1975. This was a great event of modern revolution for developing countries in Southeast Asia. Since then, Cambodia (mid-April 1975), Vietnam (late April 1975), and Laos (December 1975) have become socialist regimes under a one-party totalitarian system, which was similar to what had happened in the Soviet Union in 1917 and China in 1949. Thus, these three countries stood in the opposite direction to Thailand.

Although the student uprising in October 1973 changed Thai politics from a military authoritarian regime to liberal politics or democracy, its economy still has a capitalist regime, especially due to close relationships with the West and Japan. In addition, there is significant negative attitude in Vietnam, Laos (after the revolution 1975), and Cambodia toward Thailand due to Thai involvement in the Vietnam War guided by the United States. There have been frequent clashes of the two opposing sides in the form of speeches in public media and violent fighting at the border. Immigration offices at several border gates, including the traditional route (of local people), was closed from time to time. An example of this difficult situation is the case of Chiang Khong community of Thailand. Chiang Khong is a border district along Mekong River in Chiang Rai province in Northern Thailand. Once, it was a good place for running border trade with its opposite town in Laos, namely Houay Xay, which was a main route for distributing goods to Northern Laos. Intermittent closing of this border by the government of Laos seriously affected border trade.

The volume of trade decreased gradually. Hence, several shops had to close and move to other places. In addition, international co-operation and collaboration was hardly seen. This was a period of severe tension in this sub-region (Walker 1999; Evans 2000).

The Border under the current economic reform and political changes

However, after 10 years of running their countries under the new socialist regime, the governments of Laos and Vietnam identified several obstacles for overall development and reasons for the shortage of necessary consumption goods. Moreover, there were signs of changes in the socialist block led by the Soviet Union, such as decrease in financial and material supports and the reform policies of *Perestroika* (Economic Restructuring) and *Glasnost* (Openness) in 1985. Therefore, Laos and Vietnam needed to adapt themselves. As mentioned previously, the governments of Laos and Vietnam respectively announced the policies of *Jintanakarn Mai* or New Economic Mechanism and *Doi Moi* or Economic Reform in 1986. The policies' major concerns were opening up the country, privatization, free market, direct foreign investment, and the like.

The former Thai Prime Minister Chatchai Chunhavan declared the policy of "From Battlefield to Marketplace" a few years later. In addition, two enormous events occurred at the global level: tearing down of the Berlin Wall in 1989 and disintegration of the Soviet Union in 1991. They implied the end of the "Cold War," which had dominated the political situation and economic development throughout the world for more than four decades. These phenomena had tremendous effects on the emergence of a new direction of world development in the subsequent periods. They were also turning points of international relations in several parts of the world.

However, this drastic change did not appear in Cambodia. After the overthrow of the old regime in 1975, political conflict still dominated Cambodian society in the form of radical conflicts within the left wing itself: the left wing supported by China (known as Red Khmer) and the left wing supported by the Soviet Union and Vietnam. The conflict became obvious during the Chinese invasion into Vietnamese borders in early 1979. Finally, a UN Commission managed the first liberal general elections in 1993. Thus, Cambodia had to spend time, money, and human resources to deal with serious conflicts until nearly two decades after the revolution of 1975.

Domestic politics in Myanmar moved in a direction opposite to other countries in the same period. After the coup in 1962 led by General Ne Win, Burma was ruled by the army and was isolated from other nations. The situation was worsened by the bloody coup by the junta on August 8, 1988 (known as "8888"). Then, a group of military leaders tightened the rule of the country in the name of the State Peace and Development Council (SPDC), known as the State Law and Order Restoration Council (SLORC) from 1997. Nevertheless, border trade of local people through major routes such as Myawaddy (Myanmar)–Mae Sot

(Thailand) and Tachileik (Myanmar)–Mae Sai (Thailand) continued regularly because the majority of consumption goods in Myanmar at that time were products from Thailand.

Nevertheless, the major factor of rapid growth in GMS countries is the role of China. Geographically, China is not classified as a Southeast Asian country, but it is still a nation-state in the GMS as its southwest territory is located in the first part of upper Mekong River and occupies nearly half the length of Mekong River (2,130 out of 4,350 kilometers). The most important fact for our analysis is the active and aggressive role of China in boosting rapid change in GMS.

Today, China is a world economy leader; however, we need to look back at the start of rapid development in China. The "Cultural Revolution" that took place in China from 1966 to 1976 paralyzed the country's economy, society, and political order to a significant degree. It led to the heaviest losses since the founding of the People's Republic of China in 1949. Thus, the program of "Four Modernizations" was initiated by leader Zhou Enlai in 1963 and enacted by Deng Xiaoping in 1978. This program aimed to strengthen the fields of agriculture, industry, national defense, and science and technology in China. Its initial projects from 1979 to 1984 were supported by the United Nations Development Program and other funding agencies, including the World Bank and the Asian Development Bank (ADB). The Four Modernizations were designed to make China a great economic power by the early 21st century. Their strategies were concerned with increasing the volume of foreign trade by opening up its markets and purchasing machinery from the West and Japan to access advanced technologies. Under the situation of high political stability and strong command of the centralized state, China developed rapidly in different aspects. China showed its success as a modern state with high GDP and huge surplus of products by the late 1990s. Then, China expanded its economic activities, including social and political affairs, to different areas of the world. Certainly, GMS is a target area for China.

It can be said that the introduction of *Perestroika* and *Glasnost* in the Soviet Union in 1985 and subsequent years, respectively; operation of *Doi Moi* in Vietnam and *Jintanakarn Mai* in Laos in 1986; implementation of the policy of "Changing Battlefield to become a Marketplace" in Thailand in 1987; tearing down of the Berlin Wall in 1989; disintegration of the Soviet Union in 1991; end of Cold War; and expansion in the role of China have led to the new trend of development (liberal or neoliberal in particular) and emergence of the new face of international relations.

Economic corridor routes, physical connectivity, and changes in border communities

Emergence of GMS and changes in borders

With regard to the geographical area, the nation-states of Southeast Asia can be classified into two groups. The first group is the mainland Southeast Asia composed of Cambodia, Laos, Myanmar, Thailand, and Vietnam. The second group is the archipelago group (an island group or island chain) composed of Malaysia, Singapore, Brunei, Indonesia, and Philippines. At present, the newest country in the archipelago group is Timor Leste (which became an independent nation-state in 2002), but it is not an official member of ASEAN yet. This geographical feature implies some aspects of international connectivity, which will be discussed later.

As mentioned earlier, in the 1990s, the atmosphere of friendship and necessity of dependent development and international cooperation gradually replaced the feeling of antagonism and opposing political ideologies in Southeast Asia, particularly between Thailand, Indochinese countries, and China. Moreover, the socialist countries, Cambodia, Laos, Vietnam, China, and the isolated Myanmar, have now accepted some principles of liberal development strategy.

In 1992, with ADB's support, a group of six countries along the Mekong River, known as the GMS, entered into a program of sub-regional economic cooperation designed to enhance economic relations among the countries. These six countries include the People's Republic of China (specifically, the Yunnan province and Guangxi Zhuang Autonomous Region) as the original country of Mekong River, Myanmar, Laos, Thailand, Cambodia, and Vietnam as the last country of the river before it flows into the South China Sea. Geographically, the GMS, with the exception of China, comprises the mainland of Southeast Asia. Unlike the archipelago group, territories of GMS countries connect naturally through land and rivers. Some crucial factors of borders crossing are the relationship among nation-states and improvement of communication routes, roads, and bridges as well as utilization of modern transportation.

At the time of its founding in 1992, the aim of GMS was to launch a program of sub-regional economic relations covering nine priority sectors: agriculture, energy, environment, human resource development, investment, telecommunication, tourism, transport infrastructure, and transport and trade facilitation (ADB 2012: 3). Although GMS is not an international organization such as ASEAN, its attempts in dealing with activities of international cooperation are more obvious than those of ASEAN. Especially, the emphasis on physical or geographical connectivity of the economic corridor approach and border trade has led to rapid growth of border areas. However, it is unfair to view ASEAN's efforts as lesser than that of GMS. Several ASEAN agreements have had indirect effects on GMS economy. For example, the ASEAN Economic Community project and visa exemption for short visits (normally 30 days) for ASEAN citizens have promoted rapid growth of tourism in GMS, which has led the governments and tourist towns to enjoy increased income.

After the founding of GMS, several projects were developed and launched for the nine flagship targets areas, but the most striking impact on GMS border communities has been due to economic corridors and physical connectivity, tourism, and border trade projects (Ishida 2013).

The main purpose of the economic corridor approach and physical connectivity was to boost economic growth and trade among GMS countries and other areas. This was important in order to rectify the negative relations and poor communication during the previous period of conflicts and Cold War. However, the most active actors for these activities in the early period were China and Thailand because of their higher economic status and more successful industrial development. Particularly, China wanted to export its surplus of cheap products from agricultural and industrial sectors after nearly 20 years of the Four Modernizations policy (1978). From the perspective of international relations, it also was China's strategy to increase influence in Southeast Asia after the United States' withdrawal following the defeat in the Vietnam War in 1975 and decline of Soviet Union's influence after its disintegration in 1991.

Several programs for corridors and physical connectivity were introduced. The most effective and well-known programs were the North-South Economic Corridor (NSEC) of Road R3 and East-West Economic Corridor (EWEC) of Road No. 9.

North-South Economic Corridor of road R3

The NSEC links China, Myanmar, Laos, and Thailand. There are two routes to link these four countries:

1   Road R3A (formerly R3E): The major communities for our analysis, after its starting city, Kunming of Southwest China, are Mohan (Chinese border town), Boten and Houay Xay (two border towns in different directions in Laos), and Chiang Khong (Thai border town). If we include Bangkok, the length of this route is around 1,800 kilometers. This route was finished after the completion of the fourth friendship bridge, Chiang Khong–Houay Xay, in 2013. At present, R3A is the major overland communication route between Southwestern China and Northern Thailand including Bangkok.
2   Road R3B (formerly R3W): This road runs from Kunming city through Kengtung and Tachilek in Myanmar and links with Thailand at Mae Sai district of Chiang Rai province. Although its distance for linking Kunming with Thailand is shorter than R3A, it is a risky route because of fighting between the Myanmar military and armed ethnic groups. In addition, it requires extra expenses for the protection of different ethnic minority groups.

The river route along Mekong River from Jinghong or Xishuangbanna, the far south of China's Yunnan province to Chiang Sane district of Thailand, was operated before the overland connectivity program. However, there is a serious problem of the fluctuation of water level in the Mekong River. Particularly, the lowest level in the dry season (normally between April and May) obstructs the launch of cargo vessels. Hence, China and Thailand want an alternative route of communication, which is especially necessary to connect the land-locked Yunnan province to the sea for international trade.

Therefore, in the early period of the NSEC of GMS, commercial navigation on the Mekong River route was the main channel for border trade between China (Yunnan province) and Northern Thailand. The river route was used for physical connectivity because it provided a convenient way to transform the existing natural communication, and the investment cost for improving the route was low. For this purpose, China destroyed some rapids and islets in the river. Although China needed to negotiate with Myanmar and Laos, they were smaller bargaining powers and were dependent on China in several ways.

At that time, Chiang Saen, a small border district near the Golden Triangle of Chiang Rai province, was not only a popular ancient town for Thai and foreign tourists but also the busiest town for border trade. In only one week, caravans of more than 100 Chinese cargo vessels with agricultural products (mainly fruits, vegetables, and manufacturing goods) visited Chiang Saen Pier (or Port).

Formerly, Chiang Saen Port was a small local port run by the local municipality. The Thai government's cabinet authorized the Port Authority of Thailand to manage and operate the port on March 2003 and renovate it to serve both the modern system and manual work. Then, it was officially put into service on October 2003. At that time, the port connected not only local people but also foreign tourists who visited the Golden Triangle; Chinese workers who accompanied cargo vessels; and migrant workers from Laos, Myanmar, and Thailand. Thus, the Chiang Saen border district had three roles: a historical or ancient town (a center of power 700 years ago), a tourist town of the Golden Triangle, and the latest one—a center of border trade with China on the Mekong River route. (In addition, some land developer groups have proposed it to be an industrial zone of factories and logistic hub.) The small and sleepy town of Chiang Saen grew and changed its face very fast; for example, a traffic system was implemented in the town center, and an increase in guesthouses, restaurants, and garbage (particularly from Chinese cargo ships) was observed. Certainly, interaction among three functions or roles was not easy to manage.

A solution for the crowded Chiang Saen Port was the construction of Chiang Saen Port 2 six kilometers south of old port along the Mekong River. Modern tools and management system are used to launch the new port in a large area, but some landscape obstacles are still being addressed. The second port began service in 2011. However, the importance of Chiang Sean as the border gate from and to Southern China has gradually decreased and returned to normal since the R3A road was completed and officially opened for communication in 2008. Particularly, upon completion of the fourth international Friendship Bridge linking Chiang Khong (Thailand) and Houay Xay (Laos), the main route of overland logistics between China and Thailand moved to Chiang Khong, another border district of Chiang Rai province located around 60 kilometers east of Chiang Saen along the Mekong River.

Indeed, Chiang Khong and its opposite town, Houay Xay of Laos, have had long tradition of border trade. Once, Houay Xay was the center of French colonial occupation and an American base (during the Vietnam War) for controlling the northern part of Laos through the Mekong River route. These twin

Figure 5.1 The Mekong River area in the Chiang Khong district, Chiang Rai province (Thailand), and Houay Xay district of Laos, a well-known habitat of giant catfish, the biggest river fish in the world

Source: Taken by the author, February 28, 2017.

Figure 5.2 A quiet street near the former immigration checkpoint area in Houay Xay district of Laos

Source: Taken by the author, February 28, 2017.

border towns have been the gateway for foreign visitors in the northern part of both countries, except during the period of ideological conflict between 1975 and 1985. Hence, their town communities were rather lively because the offices of immigration and custom were located in the town centers. However, closing of Laos after the revolution from 1975 to 1985 led to silent, sleepy towns on both sides of the Mekong River (Figure 5.1 and Figure 5.2).

However, introduction of the New Economic Policy in Laos in 1986 and change in the Thai policy concerning "Changing the Battlefield to Become a Marketplace," emergence of GMS in 1992, and construction of Road R3A for logistic connectivity have facilitated the rebirth of these twin border communities. At this time, a large number of small and medium modern guesthouses, hotels and restaurants, new buildings, and other services were offered to serve a variety of people. The towns became larger, and land speculation for construction of the fourth Friendship Bridge was a major cause of this rapid growth.

The fourth Friendship Bridge across the Mekong River to connect Thai highway and Road R3A of Laos was opened in 2013. However, most local people, including those who deal with service sectors such as petty merchants along the road, were disappointed with this connecting bridge. They complained that the bridge was located 10 kilometers from the center of Chiang Khong and 12 kilometers from the center of Houay Xay, which is quite far for local people and visitors.

The immigration and custom offices on both sides had already moved to the bridge. Crossing the border at the old ports by boat was no longer allowed. Crossing the bridge means more cost of traveling. Hence, the number of local people visiting the opposite side decreased. Meanwhile, tourists, public buses, and cargo trucks do not need to travel to the center of either border town. A classic case of the downfall of business was the dissolve of the branch of Krungsri Bank in Chiang Khong. In Houay Xay, although the number of service businesses seemed to increase, the majority of those firms were run by Chinese nationals from mainland China in the name of Laotian citizens. From the perspective of the local people on both sides, they would have rejected the bridge of connectivity had they known of the difficulty they would face in their daily lives after its completion. Now, the governments of both countries are pushing the projects of a logistic hub, industrial zone, and new town near the bridge. Thus, there is a big gap between the vision of government policymakers, private companies, and international organizations and the opinion of local people concerning connectivity development projects.

The opposite end of the Chiang Khong–Houay Xay route on Road R3A of Laos is Boten–Mohan (China). Their international immigration checkpoint opened for service in 1993. Before 2000, Boten was a small, remote border village. The big change occurred in 2003 when a Hong Kong company signed a 30-year lease on 1,640 hectares of land with the Laotian government to set up a special economic zone. Since then, the encroaching development of casinos and several large hotels replaced the jungle in Boten. This was an indirect

Figure 5.3 A modern hotel with a casino and other types of gambling facilities in Boten, border town of Laos, and Mohan, the opposite border town in China, in 2007
Source: Taken by the author, December 16, 2007.

consequence of the NSEC, which encouraged the Chinese government to build a highway from Kunming to its border town, Mohan. The visa-free travel and lure of gambling, which was illegal in China, was attractive to Chinese visitors hoping to find their luck and workers for jobs. More than 10,000 Chinese tourists crossed the border to enjoy the casino and several other forms of entertainment each month. Their visit stimulated the growth of more than 150 manufacturing shops in Mohan, a border town that is situated opposite to Boten and under China's jurisdiction. The Chinese government wanted Mohan to not only be the gateway to connect its southern area with Laos, Thailand, Malaysia, and Singapore but also be a special trade zone. This was the golden age for the Boten border town, a former small jungle village (Figure 5.3 and Figure 5.4).

However, detention of some Chinese customers who could not pay their gambling debts at the casino by the gambling company led to strong pressure from Chinese government to release all hostages and shut down the company. Finally, in 2011, the Ministry of Foreign Affairs of China ordered the casinos closed, tightened border control, and cut power supply to the town (Strangio 2016). Most of the Chinese staff and concerned people returned to China. Consequently, Boten once again became a small community in terms of population but now with several empty buildings (Asieninsider 2014).

Figure 5.4 Shopping area of Mohan town at the border of China during the golden period of Boten
Source: Taken by the author, December 16, 2007.

This was not the end of the small border town. Strong efforts by China to connect with Southeast Asia (or the more popular term "ASEAN") is still a key policy for the NSEC, but this time, a high-speed train for communication connectivity was considered more suitable. After strenuous efforts and long negotiation, the stable socialist governments of China and Laos entered an agreement to build a high-speed railway that was satisfactory to both sides. The route of the high-speed train of this corridor in Laos's territory will be Boten–Luang Prabang (old capital city) and Vientiane in order to link with the Thai railway at Nongkhai, a border province on the Mekong River that already accommodated the last station of the normal train from Bangkok. The distance between Boten and Vientiane along the planned railway connectivity is around 414 kilometers. The construction began at the Laos border in late 2015. The project is expected to be completed in five years. Recently, the Thai cabinet meeting on July 11, 2017, approved a cooperation project for the development of basic infrastructure in building the high-speed train from Nongkhai to Bangkok with the distance of 647 kilometers (Vaenkeo 2016; Xuequan 2017).

Moreover, governments of Laos and China signed an agreement to establish a zone for accelerating trade, investment, and tourism at their border towns Boten and Mohan, respectively. Operations on the Chinese side were conducted through the Yunnan Xishuangbanna Mohan Economic Development Zone.

Changing borderland local communities 141

Figure 5.5 Launch of a huge development project by a Chinese business group with government support for the revival of Boten after Chinese authorities abandoned the casino in 2011
Source: Taken by the author, March 1, 2017.

Meanwhile, the Laos government operated the Boten Special Economic Zone as a cooperation project with China. This Laotian development project provided around 16 square kilometers to a Chinese company. This means that local villagers of Laos in this area have to move to a further inner area of Laos, with small amounts of compensation. In 2017, a number of large buildings are under construction by Chinese investors. They expect to transform Boten into a financial center of GMS in the near future. At present, local villagers who speak Chinese can obtain unskilled jobs such as construction workers, security guards, and cleaners in the service sector with a relatively higher salary. Most importantly, investors, traders, merchants, shop and restaurant owners, hotel staff, and local people in general are living with the hope that these projects—high-speed train for connectivity and economic development zones on both sides—will soon lead to the revival of Boten (Figure 5.5).

East-West Economic Corridor of road no. 9

Another important economic corridor is EWEC of Road No. 9 (R9), which runs from Danang (Vietnam) on the east end of the corridor through Lao Bao (border of Vietnam), Dan Savan and Savannakhet (border of Laos), Mukdahan and Mae Sot (border of Thailand), and Myawaddy and Mawlamyine (border of Myanmar) to the west end of the corridor with the distance of around 1,460 kilometers.

This corridor links the South China Sea on the Pacific Ocean and the Andaman Sea on the Indian Ocean. Unlike the NSEC, EWEC only has overland routes. There is no river route, and the Mekong River is crossed by bridges in some parts. In addition, the rail link has not been discussed seriously except in the Thai territory. It is remarkable that while China is the key actor in NSEC connectivity, Japan is the major actor in providing financial support for building the No. 9 and bridges over the Mekong River of EWEC. Concerning the map of GMS, it is not difficult to explain these countries' roles in supporting different economic corridors. Their decisions are tied to the ability to move goods and products to and from their countries. However, Korea does not play a significant role in the issue of physical connectivity but focuses on investment in the vehicle industry and social activities such as the promotion of education and culture.

The analysis of this research concentrates on three twin border towns: Lao Bao–Dan Savan, Savannakhet–Mukdahan, and Mae Sot–Myawaddy. The Lao Bao community of Quang Tri province was once a small jungle village with very few Vietnamese and three major ethnic minority groups. It is located at the border of central Vietnam, adjacent to the border of Laos at the Dan Savan town. Their border aligns with some parts of the Sepon River and the mountain range. Although, the nearest district or town to Lao Bao is around 20 kilometers away, it took nearly a day to travel there on foot in the past. At that time, neither border town—Lao Bao nor Dan Savan—had a significant implication for the economy of GMS, except as a residence for small groups of Vietnamese farmers, who were moved to this area based on a government policy after the revolution of 1975, and for some ethnic minority groups. These people could sustain their life using simple agricultural and forest products, including fish from the Sepon River. However, active response of the Vietnamese government to the introduction of EWEC and physical connectivity generated several development projects. The rapid change of this border community started in the late 1990s when the Vietnamese government introduced the special economic zone program to Lao Bao in 1998 (later, it was known as the Lao Bao Special Economic-Commercial Area) (Figure 5.6). Under the decisive plan of the strong and stable government and political regime of the one socialist party system, the encroaching development changed this small and remote border community in the jungle to a rather modern town with several buildings for factories, offices, medium-sized trading shops, asphalt roads, electric supply, and running water. The bamboo cottages of ethnic minorities were demolished and their owners moved to free concrete accommodations with basic facilities, such as electricity and running water, but they had to pay for these services themselves.[1]

The population of Lao Bao Border town has increased from less than 3,000 to more than 30,000 people, or ten times, in less than 20 years. The local people are now not only Kinh (or Vietnamese) and ethnic minorities but also workers from Laos and Thailand. For ethnic minority groups, everyday life is more convenient than in the past as they can sell more of their agricultural products at higher prices. However, all consumption goods have to be paid for in cash.

Figure 5.6 Commercial buildings at a corner of the Lao Bao Special Economic–Commercial Area
Source: Taken by the author, February 18, 2017.

Unfortunately, it has been difficult for these groups to access cash and jobs due to illiteracy or low education level and skills. Moreover, their old generation is concerned about new types of entertainment, such as karaoke, as they worry that their young generation would consume this "social evil."

As regards trade and tourism, Road No. 9 and Lao Bao international checkpoint have become the major route and gateway for border trade and foreign tourists between central Vietnam and Laos and Northeastern Thailand. This connectivity has facilitated convenient travel from Thailand and Laos to central Vietnam (Hue—the old capital city, Hoi An—ancient town, and Danang—a deep sea port in South China Sea) or vice versa. Particularly, Danang is a popular place for visiting the sea for Laotian people as theirs is a land-locked country. Moreover, at this border checkpoint, travelers sometimes face long caravans of Thai tourist buses visiting Hue, Hoi An, and Danang in Vietnam during their long holidays. The numbers of tourists on some holidays can be more than 10,000 per week. These tourists come from both middle class and grassroots, mainly from Isan or Northeastern Thailand, which are adjacent to Laos and Vietnam. Thus, road connectivity has provided the possibility of foreign overland travel to all levels of people because the cost of travel is not high. Consequently, service activities at the Lao Bao border have been lively (Figure 5.7).

Figure 5.7 A new building for single window service at the Lao Bao international checkpoint, the first place to obtain support from the ADB for a single window service project
Source: Taken by the author, February 19, 2017.

Nevertheless, completion of the third international Friendship Bridge (Nakorn Phanom province of Thailand and Thakhek of Laos) in 2011 facilitated overland travel from Thailand to Hanoi (the capital of Vietnam) and two other attractive beach towns—Hatinh and Ving—as well as Hai Phong, a deep sea port at a shorter distance. Recently, several cargo trucks moving between Thailand and Laos have shifted their transportation route from the Mukdahan–Savannakhet–Lao Bao border to the Nakhon Phanom–Thakhek–Vinh and Hanoi. This has led to a reduction in traffic and visitors in Lao Bao, although a new and progressive service called the "Single Window Inspection/Single Stop Inspection Pilot" (SWI/SSI) has begun operation with the ADB's support at the Lao Bao international border gate since 2015 (The Voice of Vietnam 2015). Changes in the traveling route have led to slow growth of the Lao Bao community, although tourists intending to travel to Hue, Danang, and Hoi An continue to travel through Lao Bao.

Originally, the cooperation agreement for border development between Vietnam and Laos was to be operated on both sides, but until now, there have been few changes on the Laos side. Dansavanh is still a small border town with a small number of shops; an old station of Lao's border bus; and a small number of car services for passengers and goods to Savannakhet, the other end of EWEC in Laos's territory. A small change is the increase in population in the past 15 years. An interesting aspect of this border area is the undocumented visitors from border villagers of both sides, particularly ethnic minorities. The

Changing borderland local communities 145

Figure 5.8 Parking area for public car services between Dansavanh–Swannakhet at the Dansavanh border town of Laos
Source: Taken by the author, February 20, 2017.

Vietnamese government has recognized them as key supporters of the liberation movement during the Vietnam War period in both countries. However, their visits are limited to the area along the Sepon River and the mountain range (Figure 5.8).

Another border town of Laos on EWEC is in Savannakhet province, located on the bank of the Makong River on the opposite side of Mukdahan province in Thailand. Both provinces have medium-size communities with a long tradition of border trade among themselves as well as a route for transporting goods and products to Vietnam. Previously, the management of trade and other business was focused around the centers of old towns, piers, or river ports on each side. After completion of the second Friendship Bridge (Thai–Laos) in 2007, all immigration and customs offices and other concerned services moved to the bridge area, which is around 10 kilometers from the town centers. Subsequently, several private business services moved to settle along the roads to the bridges. In case of Savannakhet, the Laos government established the Savan–Seno Special Economic Zone in 2003 with the area of 954 hectares, but it has not well been developed (Figure 5.9). The zone's progress was significant after completion of the second Friendship Bridge, especially in the past five years since 2012. The Savon-Seno Special Economic Zone now covers four sites: site A. Savan City

Figure 5.9 A Japanese factory in Savan-Seno Special Economic Zone
Source: Taken by the author, February 18, 2017.

(Paradise city) for entertainment and services, site B. logistic activities, site C. industrial estate, and site D. resettlement (for local people who were relocated due to the emergence of the special economic zone and for investors including foreigners). Thus, this has become the new border community of Savannakhet with a modern aspect. Meanwhile, the atmosphere of the original Savannakhet or the old center of the town is rather quiet, except for the morning market and bus station (Savan Park Savannakhet 2014; Chumnanmak, Apichatvullop, and Laphanan 2016; Thammavongsa 2016).

Although the original center of growth in the Thai border town of Mukdahan has not been significantly affected by the bridge, the trend of urban growth has moved to the area along the road toward the bridge, and the price of land has increased. However, a part of the old center along the Mekong River transformed itself with the support of Mukdahan municipality with the opening of the Indochina Market to serve Thai tourists. The main goods and products are made in China and Vietnam but the once successful guesthouses and hotels are suffering because it is more convenient to cross the border over the bridge for visiting the casino in Laos or travelling to Vietnam. In Mukdahan, like in most border towns of Thailand, the founding of a special economic zone has no clear future even though the government has officially decreed it and the price of land has risen. The reason for this situation is the

Changing borderland local communities 147

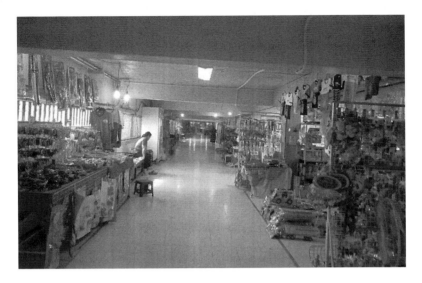

Figure 5.10 Indochina market in Mukdahan province, Thailand
Source: Taken by the author, February 21, 2017.

instability of government and people's demand for more discussion concerning the advantages and disadvantages of special economic zones as a development strategy (Figure 5.10).

Crossing the twin borders towns of EWEC on the east and west sides are the Mae Sot district of Tak province, Thailand, and Myawaddy Township of Kayin state, Myanmar. This border route also has a long tradition of border trade, but it was closed for some time due to the political situation in Myanmar, ethnic conflicts with the government, and the relationship with Thailand. The route can link with not only Mawlamyine (or Moulmein) seaport but also Pa-An, a special economic zone, and Yangon, the former capital and busiest city of Myanmar. Moreover, Mae Sot is the biggest district of Tak province in terms of economy. The rapid growth of Mae Sot started in the period of economic boom in Thailand in the late 1980s. At that time, Thailand needed a large number of workers for construction and later included several business activities and the service sector, which provided higher salaries than those in Myanmar—at double or triple the rate. The economic difficulty, suppression of the military government, and ethnic conflicts, particularly in Shan and Karen states, were the push factors of migration. Consequently, the vast number of workers from Myanmar moved to Thailand through several overland routes, both official and traditional or natural. Until today, it is estimated that 1 million to nearly 2 million (documented and undocumented) migrant workers moved from Myanmar to Thailand, and a majority of them have no plan of returning to Myanmar (Figure 5.11).

148 *Ekamol Saichan*

Figure 5.11 Cargo trucks on their way from Mae Sot (Thailand) to Myawaddy (Myanmar) queuing on the Thailand–Myanmar Friendship Bridge for customs inspection
Source: Taken by the author, February 23, 2017.

In terms of border trade, the Mae Sot and Myawaddy international checkpoint is the major route for cargo trucks carrying capital goods and products to and from Myanmar. Hence, it is the main route for the flow of labor and goods to and from Myanmar.

Here, rapid changes were observed after the introduction of EWEC, operation of physical connectivity, Myanmar political reform of 2013, replacement of the single-truck road or the alternating one-way system by the two-way system from Myawaddy to Yangon in 2015, launch of the Myawaddy Special Economic Zone, and recent facilitation of entering Myanmar overland through border checkpoints. Meanwhile, operation of several development projects by the Thai government, such as the construction of the second Thai–Myanmar Friendship Bridge across the Moei River and expansion of the main road from two lanes to four lanes between Mae Sot district and Tak province to link with the highway to Bangkok, have boosted the volume of border trade, tourists, and the flow of labor. These events and development projects have generated rapid growth of both border communities in many aspects (Naing, Chulasai, and Panthamit 2010; Saowadee, Nimsai, and Piboonrungroj 2015) (Figure 5.12).

Figure 5.12 Conversion of a two-lane road to a four-lane highway to connect Tak province to Mae Sot district, a major border town of Thailand, which is expected to be completed by 2017, including the second (bypass) Thailand–Myanmar Friendship Bridge

Source: Taken by the author, February 22, 2017.

However, after significant difficulty, Myanmar founded its special economic zone, particularly in the industrial estate of Myawaddy. This special economic zone has been established with the hope that it would help alleviate large-scale unemployment by relocating the garment industries from Mae Sot to the zone. At present, a large number of workers from Myawaddy cross Moei River every morning to reach Mae Sot's garment factories and return home the same day. They use traditional or natural routes for travelling (just five minutes by boat over the Moei River), although they are not far from the official checkpoint. With the recent positive changes from the European Union and the United States toward Myanmar, Myanmar's products will now be sent to those countries. However, the problem is the Myanmar government's restrictive policies on business, especially foreign-owned businesses. In addition, the concerned organization in Thailand would not provide power supply to Myawaddy's industrial zone without paying the cost of electricity. Another important issue is the casino business; as in many border areas in the GMS, local entrepreneurs, Chinese investors, and Thai businessmen have invested in casinos and other types of gambling to set up the businesses along the border in the past 10 years. The majority of their customers are Thai citizens. The problem is not the transfer of money

Figure 5.13 A traditional or natural crossing between the Thai–Myanmar border over the Moei River by local boat, in contrast with crossing from the official checkpoint by car, which takes around 10 minutes

Source: Taken by the author, February 23, 2017.

Figure 5.14 Crowded everyday life in Myawaddy (border) town, which is the major gateway of the overland route from the Thai border to Yangon, the former capital and business center of Myanmar

Source: Taken by the author, February 23, 2017.

Changing borderland local communities 151

abroad but the serious social problems faced by the families of people with low income. They sometimes sell their lands after losing money in gambling. Moreover, some young people, particularly young women, become involved in sex work and drug trafficking. Generally, Mae Sot and Myawaddy are the busiest border communities with a high growth rate in the present situation (Chan Mya Htwe 2015) (Figure 5.13 and Figure 5.14).

The final twin border towns discussed in this chapter are not communities on the NSEC and EWEC directly but located on the southern line of EWEC. They are the Aranyaprathet district of Sakaeo province, Thailand, and Poipet of Sisophon province, Cambodia. The Aranyaprathet–Poipet Border route is similar to the Mae Sot–Myawaddy route, and it is the busiest gateway being the main route linking Thailand and Phnom Penh, the capital city of Cambodia. Their border trade and communication was launched nearly a century ago. The old Khlong Luek (Thai border)–Poipet Railway Bridge was built in the mid-1920s for linking the two areas, although at that time, Cambodia was a French colony. However, Cambodia's civil war in the 1970s stopped the Aranyaprathet–Poipet train service, and the old bridge was closed until now. Recently, EWEC has driven the demand for both states to revive the rail link, with the expectation that it will boost trade and tourism. However, this has not occurred because construction of the new 6.5-kilometer railway line from Poipet to the border bridge has not been completed yet (MCOT 2015) (Figure 5.15 and Figure 5.16).

Figure 5.15 Modern hotels and casinos just behind the Poipet immigration checkpoint in Cambodia
Source: Taken by the author, February 25, 2017.

Figure 5.16 New area for casinos and several types of entertainment a few kilometers from the Poipet border
Source: Taken by the author, February 25, 2017.

Apart from the crowded atmosphere from the traffic of cargo trucks, tourist buses, different types of cars, and a large number of carts driven by human labor for overload goods, huge groups of transborder people, mainly Cambodian migrant workers, are common at the border. Another feature of the Poipet border is the abundance of casinos. Recently a new entertainment complex including casinos was built in a large area further inside Poipet. There is no doubt that the majority of customers are Thai people. It seems that the borders Cambodia, Laos, and Myanmar are perfect for growing a casino business. This complex is a joint venture between a Chinese company and local businesses. The consequent problems are similar to those in the Mae Sot community.

On the Thai side of the border at Aranyaprathet, the project of constructing a bypass road for heavy trucks is under way. It will lead to the emergence of a new community. An interesting event is the establishment of the biggest wholesale market called Rong Kluea Market or Talad Rong Kluea. During the day, traders and merchants from Cambodia and all parts of Thailand conduct the business of selling and buying goods and products, mainly cloth products and manufactured goods, which they carry to different places for selling. These are the reasons for the transformation of Poipet and Aranyaprathet as well as that of Myawaddy in Myanmar and Mae Sot in Thailand into boom border towns (Figure 5.17, Figure 5.18, and Figure 5.19).

Figure 5.17 A new modern shopping center at the border of Aranyaprathet
Source: Taken by the author, February 26, 2017.

Figure 5.18 Rong Kluea Market, the biggest wholesale market in Thailand, at the border of Aranyaprathet; it serves Cambodian and Thai customers from different places
Source: Taken by the author, February 26, 2017

Figure 5.19 New railway bridge at the border between Thailand and Cambodia (Aranyaprathet–Poipet) waiting for physical connectivity
Source: Taken by the author, February 26, 2017.

Conclusion

The geographical and administrative areas known as "frontier," and later "border," were perceived as remote, silent, obsolete, and static places with small number of residents for several decades. Even after the emergence of the modern nation-state with the concept of sovereignty and (fixed) territory following the end of World War II, the perception of border did not change much. Its atmosphere was not attractive to outsiders. This situation was true for all of Southeast Asia, particularly in the area called the GMS.

Until the 1990s, several factors induced changes in the border communities in GMS. These factors are as follows:

1 Political changes at the national, regional, and global levels: end of the Vietnam War in 1975, collapse of the Berlin Wall in 1989, disintegration of the Soviet Union in 1991, introduction of competitive elections in Cambodia under the supervision of the UN in 1993, and political reform in Myanmar in 2013
2 Economic changes resulting in a more liberal system: introduction of the New Economic Mechanism in Laos and the operation of *Doi Moi* or economic reform in Vietnam in 1986

3   Changes in government policy: "The Change of Battlefield to become a Market place" in Thailand
4   Atmosphere of friendship and opening up of the country for cooperation and trade
5   The notion of economic corridor and physical and transportation connectivity projects of GMS
6   Benefits from visa exemption for ASEAN citizens
7   Strong push from ADB, China, Japan, and Australia

Interactions among the aforementioned factors drove the rapid transformation of static and obsolete border communities into dynamic and modern communities. Among GMS countries, China, Thailand, and Vietnam are active actors in connectivity projects. Regarding outsiders, Japan has played a crucial role in providing financial support, but Korea has mainly concentrated on investment and assistance for educational activities. The United States, which was the former key powerful state in this area, decreased its role significantly after its defeat in the Vietnam War in 1975.

The impact of the aforementioned factors on the 12 borderland local communities discussed in this chapter can be classified as follows:

1   Founding of special economic zones at the border towns
2   Rapid growth of tourism due to the low cost and shorter time for travelling
3   Increase in the number of guesthouses, hotels and restaurants, and other service facilities, which led to changes in the shape and structure of borderland local communities
4   Increase in residents to serve the rapid growth of borderland local communities
5   Higher cost of living and land price in border towns and adjacent areas
6   Higher demand for electric supply, running water, and better management to deal with the rapidly increasing garbage and wastewater in borderland local communities

The following three points should be noted:

1   The physical connectivity approach of development can be easier to implement in mainland Southeast Asia and Southwest China or the GMS than in the archipelago Southeast Asia. As it consumes less funds and lower level of technology, we have seen rapid progress and growth of physical connectivity in the GMS since the past 25 years after its founding in 1992.
2   The term "border trade," which was once a factor affecting changes in border areas, fits the situation in the early period of the opening up of GMS countries. However, after completion and progress of several physical connectivity projects in the form of highways and bridges (and railways in the next five years), the trade routes are no longer focused on border towns and adjacent areas. Trade routes have shifted to overland connectivity with different

capital and big cities of neighboring and other countries. Therefore, the term "border trade" should be replaced by the term "trans-border or transboundary trade." Moreover, the role of border towns has become that of "transit towns" for trade and other activities. Cargo trucks, tourist buses, and other vehicles do not need to stop overnight at border towns due to better conditions of roads and higher speed of vehicles. This implies the previous success of border businesses such as hotels, guesthouses, restaurants, entertainment, convenience stores, and other service sectors will no longer be possible.

3   We have no doubt about the leading role of China in GMS development in the past 25 years. The Chinese government has invested huge amounts of funds in different activities ranging from building basic infrastructure and dams, providing loans to Chinese companies for construction, and providing a large number of educational scholarships to building a sports stadium. This is why local people in GMS always asked the author the following question at the time of the survey: "What does China want?"

The same question will be asked again in this first half of the 21st century. On May 14–15, 2017, the Chinese government organized a special conference in Beijing, and government leaders of nearly 70 countries and delegations of international organizations were invited to hear China's plan for the development of global trade (not border trade) for the 21st century. President Xi Jinping introduced the notion of the "One Belt One Road" Initiative as the strategy for the development of global trade. "One Belt" refers to the Silk Road Economic Belt, while "One Road" refers to the 21st-century Maritime Silk Road. Combination of the two terms implies a vision of revival of the ancient Silk Road trading routes geographically structured along the six corridors and the Maritime Silk Road across Asia, the Middle East, Europe, and Africa. President Xi Jinping claimed that it is "a project of the century." Although we have seen the success of China in transforming the country from a developing nation to one of the top five leading world economies in only three decades, it is too early to estimate the results of this project. Indeed, the initiative does not cover any major city of the GMS corridor, except Hanoi, the capital of Vietnam, which is located on the NSEC.[2]

However, the key question from public is, "Why does the Chinese government initiate this giant project?" There are at least two reasons for this aspiration of China. The first reason is not difficult to understand. China wants to boost the global trade for serving its massive surplus products from a variety of industries. Hence, it is necessary to expand markets throughout the world by providing a convenient, effective, and fast logistic system with a more flexible customs process. A strong point of Chinese products is that they are cheaper than products from other countries, although they may face issues of patent rights. Certainly, China will get the highest benefit from the "One Belt One Road" Initiative for increasing the strength of its economy as a leading nation. The second reason for this project concerns China's status and role in world activities. With a more powerful economy, besides having a large army and high level of technology, the voice and bargaining power of China in the international community will become louder than that of other superpowers, the United States, Russia, Germany, and Japan, and its influence will be supreme over small countries in the GMS (and Africa). Hence, the "One Belt One Road" Initiative will help create a future world under Chinese influence or hegemony by sending funds, people, technology, and products throughout the world.

Nevertheless, as regards the whole analysis, borderland local communities in the GMS are showing a new trend where once they were unattractive places for living. Now, their marginalized and peripheral status has changed, at least in terms of personal income and national revenue. They are becoming the center of land-linked areas among the surrounding countries. This is a new pattern of sub-regional relations. Therefore, not only the terms "globalization" and "regionalization" but also "sub-regionalization" should be considered when analyzing the decline of the nation-state and the new face of international relations in Southeast Asia.

Acknowledgements

I much appreciate the kindness and assistance of the following persons who provided information and opinions for my intensive survey conducted between February 16, 2017, and March 3, 2017:

1 Mr. Nguyen Van Binh (and his staff), Deputy Head, Board of the Quang Tri Economic Zones, Director of the Quang Tri Bordergate Management Center, Vietnam
2 Mr. Nguyen Vu Al, Head of the Lao Bao Representative Office, Quang Tri Provincial Economic Zones Authority, Vietnam
3 Mr. Somsak Kaveerat, Chairman, Tak Chamber of Commerce, Tak province, Thailand
4 Mr. Suchart Treeravatana, President, Maesod Tai-San Group, Tak province, Thailand
5 Mr. Satiswas Palanupap, local businessman in the Maesod district, Tak province, Thailand
6 Ms. Sary Mom, Officer, Department of Community Livelihood, Ministry of Environment, Cambodia

A very special thanks to Professor Hidetoshi Taga's research team for providing funds for the intensive survey in some border communities of the Greater Mekong Sub-region. Please accept my deep apology for not mentioning all the kind persons who have been helpful in the completion of this paper.

Notes

1 http://quangtrieconomiczone-vii.tk/2015/09/03/summary-of-15-years-of-lao-bao-special-trade-economic-zone/, accessed October 15, 2017.
2 http://news.xinhuanet.com/english/2017-05/14/c_136282982.htm, accessed October 15, 2017.

References

Asian Development Bank (ADB) (2012) *Greater Mekong Subregion Economic Cooperation Program: Overview*, Metro Manila, Philippines: Asian Development Bank (http://www.gms-eoc.org/uploads/resources/61/attachment/GMS%20Economic%20Cooperation%20Program%20Overview.pdf, accessed October 15, 2017).

Asieninsider (2014) "The Rise and Fall of Boten Golden City," June 12, 2014 (http://www.asienreisender.de/boten.html, accessed October 15, 2017).

Baramova, Maria (2010) "Border Theories in Early Modern Europe," *European History Online (EGO)* (http://ieg-ego.eu/en/threads/crossroads/border-regions/maria-baramova-border-theories-in-early-modern-europe, accessed October 15, 2017).

Bigo, Didier (2005) "Frontier Controls in the European Union: Who is in Control?," in Didier Bigo and Elspeth Guild (eds.) *Controlling Frontiers: Free Movement into and within Europe*, Aldershot: Ashgate, pp. 49–99.

Chan Mya Htwe (2015) "Myawaddy Industrial Zone Set for 2017 Opening," *Myanmar Times*, 29 September, 2015 (https://www.mmtimes.com/business/16731-myawaddy-industrial-zone-set-for-2017-opening.html, accessed October 15, 2017).

Chumnanmak, Rukchanok, Yaowalak Apichatvullop, and Patcharin Laphanan (2016) "Border Trade Area: Social Networks and Power Relations of the Thai-Lao PDR Border Trade System," *The Social Sciences*, 11 (3): 317–323.

Department of Foreign Trade, Ministry of Commerce of Thailand (2014) Statistics of Border Trade and Transboundary Trade of Thailand Report (2011–2013) (in Thai).

Department of Foreign Trade, Ministry of Commerce of Thailand (2017) Statistics of Border Trade and Transboundary Trade of Thailand Report (2014–2016) (in Thai).

Donnan, Hastings, and Dieter Haller (2000) "Liminal No More: The Relevance of Borderland Studies," *Ethnologia Europaea: The Journal of European Ethnology*, 30 (2): 7–22.

Evans, Grant (2000) *Where China Meets Southeast Asia: Social and Cultural Change in Border Region*, New York: St Martin's Press.

Evans, Grant (2002) *A Short History of Laos: The Land in Between*, Crows Nest, NSW: Allen & Unwin.

Friedeburg, Robert von (2010) "State Forms and State Systems in Modern Europe," *European History Online (EGO)*, Institute of European History (IEG) (http://www.ieg-ego.eu/friedeburgr-2010-en, accessed October 15, 2017).

Ishida, Masami (ed.) (2013) *Border Economies in Greater Mekong Sub-region*, New York: Palgrave Macmillan.

MCOT (2015) "Old Thai-Cambodia Railway Bridge Dismantled," *MCOT Online News*, January 20, 2015 (http://o.mcot.net/site/content?id=54be1de1be0470311d8b468a, accessed October 15, 2017).

Naing, Yu Yu, Luechai Chulasai, and Nisit Panthamit (2010) "Characteristics of Cross Border Trade in Myawaddy Township Kayin State, Myanmar," *Chiang Mai University Journal of Economics*, 14 (2): 100–122.

Osborne, Milton (2000) *Southeast Asia: An Introductory History*, Chiangmai: Silkworm Books.

Quoc Toan, Nguyen (2013) "Ho Chi Minh Sites in Thailand: Their Significance and Potential Problems for Thai-Vietnamese Relations," *Journal of Mekong Societies*, 5 (1): 77–96.

Saowadee, Kesinee, Suthep Nimsai, and Pairach Piboonrungroj (2015) "An Investigation and Evaluation of CrossBorder Truck Transportation from Mae Sot-Myawaddy to Yangon," *International Journal of Supply Chain Management*, 4 (4): 102–107.

Savan Park Savannakhet (2014) "Investors Head to Savan Seno Special Economic Zone," 15 August, 2014 (http://www.savanpark.com/?p=1737, accessed October 15, 2017).

Strangio, Sebastian (2016) "The Rise, Fall and Possible Renewal of a Town in Laos on China's Border," *New York Times,* July 6, 2016 (https://www.nytimes.com/2016/07/07/world/asia/china-laos-boten-gambling.html, accessed October 15, 2017).

Thammavongsa, Panyasith (2016) "Savannakhet Special Economic Zone Achieves Targets," *Vientiane Times*, September 13, 2016 (http://asianews.eu/content/savannakhet-special-economic-zone-achieves-targets-27982, accessed October 15, 2017).

The Voice of Vietnam (2015) "One-Stop-Shop Customs Piloted at Lao Bao-Densavan Border Gate," 2 June, 2015 (http://english.vov.vn/society/onestopshop-customs-piloted-at-lao-baodensavan-border-gate-287701.vov, accessed October 15, 2017).

Vaenkeo, Souksakhone (2016) "Laos-China Border Economic Zone Attracts Billions in Investment," *The Nation*, May 26, 2016 (http://www.nationmultimedia.com/detail/aec/30286723, accessed October 15, 2017).

Walker, Andrew (1999) *The Legend of Golden Boat: Regulation, Trade and Traders in the Borderlands of Laos, Thailand, China and Burma*, Hawaii: University of Hawaii Press.

Xuequan, Mu (2017) "China-Laos Railway Construction Progressing Well: Lao Officials," *Xinhua*, May 17, 2017 (http://news.xinhuanet.com/english/2017-05/17/c_136289684.htm, accessed October 15, 2017).

6 The Mekong region and changing borders

A focus on the CBTA and BCPs

Tetsu Sadotomo and Kenji Nakayama

Introduction

This chapter examines the transformation of national borders caused by the development of sub-regions. It particularly focuses on the implementation of the Cross-Border Transport Agreement (CBTA) and the recent conditions at border-crossing points (BCPs) in the Greater Mekong Sub-region (GMS). The CBTA aims to facilitate transportation, which entails the removal of intangible hindrances to the movement of humans, vehicles, and goods across the national borders of the GMS countries. Therefore, the CBTA is an important initiative, not only for promoting cross-border transportation of goods and people among the contracting countries but also for increasing cross-border traffic and creating cross-border sub-regionalism. In September 2015, after Myanmar completed its formal ratification, all six GMS countries (Cambodia, Laos, Myanmar, Thailand, Vietnam, and China) had fully ratified the CBTA, including the Annexes and Protocols.[1] For the future, the CBTA is to be implemented at each formal BCP of the GMS (a BCP is a place where formal immigration control is performed).

Nevertheless, observations at some of the borders that had implemented the Initial Implementation of CBTA (IICBTA) before complete ratification revealed many problems related to the "smoothness" of the implementation (Ishida 2014: 48–49). Moreover, there are concerns regarding negative repercussions triggered by the progress of CBTA implementation. For instance, (1) widening disparities (international, regional, and ethnic); (2) straw effects[2] in areas and countries along the border-crossing routes; (3) spread of HIV, avian influenza, and other infectious diseases; (4) human trafficking, smuggling of narcotics and arms, and spread of terrorism; and (5) deterioration of traffic safety (increase in traffic accidents) (JICA 2007: 3.10–3.12). The underlying question concerns the extent of the effect of the CBTA on the status of the borders in the GMS as significant or negligible. The formation of the regional space referred to as the GMS is considered the outcome of the changes caused by the CBTA, which created a system to manage the intangible aspects of the transportation infrastructure. This chapter aims to describe and discuss the realities of cross-border sub-regionalism promoted by the establishment of the regional CBTA system from the perspective of border transformations.

Table 6.1 On-site surveys in the border areas of the GMS

Date	Major Areas Visited
December 14–23, 2007	Houayxay (Laos)-Chiang Khong (Thailand), Mohan (China)-Boten (Laos), Nong Khai (Thailand)-Thanaleng (Laos), Savannakhet (Laos)-Mukhdahan (Thailand), Lao Bao (Vietnam)-Dansavan (Laos), Lang Son (Vietnam)-Youyi Guan (China).
December 12–19, 2009	Tachileik (Myanmar)-Mae Sai (Thailand), Kengtung (Myanmar), Golden Triangle (Thailand, Myanmar, Laos), Chong Mek (Thailand)-Pakxe (Laos).
December 12–19, 2010	Japanese textiles and electronics manufacturers with operations in Thailand and Laos, transportation companies with operations in Thailand, Laos, and Vietnam, etc.
March 9–20, 2014	Yangon (Pathein Industrial Park, Thilawa Industrial Park, and so on, Myanmar), Daluo (China)-Mongla (Myanmar), Mohan (China)-Boten (Laos).
March 7–14, 2015	Nong Nok Khiene (Laos)-Trapeang Kriel (Cambodia), Phnom Penh (Cambodia), Ruili (China)-Muse (Myanmar), etc.
March 3–13, 2017	Myawaddy (Myanmar)-Mae Sot (Thailand), Daluo (China)-Mongla (Myanmar), Mohan (China)-Boten (Laos), Houayxay (Laos)-Chiang Khong (Thailand), Golden Triangle (Thailand, Myanmar, Laos), Tachileik (Myanmar)-Mae Sai (Thailand).

Source: Prepared by the authors.

Note: T. Sadotomo participated in all on-site inspections and K. Nakayama participated in the 2017 on-site inspection. Underlined portions indicate the BCPs mentioned in this chapter.

The study's researchers conducted on-site surveys of the GMS on numerous occasions (Table 6.1). This chapter presents several findings obtained through these field surveys, which were primarily conducted by Tetsu Sadotomo and Kenji Nakayama. Data on the significance of national borders can be derived only through this type of field survey. Thus, these data offer a resource for all research at the sub-regional level. We particularly aimed to use the detailed fieldwork experiences to learn about the changes to and relations between sub-regions and national borders. However, due to space constraints, the focus of this chapter is on some of the BCPs in the North-South and East-West Economic Corridors.

Economic corridors and border-crossing points

The GMS development program, supported by the Asian Development Bank (ADB) since 1992, is currently one of the most dynamic transnational integration programs in Southeast Asia (Shrestha and Aekapol 2013). The economic growth in Southeast Asia during recent decades has increased demands for better connectivity (Bhattacharyay 2010). With ADB support, the GMS governments

Figure 6.1 Existing border SEZs, other key BCPs, and selected other SEZs
Source: Asian Development Bank, *The Role of Special Economic Zones in Improving Effectiveness of GMS Economic Corridors*, Metro Manila: Asian Development Bank, 2016, p. 12.

endorsed a 10-year strategic framework in 2001 as their blueprint for enhanced connectivity. In 2001, three economic corridors (the North-South Economic Corridor, the East-West Economic Corridor, and the Southern Economic Corridor) were approved at the Tenth GMS Ministerial Conference as flagship projects under the ADB-supported projects.

The three economic corridors were prioritized in the GMS transportation sector development plans. Economic corridors are major hubs of economic activity, exchange, and transportation (see Figure I.4 in the Introduction). These corridors were established to encourage trade, investment, and tourism in the GMS, and they were designed to link the sub-region's previously fragmented road networks to a direct outlet for trade with South, Southeast, and Northeast Asia by 2015. This step intended to further enhance the strategic location of the GMS as the land bridge among these regions (Khanal 2008: 3).

The GMS member countries always have been interested in developing Special Economic Zones (SEZs) to stimulate economic activity along the GMS economic

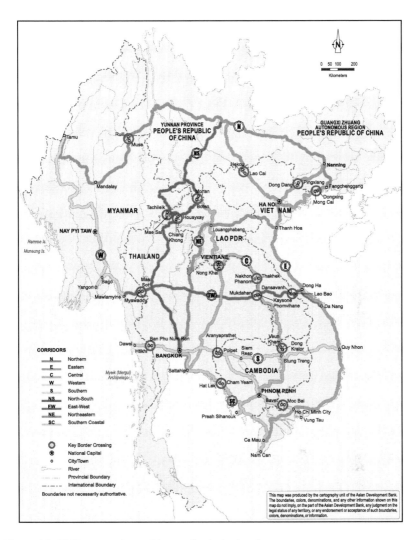

Figure 6.2 GMS economic corridors and priority border areas
Source: Asian Development Bank, *Greater Mekong Subregion Urban Development Strategic Framework 2015–2022*, Mandakuyong City: Asian Development Bank, 2015, p. 14.

corridors and, particularly, in the BCPs. By 2015, all of the GMS countries had embraced SEZs in principle, although it is not fully clear how successfully they have been implemented. Figure 6.1 shows the existing border SEZs, other key BCPs, and selected other SEZs.

Long queues of trucks are observable at the truck shipment centers of the border zones, such as Mohan (China)-Boten (Laos), Tachilec (Myanmar)-Mae Sai (Thailand), Myawaddy (Myanmar)-Mae Sot (Thailand), and Ruili (China)-Muse (Myanmar). Mohan and Boten are new small towns in China and Laos, respectively, whereas Mae Sai and Mae Sot (Thailand) and Ruili (China) are mid-sized or large towns where markets, hotels, banks, restaurants, and souvenir shops can be observed. However, it is difficult to assess the relative extent of activity of existing border SEZs because traffic data exist for some not all of BCPs except for the Thai BCPs (ADB 2016: 9).

Borders are often the weak link in a corridor, and BCPs are the focus of administrative activities regarding immigration, customs, quarantines, and other bureaucratic items (ADB 2016: 9). Therefore, the *Greater Mekong Subregion Urban Development Strategic Framework 2015–2022* (2015) included Planning and Development of Border Areas in Strategic Pillar 2 as its plan for strategically developing the border areas. It identified 17 locations to serve as important links between countries, and it indicated critical points along the GMS economic corridors as priority border areas (Figure 6.2). Numerous action plans requested the promotion of efficient development on both sides of these regions (ADB 2015: 15). Among these border areas, this chapter focuses on the following: (1) Mohan (China)-Boten (Laos), (2) Houayxay (Laos)-Chiang Khong (Thailand), and (3) Tachileik (Myanmar)-Mae Sai (Thailand), all of which are on the North-South Economic Corridor, and (4) Myawaddy (Myanmar)-Mae Sot (Thailand), which is on the East-West Economic Corridor. These priority border areas are concurrent BCPs covered by the CBTA. This chapter also discusses the Daluo (China)-Mongla (Myanmar) BCP, which is on the North-South Economic Corridor, to compare this non-CBTA border area to the CBTA border areas listed earlier.

Objectives and outcomes of the CBTA

Outline and objectives

The CBTA is a multilateral instrument that aims to facilitate cross-border transportation of goods and people by streamlining regulations and decreasing the intangible barriers to such activities in the sub-region. The CBTA is formally named *The Agreement Between and Among the Governments of the Kingdom of Cambodia, the People's Republic of China, the Lao People's Democratic Republic, the Union of Myanmar, the Kingdom of Thailand, and the Socialist Republic of Viet Nam for the Facilitation of Cross-Border Transport of Goods and People*.[3] The CBTA contains 407 articles, 44 of which comprise its main body. The specifics are presented in 20 annexes and three protocols that provide legal guidance on implementing the CBTA (Table 6.2).

The CBTA was a response to the emerging need to strengthen the related system to manage the intangible aspects to support large investments in infrastructure in the GMS so that it could benefit from increased economic connectivity. It addressed the need to enhance the sub-region's competitiveness through policies and rules to foster effective cross-border movements of people, goods, and services (ADB 2011: vi). Specifically, the goal of the CBTA was to integrate customs, immigration, and quarantine procedures for single-window

Table 6.2 CBTA annexes and protocols

Annex/Protocol	List of Annexes and Protocols	Signing Date
Annex		
1	Carriage of dangerous goods	December 16, 2004
2	Registration of vehicles in international traffic	April 30, 2004
3	Carriage of perishable goods	July 5, 2005
4	Facilitation of frontier-crossing formalities	April 30, 2004
5	Cross-border movement of people	July 5, 2005
6	Transit and inland clearance customs regime	March 20, 2007
7	Road traffic regulation and signage	April 30, 2004
8	Temporary importation of motor vehicles	March 20, 2007
9	Criteria for licensing of transport operators for cross-border transport operations	December 16, 2004
10	Conditions of transport	July 5, 2005
11	Road and bridge design and construction standards and specifications	April 30, 2004
12	Border crossing and transit facilities and services	April 30, 2004
13a	Multimodal carrier liability regime	April 30, 2004
13b	Criteria for licensing of multimodal transport operators for cross-border transport operations	December 16, 2004
14	Container customs regime	March 20, 2007
15	Commodity classifications system	April 30, 2004
16	Criteria for driving licenses	December 16, 2004
Protocol		
1	Designation of corridors, routes, and points of entry and exit (border crossings)	April 30, 2004
2	Charges concerning transit traffic	July 5, 2005
3	Frequency and capacity of services and issuance of quotas and permits	March 20, 2007

Source: Asian Development Bank (ADB), *Greater Mekong Subregion Cross-Border Transport Facilitation Agreement: Instruments and Drafting History*, Mandaluyong City: Asian Development Bank, 2011, p. 20.

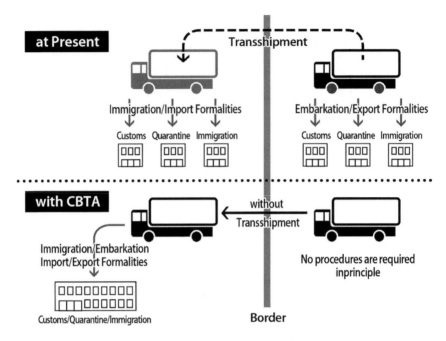

Figure 6.3 Mechanism to facilitate border-crossing formalities
Source: Japan International Cooperation Agency (JICA), *The Research on the Cross-border Transportation Infrastructure: Phase 2: Final Report*, Tokyo: Japan International Cooperation Agency and ALMEC Corporation, 2007, p. 9.

inspection (SWI). In addition, the CBTA created single-stop inspection (SSI), which reduced two procedures, one in the country of exit and the other in the country of entry, to one procedure. Therefore, under the SSI system, automobiles are not inspected in the country of exit, and an inspection is performed only in the country of entry (Figure 6.3). The SWI and SSI are key concepts of Article 4 of the main agreement and of Annex 4 (Ishida 2013: 58).

Moreover, the CBTA influenced the BCPs as crossroads of the economic corridors in the GMS. Protocol 1 of the CBTA designated 15 borders at the economic corridors (Table 6.3). The names of the borders designated by the CBTA for initial implementation (IICBTA) were Dansavan (Laos)-Lao Bao (Vietnam) (2005), Mukhdahan (Thailand)-Savannakhet (Laos) (2006), and Hekou (China)-Lao Cai (Vietnam) (2007). Furthermore, IICBTA was planned for Mohan (China)-Boten (Laos), Houayxay (Laos)-Chiang Khong (Thailand), and Huu Nghi (Vietnam)-Youyiguan (China) (Yu 2009: 7). In 2015, a Common Customs Area (CCA) was established at the Dansavan-Lao Bao border, and the first SSI formally began to operate. Revision work referred to as "CBTA2.0" was pushed forward with the support of the Australian Agency for International Development, and the aim of the full-scale enforcement of revised edition CBTA now states 2019.[4]

Table 6.3 Fifteen BCPs designated in Protocol 1 of the CBTA

List of Corridors, Routes, and Border Crossings	
North-South Economic Corridor	① Mohan (China)–Boten (Laos)
	② Houayxay (Laos)–Chiang Khong (Thailand)
	③ Tachileik (Myanmar)–Mae Sai (Thailand)
	④ Hekou (China)–Lao Cai (Vietnam)
East-West Economic Corridor	⑤ Myawaddy (Myanmar)–Mae Sot (Thailand)
	⑥ Mukhdahan (Thailand)–Savannakhet (Laos)
	⑦ Dansavan (Laos)–Lao Bao (Vietnam)
Southern Economic Corridor	⑧ Aranyaprathet (Thailand)–Poipet (Cambodia)
	⑨ Bavet (Cambodia)–Moc Bai (Vietnam)
	⑩ Hat Lek (Thailand)–Cham Yearn (Cambodia)
Other corridors/routes/border crossings	⑪ Ruili (China)–Muse (Myanmar)
	⑫ Veunekham (Laos)–Dong Kralor (Cambodia)
	⑬ Thanaleng (Laos)–Nong Khai (Thailand)
	⑭ Nam Phao (Laos)–Cau Treo (Vietnam)
	⑮ Wang Tao (Laos)–Chong Mek (Thailand)

Source: Asian Development Bank (ADB), *Greater Mekong Subregion Cross-Border Transport Facilitation Agreement: Instruments and Drafting History*, Mandaluyong City: Asian Development Bank, 2011, p. 171.

Positive and negative outcomes at the BCPs

By lowering the borders' walls, the CBTA was expected to create positive and negative outcomes at the BCPs in the GMS. Several of the most common of these outcomes are discussed in the following section.

First, an obvious positive change, which is logical given the objectives of the CBTA, is that the border regions were expected to prosper in increased trade and investment activities. The provisions of the CBTA were expected to stimulate the cross-border areas to become border trade zones because border inspection procedures would take less time, which was expected to facilitate the cross-border movements of goods (Ishida 2013: 74). In addition to a net positive influence on local standards of living in the GMS economic corridors, there has been a particularly positive influence on intra-GMS trade in mid-level commodities, such as electronic goods (Fujimura 2017).

Another positive outcome was expected to result from increased cross-border movements of people. The so-called "border pass" system enables residents in the border areas to cross back and forth without passports. They can buy food and other everyday items without paying customs duties when the purchases are not intended for business purposes. The border pass and duty-free system supports people whose incomes are not particularly high. The increase in cross-border labor-related traffic between Thailand and Cambodia, Laos, and Myanmar (CLM Countries) has been stimulated by income disparities because

168 *Tetsu Sadotomo and Kenji Nakayama*

workers cross to Thailand from the CLM Countries for work via these borders (Kudo and Ishida 2013: 11–12).

On the other hand, several problems at BCPs are evident, such as illegal workers, human trafficking, illegal tree felling, and drug abuse.[5] Most of the cross-border workers at BCPs are illegally working, which, consequently, forces them to work for unreasonable low wages, particularly at BCPs between Thailand and the CLM countries. The economies of the CLM countries cannot meet the increasing employment demands of young adults without the cross-border movement at BCPs. In 2009, the income gaps in GDP per capita between Thailand and the CLM countries were 5.7 (Cambodia), 4.2 (Laos), and 9.4 (Myanmar) times (Kudo and Ishida 2013: 12). Thailand provides job opportunities and technologies, whereas the CLM countries provide a low-wage labor force.

Furthermore, several border cities in the GMS have casinos, such as on the borders between Thailand and Cambodia, Thailand and Laos, China and Laos, China and Myanmar, and Cambodia and Vietnam, which cause concerns regarding the deterioration of public safety and their effects on young adults. Most of the casinos are in the CLM countries. In the Golden Triangle, a large casino and hotel is on Donsao Island in Laos (Figure 6.4). Casinos are good business opportunities for the CLM countries because they draw foreigners (who spend their money). Tourists and gamblers from the relatively high-income countries (e.g., China and Thailand) strongly tend to frequent the casinos because gambling is prohibited in their countries. Notably, casinos were built between the border posts at the Poipet-Aranyaprathet border of Cambodia and Thailand where tourists from Thailand can gamble without leaving Thailand or entering Cambodia.

a. Casino on Donsao Island in Laos   b. The landing for the boat used to cross to the casino

Figure 6.4 Casino at Golden Triangle on the Laos side
Source: Both photos taken by K. Nakayama on March 10, 2017.

Recent conditions in several BCPs

The North-South Economic Corridor

Mohan (China)-Boten (Laos) BCP

The Mohan (China)-Boten (Laos) BCP on the Laos route (Road R3A) of the North-South Economic Corridor is a key location for transportation and an international border gate for individuals from third countries (Figure 6.5). It is designated as a CBTA-BCP that was a planned IICBTA, which, because of its importance, has undergone major socioeconomic changes.

First, in 2003, the Laotian government established Boten as a SEZ, and the subsequent leasing of land to Chinese corporations dramatically changed this isolated mountain region. It transformed into a casino town for the Chinese. Since then, many Chinese have owned hotels and stores for the Chinese residents and tourists of the SEZ on the Laotian side (Boten), which was running in China time. Many Chinese tourists used these casinos; however, the casinos were closed in 2011 because of pressure from the Chinese government. Many problems had occurred regarding overburdened debtors, public morals, embezzlement of public monies in China, and so on. After the casinos closed, Boten again experienced a major change and became a ghost town.

However, after the November 2014 One Belt One Road Initiative of the Chinese government, this BCP began to experience new development. In late August of 2015, China and Laos entered into the *Joint General Scheme of Mohan-Boten Economic Cooperation Zone*.[6] Furthermore, construction of the China-Laos International Railway from the Mohan-Boten BCP to the Laotian

a. Border gate on the Mohan side   b. Border gate on the Boten side

Figure 6.5 Mohan-Boten BCP
Source: Both photos taken by K. Nakayama on March 8, 2017.

capital (Vientiane) is being financed with Chinese capital.[7] This BCP is in an ideal strategic location for China to exert an influence on Southeast Asia (Santasombat 2015).

When we conducted a survey in March 2017, the road from Jinghong on the Chinese side to Mohan in China had been completed, and construction to convert it into a highway was progressing with extreme rapidity (Figure 6.6). Large numbers of cargo trucks passed through the Mohan-Boten BCP (Figure 6.7). Then, small entertainment facilities for the Chinese, such as gaming centers, were built in duty-free shops in Boten (Figure 6.8). This is part of the reason that there are prospects about developing resorts (mainly golf courses) at Boten in Laos.[8]

During the 1990s, China and Laos had an agreement on overland transportation and a reciprocal use system for rolling stock. However, the simplification of the border-crossing procedures planned by the IICBTA was expected to create problems. Observations of the current situation suggest that major problems exist regarding the smooth implementation of the border-crossing procedures for cargo trucks. We believe that the most serious problem at this BCP is the

a. Jinghong tollgate   b. Mohan tollgate   c. Railway bridge

Figure 6.6 Construction of the highway and railway from Jinghong on the Chinese side to Mohan in China
Source: All photos taken by K. Nakayama on March 8, 2017.

a. The Mohan side   b. Between the gates   c. The Boten side
(Customs inspection point)

Figure 6.7 Cargo trucks at the Mohan-Boten BCP
Source: All photos taken by K. Nakayama on March 8, 2017.

Figure 6.8 Entertainment facilities in a duty-free shop in Boten
Source: All photos taken by K. Nakayama on March 8, 2017.

Figure 6.9 Large-scale environment-damaging development in Boten created by Chinese financing
Source: All photos taken by K. Nakayama on March 8, 2017.

negative effects of large-scale clearing of mountainous land that is environmentally damaging and funded by Chinese capital (Figure 6.9). These activities are expected to result in not only the devastation of the land in the region but also an increase in natural disasters, such as landslides and floods, including environmental problems and the illegal felling of trees. Thus, there is a risk of major negative effects on local residents, including minority groups.[9]

Houayxay (Laos)-Chiang Khong (Thailand) BCP

The Houayxay (Laos)-Chiang Khong (Thailand) BCP on the Laos route (Road R3A) of the North-South Economic Corridor experienced major changes. This BCP is an international gate for individuals from third countries. In the past, travel to Houayxay across the Mekong River from Chiang Khong required a short ferry ride (Figure 6.10), making this BCP the missing link in the North-South Economic Corridor for overland public transportation and logistics.

At the end of 2013, China and Thailand equally divided the construction costs to build the long-awaited Fourth Mekong Friendship Bridge (Figure 6.11), which is about 10 kilometers each away from Houayxay and Chiang Khong. It is a BCP for individuals to travel to and from third countries. Consequently, the overland transportation route of the North-South Economic Corridor connecting Kunming (Yunnan province, China) to Bangkok (Thailand) experienced major improvements, and this BCP continues to grow in importance.

172 *Tetsu Sadotomo and Kenji Nakayama*

a. Immigration b. Landing for passenger boats c. Cargo port

Figure 6.10 Boat landing and cargo port on the Chiang Khong side
Source: All photos taken by K. Nakayama on March 9, 2017.

a. Border gate on the Houayxay side b. Cross-border shuttle bus

c. Fourth Mekong Friendship Bridge d. Border gate on the Chiang Khong side

Figure 6.11 Fourth Mekong Friendship Bridge and the border region
Source: All photos taken by K. Nakayama on March 9, 2017.

However, at the time of our March 2017 survey, we saw few Chinese cargo trucks or groups of Chinese tourists crossing the Fourth Mekong Friendship Bridge. Although a modern gate and bridge were built on the site, the

Figure 6.12 Chiang Khong Newcity "Ghost Town"
Source: Photographed by K. Nakayama on March 9, 2017.

surrounding border area was surprisingly inactive. The newly built Chiang Khong Newcity on the Chiang Khong side of the bridge had deteriorated to the point of becoming a ghost town (Figure 6.12). Many of the cargo trucks we observed were queued up waiting to pass through the Mohan-Boten BCP, suggesting to us that they were related to the Chinese development projects in Laos instead of being bound for Bangkok along the North-South Economic Corridor. Although the Houayxay-Chiang Khong BCP experienced some improvements to its infrastructure to improve its suitability to overland transportation, and its management and operations were under the IICBTA plan, its influence for promoting border trade apparently remains negligible. The vast majority of traffic by local residents and commercial cargo still uses the small boats that form the cross-border residential and economic zones. Indeed, after the completion of the Fourth Mekong Friendship Bridge, cross-border trade via small boats increased rather than decreased.[10]

Tachileik (Myanmar)-Mae Sai (Thailand) and Daluo (China)-Mongla (Myanmar) BCPs

The Tachileik (Myanmar)-Mae Sai (Thailand) BCP and the Daluo (China)-Mongla (Myanmar) BCP are on the Myanmar route (R3B) of the North-South Economic Corridor. The former BCP is an international gate for individuals from third countries, and the latter BCP is a second-class gate that does not allow such passage. Observations of the former from the direction of the mountain suggest that Tachileik and Mae Sai, which are on either side of the narrow Sai River, is one town. The BCP is a lively and active residential area, with Thai shoppers, Myanmarese peddlers, migrant workers, passenger vehicles, light trucks, and

174 *Tetsu Sadotomo and Kenji Nakayama*

a. Border gate on the Mae Sai side

b. First Mae Sai Friendship Bridge across the Sai River

c. Local residents using the bridge

d. Market on the Mae Sai side

Figure 6.13 Mae Sai-Tachilek BCP
Source: All photos taken by K. Nakayama on March 10, 2017.

other vehicles frequently passing in both directions (Figure 6.13). The shops and outdoor markets on the Thai side sell copious amounts of Chinese goods and are successful enterprises. Immigration control is required, although crossing the border bridge from Mae Sai to Tachileik for a day trip is easy to accomplish without a visa.

Tachileik is a small town in Myanmar, but it has many souvenir shops near the border for tourists. However, no trucks were observed on the border bridge (First Mae Sai Friendship Bridge) because a second bridge (Second Mae Sai Friendship Bridge) had been built in the Mae Sai suburbs in 2006. The CBTA had envisioned the second bridge as a vehicular BCP. However, that type of traffic has been reported as "somewhat sparse" (Fujimura 2014: 25). Many of the roads on the Myanmar side are unpaved mountain roads, which we argue is the reason that this road is largely not a functional economic corridor. Therefore, the Tachileik-Mae Sai BCP currently has the same strong characteristics of a cross-border residential and economic zone as the Houayxay-Chiang Khong BCP.

The Mekong region and changing borders 175

a. Border gate at Daluo

b. Jade shop and Chinese tourists

c. Trading post near China-Myanmar border

d. China-Myanmar route: Inactive main road

Figure 6.14 Daluo-Mongla BCP
Source: All photos taken by K. Nakayama on March 7, 2017.

In contrast, the Daluo (China)-Mongla (Myanmar) BCP is part of the North-South Economic Corridor, with little traffic either of local people or of local vehicles. We observed Chinese tourists frequenting the jade shops and outdoor markets of Daluo and on tours in Mongla. Although the Mongla side had large crowds of Chinese tourists when it had casinos, it is now inactive. We observed no people on the main street of the Daluo shopping district (the China-Myanmar road), and we concluded that it had become a ghost town (Figure 6.14). This BCP is unable to systematically function as an economic corridor for logistics and public transportation, and we found few of the characteristics of cross-border residential zones. Furthermore, tensions are high along the China-Myanmar border because of recent internal fighting between the Myanmar military and minority groups, and we propose that this unrest is an additional reason for the stagnation of this BCP.

The East-West Economic Corridor

Myawaddy (Myanmar)-Mae Sot (Thailand) BCP

The Myawaddy-Mae Sot BCP is on the East-West Economic Corridor, which is the Asian Highway 1. The Friendship Bridge over the Moei River connecting the two areas opened in 1997, which was relatively early (Figure 6.15). The BCP was identified as a CBTA-BCP because it is a key point for logistics and transportation. At the time of the survey, about 120,000 Thai lived in Mae Sot

a. Friendship Bridge and Moei River seen from the Myawaddy side

b. Cargo trucks crossing

c. Border gate on the Myawaddy side

d. Small passenger boats crossing the Mae Sot

Figure 6.15 Myawaddy-Mae Sot BCP
Source: All photos taken by T. Sadotomo on March 5, 2017.

(including its suburbs) along with about 200,000 immigrant workers (registered and unregistered) from Myanmar and displaced persons living in two large refugee camps. The Myawaddy-Mae Sot BCP is promoted as a SEZ and as a so-called "economic dam" to prevent the flow of Myanmarese immigrants into central Thailand (Arnold and Pickles 2011).

The current situation at this BCP is particularly interesting. Immigrant workers with passports and immigration visas come to Mae Sot across the Friendship Bridge, whereas illegal workers (those without documentation) cross the river to get to Mae Sot by boat for a fee of THB one. Passage takes about five minutes because the river is only about 20 meters wide. On the Thai side of the river, Thai soldiers inspect all incoming luggage, but they do not perform immigration processing. Therefore, visitors from Myanmar without passports or border passes can easily enter Mae Sot. Most of them simply want to shop at the market along the river and return to Myanmar that day. Many commercial streets and popular restaurants are in Myawaddy along the Moei River, and we easily observed large new shopping malls, a dealer of luxury German-made cars, and commercial streets in Mae Sot. Thus, although this BCP is a key point for logistics and public transportation, it also is a major cross-border residential and economic area. Indeed, it is so busy that the BCP cannot handle the increasing vehicular traffic, and construction of the Second Thai-Myanmar Friendship Bridge is rapidly progressing toward its goal of opening in 2019.

Conclusion

This analysis of the BCPs suggests that the following characteristics can be identified regarding the transformations of the border regions caused by the development of the GMS. First, regarding intangible changes, human interactions and exchanges of goods across borders have clearly increased because of the establishment and initial implementation of the CBTA. However, at present, the infrastructure and the managerial and operational systems are uncoordinated, which has caused problems because of the negative aspects of development. It cannot yet be concluded that implementation of the CBTA has gone according to plan at each BCP.

Second, the borders are extremely diverse, and some of them have transformed while others have stagnated. According to Taga (2015: 59), three types of borders, particularly between China and Myanmar, exist: (1) conventional areas that are revitalizing and serving as trade routes (sometimes nodes of the old tribute roads) because of the modernization process under the GMS program, (2) areas that separately move people and goods because of the structure of the entry points for cargo vehicles and the main border-crossing line, and (3) unofficial border-crossing roads on which unfettered movement occurs in residential areas because the borders have recently been located in existing residential areas.

The BCPs examined in this chapter comprise these three types, and we confirmed that some, but not all, areas had experienced changes. For example, the Houayxay-Chiang Khong BCP, the Tachileik-Mae Sai BCP, and the Myawaddy-Mae Sot BCP either had friendship bridges designed for cargo transportation or such bridges were under construction. Thus, although situations as described in (2) were observed in some areas, other areas in the same BCPs seemed unchanged in some ways by the CBTA, which fits the description of (3), through, for example, the active use of small boats in cross-border residential areas. In addition, the case of the Mohan-Boten BCP might be as described in (1).

This chapter provides a sketch of the development of the GMS program by examining the CBTA and BCPs because the progress of the GMS seems to be based on network-oriented regionalism. The general movements and knowledge of GMS regionalism are supported by intergovernmental organizations, such as the Mekong River Commission, the Mekong Institute, and the ADB. These regional intergovernmental organizations have promoted the so-called "Track 2" dialogue, which is a forum among ministries, offices, researchers, citizens, and nongovernmental organizations, to enhance and rationalize cross-border economic activities.

GMS regionalism differs from conventional legal-political regionalism, which is found in the European Union (EU) (Arnold and Pickles 2011). However, the GMS is similar to the EU because, just as the integration of Europe is an experiment in world history, the GMS is an experimental model of sub-regionalism. Characteristics of GMS regionalism are similar to those of the previous eastern European sub-regionalism in terms of socialism, extent of development, ethnic diversity, disparity, poverty, migration, and human trafficking. During the formation of a sub-region, the activities and exchanges among various actors are vital to their abilities to understanding each other at various levels. Moreover, Southeast Asia could learn from the INTERREG (a series of five programs to stimulate regional cooperation in the EU funded by the European Regional Development Fund) experience in cross-border cooperation. Very soon, a new sense of identity and people's perceptions of "our region," "imagined region," and the "Mekong citizen" might emerge in the GMS countries.

Notes

1 Initially, the six GMS countries fully ratified the CBTA main agreement (Laos, Thailand, and Vietnam in 1999; Cambodia in 2001; China in 2002; and Myanmar in 2003), and four of the countries (China, Cambodia, Laos, and Vietnam) fully ratified the Annexes and Protocols with Thailand and Myanmar in the process of such ratification (http://www.gms-cbta.org/cross-border-transport-agreement, accessed October 8, 2017).
2 The straw effect is that regional economy has deteriorated albeit trading has become facile (JICA 2007: 3.10).
3 https://www.adb.org/countries/gms/main, accessed October 8, 2017
4 https://www.jetro.go.jp/biznews/2017/09/531e0e4a2827f2da.html, accessed October 8, 2017
5 Regarding human trafficking, see Kneebone and Debeljak (2012) for their comprehensive analysis of the development of anti-human trafficking movements in the Mekong region and of the discourse that promoted these efforts.
6 http://english.mofcom.gov.cn/article/newsrelease/significantnews/201509/20150901109922.shtml, accessed October 8, 2017
7 http://www.vientianetimes.org.la/FreeContent/FreeConten_Laos284.htm, accessed October 8, 2017
8 Interview with a local Laotian guide at Boten, March 8, 2017.
9 The fact that Laotian resistance to this type of so-called "Chinese-style development" continues to broaden in scope is increasingly becoming a social issue. See https://www.japantimes.co.jp/news/2017/06/19/asia-pacific/crime-legal-asia-pacific/china-issues-security-alert-laos-national-fatally-shot/#.Wdzm91u0OUk, accessed October 8, 2017.
10 Interview with a local Thai guide at Chiang Khong, March 9, 2017.

References

Arnold, Dennis, and John Pickles (2011) "Global Work, Surplus Labor, and the Precarious Economies of the Border," *Antipode,* 43 (5): 1598–1624.
Asian Development Bank (ADB) (2011) *Greater Mekong Subregion Cross-Border Transport Facilitation Agreement: Instruments and Drafting History*, Mandaluyong City: Asian Development Bank.

Asian Development Bank (ADB) (2015) *Greater Mekong Subregion Urban Development Strategic Framework 2015–2022*, Mandaluyong City: Asian Development Bank.

Asian Development Bank (ADB) (2016) *Role of Special Economic Zones in Improving Effectiveness of GMS Economic Corridors*, Metro Manila: Asian Development Bank.

Bhattacharyay, Biswa Nath (2010) "Infrastructure for ASEAN Connectivity and Integration," *ASEAN Economic Bulletin*, 27 (2): 200–220.

Fujimura, Manabu (2014) "Transport Infrastructure in the Greater Mekong Subregion: A Fieldtrip Report," *Report of the Institute of Developing Economies*, 4: 1–89 (in Japanese).

Fujimura, Manabu (2017) "Evaluating Impact of Cross-Border Transport Infrastructure in the Greater Mekong Subregion: Three Approaches," *ADBI Working Paper 771*, Tokyo: Asian Development Bank Institute.

Ishida, Masami (2013) "What is the Cross-Border Transport Agreement (CBTA)?," in Masami Ishida (ed.) *Border Economies in the Greater Mekong Subregion*, Basingstoke: Palgrave Macmillan, pp. 53–76.

Ishida, Masami (2014) "Assessment of Cities and Border Regions Along Three Economic Corridors," in Kiyokatsu Nishiguchi and Nobuyoshi Nishizawa (eds.) *Mekong Regional Development and ASEAN Community*, Kyoto: Koyo Shobo, pp. 33–50 (in Japanese).

Japan International Cooperation Agency (JICA) (2007) *The Research on the Cross-border Transportation Infrastructure: Phase 2: Final Report*, Tokyo: Japan International Cooperation Agency and ALMEC Corporation.

Kneebone, Susan, and Julie Debeljak (2012) *Transnational Crime and Human Rights: Responses to Human Trafficking in the Greater Mekong Subregion*, Oxfordshire: Routledge.

Khanal, Bhoj Raj (2008) "Challenges and Opportunities of the Implementation of Cross Border Transport Agreement in the Greater Mekong Sub-region," *Review of Development and Cooperation*, 2 (1): 1–16.

Kudo, Toshihiro, and Masami Ishida (2013) "Prologue: Progress in Cross-Border Movement and the Development of Border Economic Zones," in Masami Ishida (ed.) *Border Economies in the Greater Mekong Subregion*, Basingstoke: Palgrave Macmillan, pp. 3–28.

Santasombat, Yos (ed.) (2015) *Impact of China's Rise on the Mekong Region*, New York: Palgrave Macmillan.

Shrestha, Omkar L., and Aekapol Chongvilaivan (eds.) (2013) *Greater Mekong Subregion: From Geographical to Socio-economic Integration*, Singapore: ISEAS Publishing.

Taga, Hidetoshi (2015) "Myanmar's Position in the GMS: Present and Future of the Border Treaty Between China and Myanmar," *Waseda Studies in Social Sciences*, 16 (1): 41–94 (in Japanese).

Yu, Shu Feng (2009) Implementation of GMS Cross-border Transport Agreements (CBTA) (http://cleanairasia.org/wp-content/uploads/portal/files/presentations/ADB_Yushu_Feng_-_CBTA_Implementation.pdf, accessed October 8, 2017).

Part III
Sub-Regionalism in Europe

7 Normative politics in the European Union's external actions
The case of ENI Cross-Border Cooperation

Yoichiro Usui

Introduction

The European Union (EU) has created shared norms among its 28 Member States and attempted to transplant those norms externally through a long-term process of repeating its normative discourses. By focusing on this practice, this chapter intends to elucidate various aspects of normative politics in the EU's external actions. The empirical case for this is the EU's cross-border cooperation (CBC) with its neighboring countries. This project has been carried out as part of the European Neighbourhood Policy (ENP). The ENP is a prototypical example of the EU's external strategy, which seeks to project an EU governance model as an outcome of European integration beyond EU Member States. Ever since its 2004 eastern enlargement, the EU has in practice distinguished between countries it will and will not permit to join the EU. In order to support the democratization of countries that will be permanently excluded from the EU, and construct lasting cooperative relationships with them, the EU has implemented the Euro-Mediterranean Partnership (EUROMED) in the Mediterranean region to the south, and the Eastern Partnership (EaP) with the former Soviet region to the east. Thus, the ENP supports efforts to build socioeconomic relationships with regions in the so-called "arc of instability" (Bertelsmann Stiftung 2015: 3), which would conventionally be targets of security policies. The European Neighbourhood Instrument's Cross-Border Cooperation (ENI CBC) program is one aspect of these wide-ranging efforts.

CBC promotes cooperation between regional and municipal governments and social organizations active on a wide range of cross-border socioeconomic projects at the local level, from cultural and administrative interactions to infrastructure improvements. Similar initiatives have long been promoted within the EU, through the formation of Euroregions (CBC structures) and Macro-Regions (much larger CBC areas). Together, these EU projects are referred to as INTERREG, and are viewed as one method for dismantling national borders and constructing a single Europe. CBC represents an effort to incorporate these strategies into the ENP. It can therefore be understood as an attempt to transplant the EU's distinctive cross-border governance model outside the EU area.

The norms that define this model are based on EU law (Regulation 232/2014). The projects commenced in earnest between 2006 and 2013, and currently the 2014 to 2020 round of projects is being initiated. With a total budget of about one billion euros for the seven-year EU funding period, the subsidies for these projects are certainly not large, but the distinctive stamp of EU normative politics is visible in the durability of the governance model that has been constructed through the process of European integration. By analyzing CBC policy papers, this study focuses on the EU's repeated long-term projects, which are aimed at encouraging neighboring countries to accept EU norms, and attempts to elucidate the normative strategy responsible for putting these projects in place. However, while many examples of CBC exist, this chapter does not examine the details of individual projects. Its main purpose is rather to present a theoretical discussion, based on an analysis of policy papers.

Part 1 provides an overview of the ENP and clarifies the political context of CBC implemented by the EU in its boundary regions. While the ENP has been the subject of a comparatively large quantity of research within the field of EU studies, most of this research concludes that it has achieved limited results. In contrast, this section focuses on the unintended pacifist practices that have come about because the EU has been forced to respond to regions that would conventionally be the target of security policy, with a policy of sustained socioeconomic cooperation. Following this discussion of CBC's political context, Part 2 describes the ways in which various EU norms are projected beyond the EU area, given its large geographical scale and the CBC's extremely small budget. This is not a true case study and is limited to an analysis of policy papers that serve the theoretical discussion. This analysis brings to light the long process of policy replication that results in the transfer of EU norms beyond the EU area. Finally, Part 3 discusses the political significance of this process and considers the possibility that the long, repetitive project of standardizing the EU's basic values may construct a value discourse that differentiates between European and non-European regions.

Studies of the ENP from the viewpoint of normative politics

Great Powers are used to taking pride in the qualitative superiority of their own norms and attempt to disseminate them broadly to other nation-states in order to expand their spheres of influence; therefore, these behaviors by Great Powers in themselves do not merit special mention from a historical perspective. However, when carried out by a regional integration organization such as the EU, it is by no means easy to accomplish. This chapter focuses on this point. Shared norms must be established and maintained in 28 Member States, with a combined population of 500 million people. Europe has been created by establishing a legal framework that ensures collective action based on these shared norms, and implementing action plans in as many policy areas as possible, to coordinate cooperative responses to common problems. This accumulated historical experience provides a reference point for transplanting EU norms externally. The distinctive characteristics visible in the EU's external actions reflect the style in which Europe was constructed. The ENP is a direct and concrete example of this process.

According to the EU law that regulates these policies (Regulation 232/2014), the goal of these policies is to develop special relationships with neighboring countries (Preamble Para. 3), and, through the participation of regional governments, municipalities, and civil society organizations (Preamble Para. 6), to achieve EU standards for values and norms consistent with a democratic system of government, the recognition of human rights, the rule of law, good governance, the market economy, sustainable development, social inclusion, people-to-people contacts, gender equality, minority rights, and non-discrimination (Preamble Paras. 3 and 21). Promoting CBC and Macro-Regional Strategies (MRS) is an element of these goals (Preamble Paras. 5–6.). As is evident from the breadth of its programs, the ENP cuts across many policy areas, from security and trade to the environment and development (Khasson, Vasiyan, and Vos 2008). The gist of the policy is to hold out the carrot of access to the single EU market, while using political dialogue, funding, and technological support to disseminate EU-style good governance, market economy reforms, and the *acquis communautaire*, which embodies EU norms (Khasson, Vasiyan, and Vos 2008: 236).

The basic aim of this policy is to stabilize the aforementioned "arc of instability" that surrounds the EU. The EU classifies the neighboring states into two broad groups. The EaP includes Armenia, Azerbaijan, Belarus, Georgia, Moldova, and Ukraine (Russia, however, is given special status), while the Union for the Mediterranean includes Algeria, Egypt, Israel, Jordan, Morocco, Lebanon, Libya, Palestine, Syria, and Tunisia. As is immediately evident from this list of countries, the policy is targeted at regions that would conventionally be dealt with primarily in terms of security concerns.

However, the measures the EU is pushing forward through this policy are uniformly related to socioeconomic cooperation. Annex II of Regulation 232/2014 includes a list of goals, such as administrative collaboration, participation by civil society organizations, economic growth, youth employment, small and medium-size businesses, agriculture, natural resources, renewable energy, transportation infrastructure, support for education and employment, management of immigrants, and post-conflict confidence-building. Security is mentioned as a goal (Regulation 232/2014, Article 1), but it is not emphasized. The policy was launched in 2004, reviewed in 2010, and a revision was scheduled for 2015. For the 2014 to 2020 funding period, 15.4 billion euros have been appropriated (Article 17 (1)), which represents 26% of the EU's total foreign relations expenditures (European Commission 2013: 7). It is exactly the EU's most significant external action program. Nevertheless, considering the political situations in the countries targeted by the policy, the available funds are hardly adequate. We must remember that these policies are not military in nature, and even in regions where political instability is spreading; neither military operations nor police missions are planned within the framework of the ENP (Bertelsmann

Stiftung 2015). Instead, the framework emphasizes socioeconomic initiatives and depends on the existence of North Atlantic Treaty Organization (NATO).

However, while the ENP may be meaningless from the perspective of international politics, it cannot be ignored. The diffusion of norms does not necessarily require large-scale financing nor is a military presence a prerequisite to achieving this diffusion. The very existence of the EU, with its single market of 500 million developed nation residents, is appealing for the countries surrounding it. The administrative system that maintains and manages this market through a comparatively high-quality regulatory system even serves as a benchmark for other countries, as they modernize. To say, however, that the diffusion of EU norms to neighboring countries does not depend on a military presence or substantial funding would be inaccurate; rather, it is precisely because the scale of funding is small and there is no military presence that the EU has been forced to advance a form of politics that makes use of norms. This point is exactly what this chapter will focus on.

After the EU expanded eastward in 2004, it promoted the Europeanization of countries to which it would definitely not grant membership. The EU conceived of the countries surrounding it as "a wider Europe," and adopted a policy of transplanting EU norms to these territories. The ENP is a concrete expression of this policy. It is truly a project intended to spread the accomplishments of European integration to countries that will never be granted EU membership. This has led some to regard the EU as Europe's "protector" or "sponsor," while others view it is "a regional hegemon" or "big brother." (Bechev and Nicolaidis 2010: 476)

However, it has never been recognized that the EU has real power. Certainly, the ENP has been a popular target for EU studies; however, EU enlargement studies have focused primarily on examining distinctions between neighborhood policies and enlargement processes from the perspective of the influence of EU norms. Furthermore, Normative Power Europe theorists have debated the successes and failures of the diffusion of norms. While norms have attracted attention, preceding studies has emphasized their failure as a policy instrument. These studies espouse counterexamples to the existence of normative power; focus on limits to the power of norms diffusion as compared with enlargement; and note the necessary conditions for the successful transfer of norms, observing constitutional reforms as failures and policy cooperation as successes. These studies furthermore judge the EU's "soft" responses to conflict prevention, conflict resolution, and peace-building—such as responding to security issues with low-budget economic policies—as failures and emphasize the tribulations of a wider Europe, including the Arab Spring, tensions with Russia, and the euro crisis (Whitman and Wolff 2010; Haukkala 2011; Whitman and Juncos 2014). Of particular note is the research that argues for the need to carefully examine how, in the process of norm diffusion, neighboring countries in actuality employ evasion, deception, distortion, and reinterpretation of EU norms (Parmentier 2000).

So, what significance can we find with regard to the ENP, especially in EU's existential crisis?

EU norms in ENI CBC

The ENP is the EU's external normative politics in practice. In this politics, the stability of the value content of EU norms deserves closer attention. As discussed earlier, preceding studies confirm that the EU has behaved precisely as the leader of a wider Europe, whereas the limited policy results of the EU's attempts to diffuse its own norms have also been emphasized. The point that merits greater attention here, however, is the stability of EU norms. Simply put, regardless of whether it has achieved successes or failures, the EU has endlessly repeated concrete projects aimed at convincing various countries to adopt its own norms. The dispersion of norms and the implementation of projects through this process of repetition is an attempt by the EU to transplant its own governance model it has constructed over many years through the European integration process. A prime example of this is CBC. This program is an attempt to apply the system of CBC that has existed for a quarter of a century in the EU to territories that border it, which equates to nothing less than transplanting measures used to construct Europe. In financial terms, each CBC project is small, and far from being a meaningful phenomenon in international politics. Within the EU, these projects were advanced starting in 1990, under the name of INTERREG. The important point with regard to the implementation of these projects is the repetitive and long-lasting nature of the process. The EU has repeated this process across Europe numerous times and eventually accumulated results. INTERREG has been in place for more than 25 years. As will be discussed, ENI CBC is a sustained and repetitive effort to project this style of constructing Europe beyond the EU territory.

In this context, the EU's "internal" MRS should also be paid attention to. Currently, the EU is planning to expand and develop the INTERREG program under the banner of MRS, which builds on INTERREG's accomplishments. One aspect of the MRS program intersects with CBC, whose target is the "external" zone. The EU regulations established for ENP take into account the external aspects of MRS and stipulate the obligation to ensure consistency between the two programs (Regulation 232/2014, Preamble Paras. 5 and Article 8 (5)). While the duplicate funding of these two programs is undeniably a sign of waste in the EU's regional policies, the EU Council of Ministers has officially acknowledged that the MRS is a means of achieving multi-level governance (MLG). In doing so, it officially recognizes that the EU is not only an intergovernmental organization but also a multidimensional, multilayered, composite body that includes subnational bodies. ENI CBC, including the external aspects of MRS, can be interpreted as a transfer of the EU's MLG system to regions outside of its territory.

Cross-Border Cooperation

As discussed earlier, the EU's intra-territorial INTERREG program has been applied to neighboring regions. This INTERREG is a program of the European Regional Development Fund (ERDF) that was initiated in

1990. It marked its 25th anniversary in 2015. Events were held throughout Europe to celebrate and promote this anniversary. However, CBC between municipalities in border regions existed even before the EU's predecessor, the European Economic Community, officially established a policy framework for such cooperation. For example, cooperative agreements between Germany and the Netherlands (the EUREGIO region), and between France, Germany, and Switzerland in the 1950s, and between France, Germany, and Luxembourg in the 1960s are recognized as predecessors of INTERREG (Wassenberg and Reitel 2015: 8). The joint border projects that the EU has advanced in its attempt to adapt this program to neighboring regions and build extraterritorial cooperation is thus based on accumulated experience that reaches back half a century.

The direct aim of CBC is to build stable cross-border cooperative relationships through programs that include providing support for small and medium-sized businesses, joint programs related to education and culture, measures to address poverty, experience-sharing to encourage good governance, environmental measures, improvements to transportation infrastructure, the promotion of renewable energy, and administrative cooperation on border management. Table 7.1 lists projects for the 2014–2020 funding period, together with their budgets. All of the individual programs implemented under each project are submitted to the European Commission and shared, via the Commission, with Member States, neighboring countries, and the European Parliament (European External Action Service [EEAS] and European Commission 2014).

As a model example, the European Commission presents CBC between Russia and Finland (EEAS and European Commission 2014: 5). In the 2007–2013 funding period, related projects were categorized as Priority 1, comprising 21 economic development projects; Priority 2, comprising 18 projects related to problems shared across the border zone; and Priority 3, comprising eight projects related to social development and civil society, plus eight comparatively large infrastructure projects (Joint Managing Authority Regional Council of South Karelia 2014). Economic development projects included support for small and medium-sized businesses in the renewable energy sector, and cooperation in developing forestry resources; projects related to shared problems in the border zone included the preservation of biodiversity, and the prevention of marine accidents; social development and civil society projects included cooperation between municipal governments on sports, support for youth, education, and culture; and infrastructure projects included the improvement of roads at border crossings (Joint Managing Authority Regional Council of South Karelia 2014).

CBC comprises a collection of these small individual projects. The budget for the 2014–2020 funding period is 1.5265 billion euros, approximately half of which is appropriated from the ERDF (EEAS and European Commission 2014: 9). The EU's strategy is to extend the internal policy that engendered CBC beyond EU territory, through the accumulation of countless cooperative projects that cross national borders.

Table 7.1 The European Neighbourhood Policy's Cross-Border Cooperation: funding allocations for projects in the 2014–2020 funding period

Participating countries	Number of participating local governments	Apportioned funds (million euros)*
Finland, Sweden, Norway/Russia (Kolarctic)	8	35.07
Finland/Russia (Karelia)	4	29.61
SE Finland/Russia	5	45.50
Estonia/Russia	5	18.63
Latvia/Russia	3	24.04
Lithuania/Russia	3	32.53
Poland/Russia	8	72.19
Latvia, Lithuania/Belarus	4	74.00
Poland/Belarus, Ukraine	11	175.80
Hungary, Slovakia, Romania/Ukraine	7	73.95
Romania/Ukraine	9	60.00
Romania/Moldova**	5	81.00
Italy/Tunisia	14	33.35
Macro-Regional Strategies		
Baltic Sea Region*** (11 countries)	27	8.80
Black Sea Region**** (10 countries)	26	39.04
Mediterranean Sea Region***** (19 countries)	107	290.60
Mid-Atlantic Region (4 countries)	16	149.87

Source: Created by the author from EEAS and European Commission, Programming of the European Neighbourhood Instrument (ENI) – 2014–2020, Programming Document for EU Support to ENI Cross-Border Cooperation (2014–2020), Annex 2 and 3.

Notes: *Total of ENI and ERDF funds, 2014–2020. **Moldova is counted as one government. ***Finland/Sweden, Denmark, Estonia, Latvia, Lithuania, Poland, Belarus, and Norway are each counted as one government. ****Moldova, Georgia, Armenia, and Azerbaijan are each counted as one government. *****Malta, Palestine, Israel, and Lebanon are each counted as one government.

Through this accumulation of low budget projects that are quite separate from security measures, the EU is, in effect, politically mobilizing MLG. It is worth pausing to consider this point. This strategy signifies the incorporation of regional governments, municipalities, and local civil society groups into relationships between central governments, and key roles are assigned to subnational actors. Table 7.1 shows the extent of participation by subnational actors in the projects planned for the 2014–2020 funding period, in terms of the number of local governments involved centrally. The EU's goal is to disseminate its norms through accumulated interactions between these so-called "third level" actors over many years. The European Commission is attempting to use existing forums and networks where these actors gather. The Council of the Baltic Sea States (CBSS), the Barents Euro-Arctic Council (BEAC), the Black Sea Economic Cooperation (BSEC), the Association of European Border Regions (AEBR), and the Network of Eastern External Border Regions (NEEBOR) are among the existing networks the Commission has used (EEAS and European Commission 2014: 7–9). Regional and municipal government staff members from various countries gather at these forums to promote CBC. This policy takes the same approach as MRS, which the EU has promoted within its territory. MRS also incorporates relationships with the EU's neighbors and represents an effort to further evolve INTERREG's quarter-century of accomplishments.

Macro-Regional Strategies

The essence of European unification is reflected in the effort made to avoid partitioning EU territory by the national borders of its Member States. The MRS program implements projects across national borders and represents an evolution of INTERREG, which was initially implemented on a comparatively small scale; it is a method of integration that promotes CBC on a larger scale. As shown in Table 7.2, some initiatives have been launched in the Baltic Sea and Danube regions, others are underway in the Adriatic and Ionian region and the Alpine region, and are being planned for the North Sea, the Atlantic Arc, the Carpathian, Black Sea, and Mediterranean regions (European Parliament 2015). By establishing Macro-Regions that cut across multiple countries inside EU territory, this program creates intergovernmental socioeconomic joint project groups financed by the EU and sets up systematic frameworks for drawing in regional governments, municipalities, and civil society organizations. It is exactly a concrete expression of multilevel governance within the EU (Regulation 1303/2013, Article 5) (European Commission 2009: European Commission 2014).

Funding for the MRS project depends on the budget allocated to the EU's regional policies. In its regional policy budgetary framework, it is the European Commission that has been in charge of using funds for the INTERREG project, which is slated for expansion. Beginning with the Baltic Sea Cooperation strategy in 2009, various industrial, environmental, transport, and personnel exchange projects that had been advanced under an official program called the European Territorial Cooperation have been officially recognized as MRS by the leaders of EU Member States. This means that a new budgetary provision has not been made for MRS nor has a new regulatory system been created for it. The entire project is designed as an extension of the existing INTERREG project, advanced through self-initiated cooperation within the designated Macro-Regions. Its effectiveness is questionable. A report on the project submitted to the European Parliament was critical of these "three NOs": no new budget, no new law, and no new system (European Parliament 2015: 22).

Nevertheless, the MRS is more than rhetoric. Through the process of officially recognizing MRS, the three goals have been posited: reducing disparities, linking regions, and advancing foreign policy. And these three goals are guided by the principle of MLG (European Parliament 2015; European Commission 2014). Focus in this chapter is on foreign policy. As shown in

Table 7.2 The European Union's Macro-Regional Strategy

Currently implemented
EU Strategy for the Baltic Sea Region (EUSBSR) ⇐ Led by Sweden, launched October 2009
   EU Member States: Denmark, Sweden, Finland, Germany, Estonia, Latvia, Lithuania
   Neighbor countries: Norway, Russia, Belarus
EU Strategy for the Danube Region (EUSDR) ⇐ Led by Austria and Romania, launched June 2011
   EU Member States: Germany, Austria, Czech Republic, Slovakia, Hungary, Bulgaria, Croatia, Slovenia
   Neighbor countries: Bosnia and Herzegovina, Montenegro, Serbia, **Ukraine, Moldova**

In preparation
EU Strategy for the Adriatic and Ionian Region (EUSAIR) ⇐ Led by Italy, adopted September 2014
   EU Member States: Italy, Croatia, Slovenia, Greece
   Neighbor countries: Montenegro, Serbia, Bosnia and Herzegovina, Albania
EU Strategy for the Alpine Region (EUSALP) ⇐ Led by France
   EU Member States: France, Germany, Austria, Italy, Slovenia
   Neighbor countries: Liechtenstein, Switzerland

In planning
North Sea Region ⇐ No lead country
   EU Member States: Sweden, Denmark, the Netherlands, Belgium, France, Germany
   Neighbor countries: Norway
Atlantic Arc Region ⇐ No lead country
   EU Member States: Ireland, United Kingdom, Portugal, Spain, France
   Neighbor countries: Iceland, Norway, Greenland, Faroe Islands
Carpathian Region
   EU Member States: Poland, Hungary, Slovakia, Romania
   Neighbor countries: **Ukraine**
Black Sea Region ⇐ No lead EU country
   EU Member States: Greece, Bulgaria, Romania
   Neighbor countries: Russia, **Ukraine, Moldova, Georgia**, Turkey, **Armenia, Azerbaijan**
Mediterranean Region ⇐ Led by Cyprus and Malta
   EU Member States: Portugal, Spain, France, Italy, Cyprus, Malta, Croatia, Slovenia
   Neighbor countries: **Israel, Palestine, Jordan, Lebanon, Syria, Egypt,** Libya, **Algeria, Morocco, Tunisia**, Montenegro, Albania

---

Source: Created by the author from European Parliament, New Role of Macro-Regions in European Territorial Cooperation: Study Part I, January 2015, pp. 29–44.

Note: Bold lettering indicates countries targeted by the ENP.

Table 7.2, MRS incorporates countries that are targeted by the ENP. Within its borders, the EU has contacted subnational actors and made them the prime movers in promoting joint socioeconomic projects straddling national boundaries; that method is now being employed outside EU external borders. The European Commission has developed a policy of involving countries outside EU external borders in various dimensions and is addressing the issue of improving mechanisms for doing so (European Commission 2014: 10). In this way, basic EU norms that are prerequisites for any project inside EU borders—such as gender equality, environmental conservation, social justice, and participation from all levels of society through partnerships that observe the European Code of Conduct (Regulation 2303/2013)—are diffused outside the EU. The aim of the EU is clearly to link projects for European integration with projects for ENP.

A MLG style forms the foundation of European Integration, and the style has been tried to be implanted into external regions. The Council of Ministers emphasizes MLG as the basic norm that defines partnership between government bodies:

> the Commission and the Member States to actively support the multi-level governance approach recognizing the potential substantial contribution from all levels of society in implementing the macro-regional strategies
> (Council of the European Union 2014: 13)

The intention of EU Member States to involve actors other than central governments in international politics can be observed in this statement. Participation by subnational actors such as regional and municipal governments is one of the basic norms of the EU. By involving these in the formulation of MRS, the EU aims to construct and spread this norm of participation. This also implies that the EU is advancing a policy of creating various channels for neighboring country actors other than central governments to participate in EU projects and, through those channels, transferring the EU's basic norms outside its territory. This interpretation enables a reassessment of the political significance of MRS with regard to the ENP.

The political significance of ENI CBC

As mentioned earlier, CBC is quite distinct from security policy and the budget of each CBC is small. However, the EU has carried out the long-term accumulation of numerous CBC projects internally and externally. What is the significance of this for international politics? Can we ignore it as a meaningless episode? The answer, of course, is no. The ultimate aim of CBC is EU security, achieved through the diffusion of EU norms to neighboring countries. Preceding studies have also argued that the basic goal of the ENP is to prevent conflict by actualizing the values of the EU (Tocci 2007: 6). This goal is expressed in the transfer of the EU governance mode, which is both the method and the result of European integration, to exterior territories. CBC is a typical model of this EU governance mode, in which nongovernmental actor participation becomes a norm. This norm dictates that states engage in dialogue on the international stage, not only with sovereign nation-states, but also with non-state actors. The official and unofficial systems that create networks of these non-state actors and promote partnership with them serve as particularly good channels for disseminating the other basic EU norms, such as democracy, human rights, the rule of law, good governance, market economics, sustainable development, social inclusion, people-to-people contacts, gender equality, minority rights, and anti-discrimination. This is the philosophy that defines the CBC initiative.

Here the structures of international politics around the ENP deserve further attention. These structures are comprised of three types of relationships. The first type is relationships between international organizations. NATO virtually monopolizes military functions, while the EU offers only the carrot of market access. Projects that prioritize socioeconomics in the aforementioned "arc of instability" have been promoted in a context in which NATO's military power exists. The second type is relationships between public institutions within internal EU area. In the realm of security, views of the "big three" (France, the United Kingdom, and Germany) play a major role. The field of activity for the European Commission, a supranational institution, lies in policy measures related to socioeconomic issues such as targets of CBC projects, while the European Council, an intergovernmental institution, decides and implements foreign and security policy. The third and final type of relationship is that of CBC between non-state actors. With leadership from the European Commission, regional governments, municipalities, and local socioeconomic organizations are incorporated across borders into relationships between central governments. This arrangement is referred to as MLG, which can be said to be a method, style, goal, and outcome of European integration. The international political structure that defines the ENP represents the sum of these three relationships. The cross-border connections between non-state actors brought about by CBC have been promoted by the European Commission under these structural circumstances. Here, there is a need to keep in mind that, while CBC projects have been embedded into big powers' politics based on NATO, a nonmilitary stabilization policy of the EU has emerged, despite the fact that these regions would conventionally require security measures. It is by no means easy to begin or sustain CBC projects in these regions.

A report of the Bertelsmann Foundation, a German think tank, criticized the EU for neglecting international political arrangements. The ENP is a policy to respond to issues that would conventionally be addressed through low-budget socioeconomic policy measures. These measures are primarily planned and implemented by the European Commission, and therefore they are not incorporated into missions of the EEAS, which is responsible for strategically important aspects of the EU's external relations. While missions of the Common Security and Defense Policy (CSDP) are definitely necessary given the current situation, such missions have never ever been dispatched to these ENP regions. A policy paper from the Bertelsmann Foundation argues that the ENP should be transferred to the framework of the Common Foreign and Security Policy, and that it should be made an instrument of external action with real power, and should not hesitate to dispatch CSDP missions (Bertelsmann Stiftung 2015). This type of proposal, however, also serves to emphasize the nonmilitary orientation that pervades the ENP.

MRS has often been criticized for its dependence on the European Commission for achieving cooperation between subnational actors. These critics have pointed out problems related both to the political will of Member States' governments and to the capacity of regional and municipal governments and raised alarms regarding their "over-dependence" on the European Commission (European Commission 2014: 4). If CBC is viewed as a strategy for external action, however, this is not entirely problematic. CBC displays a strategic orientation towards EU norms. The EU has sought to build relationships in border zones through a governance model that it has repeatedly implemented over a period of many years within its internal area. This strategy reveals the EU's intention of using values and norms as a strategic tool for security. While diffusing the norm of participation by non-state actors in border regions, through the creation and utilization of channels of interaction between regional and municipal governments, the EU is strengthening cooperation around non-traditional security threats such as organized crime, contagious diseases, and environmental degradation (EEAS and European Commission 2014).

CBC makes the further strategic contribution of creating discourses of values and norms, according to which the acceptance of EU norms as a matter of course serves as proof that a nation is civilized. Representing the EU as the bearer of civilization is a strategic outcome of the ENI CBC. The EU's project of making a MLG system, which not only allot a central role to subnational actors such as regional and municipal governments but also mobilize civil society organizations, are also significant in terms of confidence- and peace-building in external border areas. These programs can indeed be interpreted as the EU's pursuit of an ideal, in which politics exist to serve norms. The norms of human rights, democracy, rule of law, good governance, free markets, sustainable development, accountability, partnership, and rejection of uniformity (respect for the diversity of each nation) form a base for EU policy programs. These are values that the EU has espoused innumerable times in various venues. The EU has employed a similarly repetitive process for building these normative values, transforming them into legal norms, and using them to establish its own normative discourse as a given. The ENI CBC can be interpreted as a political apparatus for replicating the European normative discourse. However, we must also note that the construction of this discourse clearly distinguishes between "a civilized (European)" and "an uncivilized (non-European) regions".

Conclusion

The CBC initiative discussed in this chapter rests upon 25 years of INTERREG experience within the EU internal area. The path that the EU is treading with the ENI CBC is unchanging. The immediate goal of the project is to construct channels between regional and municipal governments and national governments, with guidance from the European Commission, and it is precisely during this process that we may observe the EU's self-replicating norms. Participation based on multilevel partnership has been emphasized innumerable times as one of the important EU norms, and project participants are required to accept this norm. Rooted in this norm of participation, local entities linked in cross-border relationships seek to realize the universal norms of civilized nations, such as human rights, anti-discrimination, gender equality, environmental conservation, and social justice. This is the ideological vision of ENI CBC that has been pursued as one component of the ENP.

The international political environment that surrounds ENI CBC is truly tumultuous. EUROMED cooperation has taken place in the context of chaos stemming from the Arab Spring, while in the EaP region, conflict has erupted in Georgia and Ukraine. Then, in 2015, the program faced a decisive crisis, with the massive inflow of refugees from Midlle East. However, we must also not allow our image of the ENI CBC projects to be shaped solely by the fluid aspects of the current situation. Rather, we must focus our attention on the EU as the long-term backdrop for these fast-moving current events.

References

Bechev, Dimitar, and Kalypso Nicolaidis (2010) "From Policy to Polity: Can the EU's Special Relations with its 'Neighbourhood' be Decentred?," *Journal of Common Market Studies*, 48 (3): 475–500.

Bertelsmann Stiftung (2015) *The EU Neighbourhood in Shambles: Some Recommendations for a New European Neighbourhood Strategy*, Gütersloh: Bertelsmann Stiftung.

Council of the European Union (2014) Draft Council Conclusions on the Governance of Macro-Regional Strategies, 13374/14. Brussels, October 9, 2014.

EEAS and European Commission (2014) Programming of the European Neighbourhood Instrument (ENI) – 2014–2020, Programming Document for EU Support to ENI Cross-Border Cooperation (2014–2020) (http://eeas.europa.eu/archives/docs/enp/pdf/financing-the-enp/cbc_2014-2020_programming_document_en.pdf, accessed July 8, 2017).

European Commission (2009) European Union Strategy for the Baltic Sea Region, COM (2009) 248 final.

European Commission (2013) *Multiannual Financial Framework 2014–2020 and EU Budget 2014: The Figures*, Luxembourg: Publications Office of the European Union.

European Commission (2014) Concerning the Governance of Macro-Region Strategies, COM (2014) 284 final.

European Parliament (2015) New Role of Macro-Regions in European Territorial Cooperation: Study Part I. Policy Department B: Structural and Cohesion Policies, Directorate-General for Internal Policies. IP/B/REGI/FWC/2010_002/LOT02-C01/SC01, January 2015.

Haukkala, Hiski (2011) "The European Union as a Regional Normative Hegemon: The Case of European Neighbourhood Policy," in Richard G. Whitman (ed.) *Normative Power Europe: Empirical and Theoretical Perspectives*, New York: Palgrave Macmillan, pp. 45–64.

Joint Managing Authority Regional Council of South (2014) South-East Finland-Russia ENPI CBC 2007–2013 Cross-border cooperation programme supporting EU's external actions with the financing from the European Union, the Russian Federation and the Republic of Finland: Sharing Borders – Growing Closer (http://www.southeast-finrusnpi.fi/wp-content/uploads/sites/2/2013/10/South-East-Finland-Russia-ENPI-CBC-brochure2014_lowresweb.pdf, accessed July 8, 2017).

Khasson, Viktoriya, Syuzanna Vasiyan, and Hendrik Vos (2008) "Everybody Needs Good Neighbours: The EU and its Neighbourhood," in Jan Orbie (ed.) *Europe's Global Role: External Policies of the European Union*, Aldershot: Ashgate, pp. 217–238.

Parmentier, Florent (2000) "The Reception of EU Neighbourhood Policy," in Zaki Laïdi (ed.) *EU Foreign Policy in a Globalized World: Normative Power and Social Preferences*, London: Routledge, pp. 103–117.

Tocci, Nathalie (2007) *The EU and Conflict Resolution: Promoting Peace in the Backyard*, London: Routledge.

Wassenberg, Birte., and Bernard Reitel (2015) *Territorial Cooperation in Europe: A Historical Perspective*, Luxembourg: Publications Office of the European Union.

Whitman, Richard G., and Ana E. Juncos (2014) "Challenging Events, Diminishing Influence?: Relations with the Wider Europe," *Journal of Common Market Studies*, 52 (1): 157–169.

Whitman, Richard G., and Stefan Wolff (eds.) (2010) *The European Neighbourhood Policy in Perspective: Context, Implementation and Impact*, Basingstoke: Palgrave Macmillan.

8 Sub-regionalism in the border regions between the EU and Russia

Kazu Takahashi

Introduction

Instances of micro-level cross-border cooperation (CBC) by local governments and other actors in Europe, called Euroregions, increased dramatically in the 1990s. Previously, only a handful of Euroregions existed. The number reached 70 in 2000, 137 in 2006, and is currently at more than 180.[1]

Until the eastward expansion of the European Union (EU) in 2004, Euroregions served to create the geography-based horizontal integration of the EU. They also served to enhance vertical integration in terms of decision-making as they allowed the involvement of representatives from local governments, corporations, non-governmental organizations (NGOs), central governments, and international organizations. Meanwhile, the EU actively established Euroregions in regions outside but adjacent to the EU. This operation had the strategic objective of integrating geographically crucial regions in advance of their joining the EU. Another more technical objective was to acquaint future EU countries with the EU system, including practical knowledge of its systems (Takahashi 2012).

From this perspective, Euroregions had completed their original purposes toward regional integration in 2004. Nonetheless, Euroregions continued to be established outside the EU territory. The Russia–Ukraine border region stands out as an example. Euroregions Dnieper and Slobozhanshchyna were set up in 2003 and followed by Euroregion Yaroslavna in 2007 and Donbass in 2011, which meant that the entire Russia–Ukraine border region was at the time covered by four Euroregions. Further, Euroregion Dniester, which includes Transnistria, was established in 2012. Transnistria/Pridnestrovie declared its secession from Moldova in 1990, but it was not recognized as a sovereign state in the international community. These Euroregions do not share borders with the EU.

Establishing a Euroregion is based on the legal framework provided by the Council of Europe's Madrid Agreement. Thus, creating one outside the EU is not necessarily a unique occurrence, as Russia and Ukraine are both members of the Council of Europe. Usually, the expansion of CBCs is explained through the theory of multi-level governance (MLG), which underlines the transfer of power from the central government to the regional or local government. Therefore, when an unrecognized state, such as Transnistria, whose border has not been determined, establishes a Euroregion, it is rather unique and difficult to explain according to the theory of MLG. In addition, the local governments in Ukraine and Russia are typically weak and tend to limit the local residents' political activities. Thus, it is highly unlikely that their central governments would share power with actors other than those at the state level. This situation raises the question on why Euroregions continued to be established in the region outside of the EU. The present study aims to examine the role of Euroregions in these regions from the viewpoint of the regional policies of the EU and Russia. This investigation may contribute to the theories of regional integration that used to pay no attention to the relationship with the policies of actors outside of the region.

Euroregions obtain subsidies through the EU's regional policy program INTERREG instead of going through its own central government (Inoue 2005; Sengoku 2007; Shiba 2007; Wakamori, Yagi, Shimizu, and Nagao 2007). It is a unique scenario because the EU's subsidies are distributed to each government first; such a scheme fueled the development under the system. Against this backdrop, research on Euroregions as well as micro-level CBCs often tends to be discussed from the viewpoint of the EU's regional integration and in relation to the INTERREG program. These studies analyze Euroregions from the viewpoint of "the principle of subsidiarity" and MLG and consider Euroregion formation as a form of EU integration. For this reason, analysis of Euroregions outside EU territories has not garnered much attention.

Meanwhile, studies on Euroregions in the border regions of the EU attracted interest as these areas may promote the EU's expansion. As the EU's eastward expansion between 2004 and 2007 ended, and the concern for the drawing of the new east–west line persisted, studies analyzing these particular Euroregions as a tool for the EU to integrate these surrounding areas began to emerge (Scott 2006). However, few have focused on the logic of regionalism (Popescu 2006). Studies on Euroregions outside the EU territory have been sparse, perhaps owing to the presumption that building an independent cooperative relationship crossing the national framework seems unlikely, in the context of the strong state power in Russia and Ukraine. That is to say, many scholars questioned the feasibility of a Euroregion cooperative structure in these regions led by actors who act as agents not for the regions but for the central government.

Certain studies on Euroregions outside EU territory have been presented in relation to the EU's Eastern policies, the Eastern Partnership (EaP), which will be discussed later in this work, or Russian foreign policies (Delcour 2011; Gower and Timmis 2011; Herrschel 2011; Koresteleva 2012; Stadtmuller and Bachmann 2012), but none focused on the Euroregions themselves. With this in mind, this study focuses on Euroregions outside EU territory and examines the meaning of sub-regionalism in this part of the world.

Euroregions in the region between Russia and Ukraine

Ukraine is a non-EU member country with which Russia has established Euroregions. In Western Ukraine, two Euroregions began cooperating in the 1990s: Euroregion Bug along the border with Poland was established in 1995 and

Sub-regionalism between the EU and Russia 199

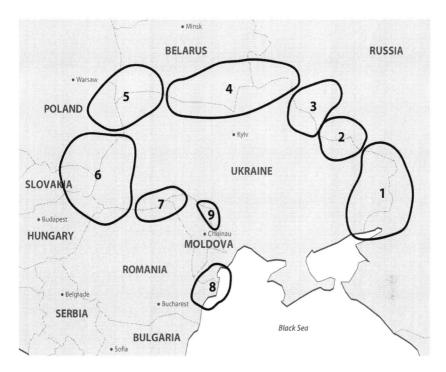

Figure 8.1 List of Euroregions located at the border of Ukraine
Source: Created by the author.

Note: 1=Euroregion Donbass; 2=Euroregion Slobozhanschina; 3=Euroregion Yaroslavna; 4=Euroregion Dnieper; 5=Euroregion Bug; 6=Carpatian Euroregion; 7=Euroregion Upper Prut; 8=Euroregion Lower Danube; 9=Euroregion Transnistria.

Euroregion Carpathian, which includes regions in Poland, Hungary, Slovakia, and Romania, in 1993. Two Euroregions named the Upper and Lower Prut River were also added as a step toward preparing Romania to join the EU.

In Russia's eastern border region, Euroregions Dnieper and Slobozhanshchyna, Yaroslavna, and Donbass were established in 2003, 2007, and 2010, respectively. This means that Ukraine's entire border with Russia was consequently covered by four Euroregions. These Euroregions in Eastern Ukraine were established as the eastward expansion of the EU and covered a considerably large area (see Figure 8.1). Euroregion Dnieper includes the Bryansk region in Russia, the Chernigov region in Ukraine, and the Gomel region in Belarus. The area is where the Chernobyl Nuclear Power Plant was located. It was a fertile farmland prior to the Chernobyl disaster, which caused severe environmental damage that eventually resulted in a dramatic population decline in the area. The population decline was especially true in the working-age population, causing the regional economy to stagnate. The decision to establish a Euroregion in the area plagued with environmental aftereffects of the disaster can be traced back to 1997, when leaders of the neighboring border regions discussed potential CBCs in the area with respect to the economy, science, technology, and culture. Environment ministers from Belarus, Ukraine, and Russia signed a document as regards environmental improvement of the Dnieper River Basin region in 2002. It was followed by the establishment of Euroregion Dnieper on April 29, 2003 based on previous discussions and documents.

Euroregion Dnieper's objectives include comprehensive development in the economy, telecommunication, education, healthcare, sports, tourism, regional environmental protection, emergency rescue in case of natural disasters, and expansion of cooperation among residents of the border regions. This Euroregion has also implemented such projects as hosting conferences for promoting cooperation, creating a model for managing local education and developing tourism, creating measures to resolve water rights issues within Euroregion Dnieper, and establishing an international research institute for Slavic Studies.[2]

Projects in Euroregion Yaroslavna include the following: repair work on the floodgate of the reservoir at the Sinyak River hydroelectric power station in the Korenevsky district of Kursk region; environmental protection in the Psel River basin situated in the Ukraine–Russia border region; studies on folklore in the border region in Sumy and Kursk; development of the information and technology (IT) competence of specialists as means of ensuring their competitiveness in the regional labor market; establishment of a network cross-border (open) university in Euroregion Yaroslavna; analysis of the social situation for further development of welfare programs for the youth; and population research in the area between Sumy and Psel Rivers from the 8th to the 13th centuries (AEBR 2012).

Euroregion Slobozhanshchyna was established in 2003, prompted by the urging of Russian economists at the National University of Kharkiv. It aims to revitalize the economy, develop small- to medium-size businesses, and promote the interdependency between Russia and Ukraine. Regional development programs were created in 1999. (Velychko 2012: 133)

Euroregion Donbass was established by joining Donetsk and Luhansk in Ukraine with Rostov on Don in Russia. This region includes a rich coalmine in Donetsk, Ukraine, as well as fossil fuel such as petroleum, and a rich deposit of rock phosphate. As it is a relatively new Euroregion, its main activities have been focused on building its internal structure. Its objectives also include conservation efforts in its national parks. As a step toward expanded function, it has also hosted an international investment forum (Velychko 2012: 133; AEBR 2013).

Although these Euroregions have followed a similar path as Euroregions Carpathian and Bug when they were established, exchanges at the citizen level and participation of citizen organizations seem to be lacking. Meanwhile, their websites tend to post many announcements as regards border-crossing points, resource management, and relevant laws and regulations. The location of these Euroregions is a crucial point of dimension. Kursk, the main city of the Russian side in Euroregion Yaroslavna, and Kharkiv, its Ukrainian counterpart, are located at a strategic point that links Moscow and Sevastopol, where the Russian naval base is located. Although Donetsk, the main city on the Ukrainian side in Euroregion Donbass, has rich mineral resources, there is no major railway that goes directly from the Sea of Azov to the Black Sea. Rather, the major road and railway have to first enter Russian territory and leave from Rostov. This makes it essential for Donetsk to gain the cooperation of Russia. This situation illustrates the fact that if the region were not to be kept as a Euroregion in this area, it will be restricted by the infrastructure in Russia and Ukraine, such as roads and railways built during the Soviet era.

The EU/Russian regional policy in Eastern Europe

The area between the EU and Russia has a wide variety of names. The area between the Soviet Union and the European Community (EC) was called "Eastern Europe" during the Cold War. When the Cold War ended and "East European" countries began to join the EU, the phrase "Eastern Europe" signified the area sandwiched between Russia and the EU. This new meaning includes an extra layer of nuance: rather than a simple geographical designation, it connotes that this area finds itself outside West European civilization. The dissolution of the Soviet Union gave birth to independent countries in the area, but these new countries had never been independent states prior to 1991, as they had existed within the Soviet system politically and economically. Joining an international organization as sovereignty states was a novel experience. Further, amid the economic and political confusion in the 1990s, Russia neglected to address the issue of the Soviet Union's former republics. Meanwhile, concerned that this turmoil might spread into the EU, the EU began implementing its own regional policy targeting this particular region. After overcoming the economic crisis of 1998, Russia also began rebuilding its relationship with the EU and its neighboring countries.

In addition to "Eastern Europe," this area is called "Shared Neighborhood" (Gower and Timmins 2011), "Post-Soviet Space" (Delcour 2011), "Post-Socialist Europe" (Herrschel 2011), "Lands Between" (Hill 2012), and "Common Neighborhood."[3] The term "Eastern Europe" is mainly a geographical concept, whereas the terms "Shared Neighborhood" and "Common Neighborhood" hint at the EU's opinion on this region. Terms such as "Post-Soviet" and "Post-Socialist" suggest that this region is still considered one entity or a group even after the Soviet Union's dissolution. Hence, both the EU and Russia accept that the countries in this region share a certain commonality and feel a certain level of responsibility toward them.

The next section presents an examination of regional policies of the EU and Russia toward these countries.

EaP

The EU's regional policies in the past were based on the objective of closing the economic gap among the regions to ensure smooth integration with the EU. However, many have argued that the EU should move away from a uniform regional policy and shift toward policies that account for the characteristics and historic links of various regions as their integration within the EU progresses. Focusing on the area that includes the Mediterranean, France, and Spain hosted the Barcelona Process in 1995 and demonstrated their intention to emphasize the cooperative relationships in the Mediterranean. The Barcelona Process, which began with the urging of then Spanish foreign affairs minister Javier Solana, aimed at ensuring the security and cooperation in the Mediterranean by implementing measures dealing with illegal immigration and economic development. The Barcelona Process was later established as the Euro-Mediterranean Partnership.

In reaction to this movement in the Mediterranean, then EU Chair Paavo Lipponen, Finnish Prime Minister, proposed the Northern Dimension as an embodiment of the EU's regional policies, represented by cooperative relationships in the Baltic and Barents Seas regions. Its aim was to protect the environment and address social issues in the Baltic Sea Region. The Northern Dimension also intended to be a measure for Finland, the only EU country that shared a border with Russia, to ensure that the regional interests of Northern Europe are protected within the EU by emphasizing the importance of building a cooperative relationship with Russia (Oshima 2007).

These events demonstrate that Northern and Southern Europe have different interests in relation to the EU's regional policy, nonetheless integrated into the European Neighbourhood Policy (ENP). The ENP was adopted to rationalize the EU's regional policies that had come to reflect regional interests in the Barcelona Process and the Northern Dimension; the ENP had come under fire for ignoring various regional characteristics. The EU, however, argued that ENP would not serve to sever the member countries' relationships with their neighbors (Takahashi and Akiba 2010: 88–90). CBCs, in this sense, were expected to play an important role in ensuring that the EU's outer edges do not serve as the cutoff line, lest they are excluded.

ENP provides aid funds to neighboring countries for them to enjoy the economic/social development along with the EU. Funds were provided on the condition that these countries cooperated with the EU on issues such as democratization, environmental protection, and border security. The neighboring countries, however, viewed this as the drawing of a new cutoff line as the EU expansion came to an end. Former "East European" countries were willing to exert an effort to improve and implement systematic reforms demanded by the EU, such as democratization, good governance, environmental protection, and border security, on the assumption that they be allowed to join the EU. With the ENP, not only are countries not guaranteed membership to the EU, the program also seems to be the EU's attempt to impose its values on joining countries. Reception of the ENP was therefore cool. Ukraine and Moldova expressed dismay at seeing their chance of joining the EU reduced to nil, especially after they had earned the support of Poland and Romania. Further, the Mediterranean countries that were hoping for the EU's involvement in the Palestinian issue through the Euro-Mediterranean Partnership also worried that the EU would withdraw from its engagement after the ENP was adopted.

Streamlining of the EU's policies by the ENP also hit former East European countries, especially Poland and Romania, which had been newly accepted into the organization. Poland was pushing for Ukraine to be accepted into the EU as Ukraine has a large Polish population. Poland was also concerned that the EU might become more pro-Russia as the possibility for Ukraine to join the EU was no longer viable and the EU policies would be mainly driven by the European Commission. Although the EU was in dispute with Russia over the Orange Revolution in Ukraine in 2004, Germany's policy was firm in its "Russia First" stance that clearly indicated it would favor Russia over Ukraine.[4] Poland was alarmed by the possibility that this "Russia First" policy would become the main stance of the ENP and proposed the creation of EaP as the Eastern Dimension within the ENP, and the Polish proposal was confirmed at the ENP's Prague Summit in 2009.[5]

The EaP includes Armenia, Azerbaijan, Belarus, Georgia, Moldova, and Ukraine as its members. It aims to promote a cooperative political relationship between the EU and its members as well as ensure the EU's support for political and economic reforms in member countries so as to further accelerate economic integration. The members also agreed to a long-term objective to promote citizens' cross-border movement by eliminating the travel visa if and when the conditions for a safe cross-border travel can be maintained and if the borders are sufficiently controlled. These agreements were later confirmed at the Warsaw Summit in September 2011 (European Union 2012: 6).

The EaP provides bilateral and multilateral initiatives based on the EU's associate agreement. The support toward Ukraine and Moldova on their border control is especially worth noting. The EU Border Assistance Mission to the Republic of Moldova and Ukraine (EUBAM) coordinated and modernized the border control of these two neighbors while ensuring that the process is in accordance with EU standards. Its ultimate goal is to increase the capacity of these two nations to control their own borders. Although the EU had been providing EUBAM with aid funds within the framework of the European Neighbourhood and Partnership Instrument (ENPI) since November 2007, the adoption of the EaP allowed experts in the field of border security and customs from 19 EU countries to contribute as well. The headquarters of the EUBAM is located in Odessa, Ukraine, and its activities are concentrated on six border regions between Ukraine and Romania as well as the Port of Odessa. There were more than 200 staff members from the EU spread over 1,222 km between Ukraine and Moldova along with more than 100 experts in customs and border security. These staff members worked alongside local personnel in Ukraine and Moldova. It was agreed that their work would continue until December 2015 (European Union 2012: 6).

The support for these border security measures was not limited to Ukraine and Moldova, which share direct borders with the EU. Rather, the EU provided EUR 2.7 million to the border points for Belarus and Ukraine and EUR 2.9 million to those in Georgia and Armenia to improve their ability to control their borders. The initiative of the ENP/EaP that provides funds for border security on a country basis, called Flagship, was allotted a budget of EUR 44 million, which is an indication of the level of the EU's concern on the issue (European Union 2012: 6).

The EU provides funds to strengthen border security in these regions as Ukraine and Moldova are the biggest source of illegal immigrants in the EU. The other aim of the EaP, apart from sharing the domains of "freedom, security, and justice" with partner countries, was to reduce the flow of illegal immigrants, drugs, and other harms from these countries to EU community.

Poland and Sweden made the first suggestion to create the EaP within the framework of the ENP. As mentioned previously, the ENP quashed the possibility for Ukraine to join the EU, and Poland and Sweden were concerned that, as a result, the EU would reduce the level of involvement in East European countries, under the influence of the rhetoric of "Russia First." Meanwhile, the EU did not feel it necessary to change Germany's "Russia First" rhetoric but rather concentrated on the immediate task of addressing the issue of illegal immigrants from Eastern neighbors. It therefore made sense to the EU to be motivated in involving itself through the EaP in the region sandwiched between itself and Russia and bringing reforms to create democratic nations that share the EU's political values. In this sense, the ENP/EaP reflected more the self-interest of the EU as well as of Poland, Germany, and Ukraine than the consideration for these regions. Although these EU countries' intentions differed, they agreed on Eastern Europe's strategic importance, on which they were able to form a cohesive set of regional policies.

Russia's regional reorganization

According to Delcour, the EU considers Russia as one of two pillars of continental Europe together with the EU. As a consequence, it also believes that Eastern Europe would be reorganized by Russia (Delcour 2011: 42). However, Russia only became interested in this region after its economic crisis had ended in 1998 and it had entered a period of economic recovery. Russia announced its midterm strategies with the EU in 2000 and signed "Action Plan for Combatting Organized Crime" along with the EU. Further, at the EU–Russia Summit held in Saint Petersburg in 2003, the two entities jointly pledged a cooperation on four "common areas": (1) Creation of an open and integrated market as a shared economic space; (2) Issues as regards human rights and rule of law, the common threat of terrorism and organized crime, and visas in relation to freedom, security, and justice; (3) Recognition of shared interests in various international issues, especially in the area of border security, for cooperating on crisis management within the "Common Neighbourhood"; and (4) Areas related to research, education, and culture (Delcour 2011: 54). They signed the Partnership and Cooperation Agreement (PCA) in 2006 as well as the Visa Agreement and Readmission Agreement in 2007.

However, the EU rejected Russian President Dmitry Medvedev's proposal of "Pan-European Security Agreement" in 2008. Russia inversely refused to sign the "Energy Charter" proposed by the EU in 2009. Although they were seemingly in conflict with each other in these points, they were able to cooperate on issues unrelated to European territory. For example, Russia sent its troops to Chad on a peacekeeping mission at the EU's request.

Russia seems to take a selective approach to the EU policies. It is willing to cooperate on issues it shares with the EU, such as illegal immigration, organized crime related to drug, trafficking, and terrorism. It also agrees to strengthen cooperative relationship on the "common areas" shared with the EU. However, Russia has a different standpoint with the EU on energy issues, which the EU considers as crucial as "freedom, security, and justice." Further, Russia felt threatened by the EU's "involvement" in Ukraine's Orange Revolution in 2004 and cut off exports of natural gas to Ukraine, also partly owing to Ukraine's nonpayment for previous purchases. Russia has also complained repeatedly that Ukraine is stealing Russia's exports of natural gas to the EU.[6] Although Russia was exporting its natural gas to the former Soviet republics at the "domestic rate" rather than the "international rate," it raised the price charged to Ukraine 4.5 times in 2006 compared with the previous year (Delcour 2011: 117). In 2008, Ukraine officially submitted the request to join the EU/North Atlantic Treaty Organization (NATO), which indicated its strong inclination toward the EU and, as a consequence, escalated the conflict with Russia.

Meanwhile, in August 2008, the conflict between Georgia and Russia over South Ossetia was reignited. Although a ceasefire was reached, with France serving as mediator, Russia was eventually allowed to station its troops in South Ossetia. This move was viewed among East European countries as the EU's "favoritism toward Russia." Most of these countries understood that the EU would not intervene in issues in Eastern Europe. When pro-Russia Viktor Yanukovych assumed office as president of Ukraine in 2010, he was able to negotiate with Russia a new agreement that would reduce the price of natural gas. Further, Ukraine defined its border with Russia and signed "Russia–Ukraine Border Resident Cross-border Travel Agreement" to ensure free movement of residents within Euroregions. In 2011, Russia signed a free trade agreement (FTA) with former Soviet republics and began its attempt to reorganize the region. This FTA includes Russia, Ukraine, Belarus, Moldova, Kazakhstan, Armenia, Kyrgyzstan, and Tajikistan. Although the ENP/EaP created by the EU functions based on bilateral relations, it does not offer any strategies that consider the Eastern Europe as one region. It is different from Russia that is now attempting to reorganize the region based on multilateral relations with former Soviet countries through FTAs.

Ukraine's reaction

Even after the Commonwealth of Independent States (CIS) was established, Ukraine continued to be plagued with issues as regards its relationship with Russia. Among the issues was Crimea. Sevastopol, which is home to the Black Sea Fleet Base, is located on the Crimean Peninsula that also hosts a large number of

Russian residents (Hill 2012: 148–149). Crimea was against the independence of Ukraine, which was gained in 1991, and declared its own independence as a response. In the end, although Ukraine's central government maintained its power over Crimea, it allowed Crimea to govern itself almost autonomously. The problem, however, was far from resolved and continued to simmer during the dispute over the Black Sea Fleet Base. Resolution came finally in 1997 when Russia and Ukraine agreed to divide Black Sea Fleets. In addition, Russia recognized Ukraine's power over Crimea and, in exchange, was allowed to lease Sevastopol for 20 years. The Orange Revolution in 2004 prompted the Ukraine government to favor the EU; the Ukrainian government eventually made an official request to join the EU/NATO in 2008. However, the country's mood shifted once again against the EU as there seemed to be no real prospect of joining the union. The election of pro-Russian President Yanukovych in 2010 served as an opportunity to revisit Ukraine's relationship with Russia. The lease of Sevastopol was then extended for another 25 years, and Russia agreed to provide discounts on the price of natural gas that it exports to Ukraine (based on the Kharkiv Pact) (Hill 2012: 149).

Another of Ukraine's issues was border security, which stems from the chronic illegal immigration problem and the uncertain border between Moldova and Transnistria. In the context of the eastward expansion of the EU in 2004, the border between Poland and Ukraine, which used to be a visa-free zone, now required a traveling visa. As entry into the EU became more difficult, the number of illegal immigrants in the EU increased, and Ukrainians were the largest group among detained illegal immigrants. There were 15,438 Ukrainian illegal immigrants detained when Poland joined the EU in 2004 and 14,441 in 2005. Although the number dipped to 11,295 in 2006, it increased again to 12,660 in 2007 (Leoncilcas and Zibas 2009: 75). Further, Ukraine is also a passage/host country to other illegal immigrants headed toward the EU; thus, Ukraine is under a heavy burden as well. The EU, Russia, and Ukraine share this problem.

Another border security issue faced by Ukraine is the border with Moldova. Transnistria declared independence from Moldova in 1990, but Moldova did not recognize the authority of Transnistria, leading to a civil war in 1992. The war reached ceasefire under the intervention of the CIS Military Division; however, Tansnistria was not recognized and stayed as a de facto state. Therefore, the border between Moldova and Ukraine remained undefined, which made it difficult for Ukraine to implement strict border control in the region. This situation also allowed an uncontrolled flow of illegal immigrants, organized crime, and smuggling. Shortly after the civil war, these two countries initially allowed Russian Army troops to be stationed within their territory to alleviate this situation. However, they recognized that such a scheme was not a desirable option for nations that gained independence from Russia. Thus, their joining of EUBAM may have been motivated by their hope to learn the knowhow of border security based on the EaP.

Even after the EU declared its eastward expansion completed, Ukraine seemed to not have given up on the idea of joining the organization and continued to improve their domestic reforms in accordance with the EU's values and standards. However, Ukraine's dissatisfaction toward the EU also continued to grow while its membership in the EU remains pending. Border security is an issue the EU is especially keenly focused on and one of the objectives of the EaP. A few experts, however, have criticized the EU's tendency to increase the freedom of movement within the EU by eliminating borders based on the Schengen Agreement, while requiring outside countries to strengthen their border control within their territory, creating an entity akin to a "European Fortress." This criticism is based on the observation that requiring neighboring countries to act according to the EU's values on issues that may invade their sovereignties, such as the border control, is a form of indirect expansion of its power.

Although Ukraine had implemented domestic reforms according to the EaP, it never prospered "along with the EU" as was suggested. Although exports from the EU to Ukraine increased by 30% after the adoption of the ENP, exports from Ukraine to the EU decreased by 7%, which resulted in a trade deficit for Ukraine. Meanwhile, Ukraine's exports to Single Economic Space (SES) countries, including CIS and Kazakhstan increased twofold, which suggests that Ukraine failed to achieve anything of substance by joining the ENP (Stegnity 2012: 56).

After Russia's complaint that Ukraine stole natural gas was lodged, Ukrainians' dissatisfaction with the pro-EU government grew, resulting in the election of pro-Russia Yanukovych as president on February 25, 2010. As previously mentioned, Yanukovych signed the Kharkiv Pact with Russia in April 2010 and authorized the lease of Sevastopol until 2042. He also signed the border agreement with Russia. Ukraine's relationship with Russia was further cemented with the two countries' cooperation in the joint satellite navigation system called GLONASS and the agreement stipulating mutual investment between Ukreximbank and VTBbank, Ukrainian and Russian banks, respectively.

As Ukraine's economic relationship with the EU showed no sign of improvement, Yanukovych strengthened his inclination toward Russia and suspended the "EU Association Agreement" scheduled to be signed in November 2013. Those who viewed that this association agreement was not only an economic index but also indispensable for implementing reforms toward democratization in Ukraine felt that Yanukovych's EU policies were a step back for democracy. Citizens began protesting in Kiev against the president's decision, and protests spread rapidly in the nation. Amid the confusion of the chain of events, the president went into exile.

The situation was no longer contained within Ukraine and began involving Russia. On February 27, 2014, soldiers occupied Crimea. Subsequently, the Crimean Parliament dismissed its prime minister and nominated pro-Russian Sergey Aksyonov as his replacement. The Russian Army took this opportunity to enter Crimea under the pretext of protecting Russian residents in the area. On March 16, a referendum was held in the Crimean Autonomous Republic as well as in Sevastopol, with the majority supporting Crimea's entry into the Russian Federation. This result then led to Crimea declaring its secession from Ukraine and submitting a request to join the Russian Federation. Russia followed it by signing a treaty incorporating Crimea and Sevastopol into Russia on March 18. In April, large-scale assemblies and occupation of government buildings took place in Donetsk and Luhansk. As a result, two "People's Republics" were established. The Ukrainian government, as its "anti-terrorism strategy," sent in the Ukrainian army to maintain public safety and prevent the separatist movement in Eastern Ukraine from spreading elsewhere. This move, as a consequence, threw the region into a state of civil war.

A presidential election in Ukraine took place amid the confusion on May 25; Petro Poroshenko was elected. However, the clash between the anti-government movement and the Ukrainian Army as well as the instability in the border region of Eastern Ukraine continued. Meanwhile, Russia mocked the Ukrainian government by calling it "Nazi fascist" and continued its criticism as the armed conflict escalated. Although a ceasefire agreement was reached in September 2014, small clashes continued to occur and an actual ceasefire failed to be achieved. German chancellor Angela Merkel played a central role in hosting a ceasefire conference, which led to the eventual signing of the "Minsk Accord" among Russia, Ukraine, the representatives of the pro-Russian forces in the Donbass region, and the Organization for Security Co-operation in Europe (OSCE).

Areas where Euroregions were established became a battleground and the stage on which international power politics played out. It seemed as if CBCs would not survive. According to an article on the website of the Association of European Border Regions (AEBR) in 2016, 30 representatives from Krusk, a Russian city in Euroregion Yaroslavna, visited Euroregion Spree-Neisse-Bober to exchange views on trade relations and medical cooperation. Although it was a visit only from the Russian side of the Euroregion, it cannot be ignored that the people representing the Euroregion visited and toured another and that Euroregions as organizations still remain (AEBR 2015).[7]

Conclusion

The reason for which Euroregions were established along the Russia–Ukraine border was Russia's reaction to the EU's eastward expansion and the subsequent expansion of the Schengen Area. Although the initial objective of the Schengen Agreement was to eliminate borders that prevent freedom of movement and thus promote regional integration, after the Amsterdam Treaty, the objective gradually changed to the protection from outside threat. The EU not only strengthened its border control in its own territory but also required neighboring countries to implement stringent border control as a preventative measure. The increase in illegal immigration from outside the EU and the fact that the main gateways for these immigrants were Ukraine and Moldova caused the EU to act accordingly. To this end, the EU created the EaP targeting East European countries within the ENP to support these regions with border security issues. These steps taken by the EU, however, caused resentment in both Russia and Ukraine.

In Ukraine, critics pointed out repeatedly that the EU's demand toward its neighbors to respect the EU's values and standards did not lead to their being allowed to join the EU. Ukraine was continuously rejected membership. The EU, meanwhile, maintained that its desire to strengthen its border control is not based on the rejection of others and increased its support for CBCs. The ENPI, which provides concrete policies for the ENP, also emphasizes the importance of CBCs in its paper "Cross-Border Cooperation Strategy Paper 2007–2013." The purposes of CBCs are to (1) promote economic and societal development in regions sharing common borders; (2) address challenges such as protection of the environment, public health, and organized crime; (3) create efficient yet secure borders; and (4) promote exchange activities among local residents. Following the Strategy Paper, Slovakia and Ukraine signed an agreement as regards cross-border movement, which enabled Ukrainians residing in the border region with Slovakia to travel freely across the border with only their passports and permission papers; they would not be required to obtain a visa. Ukraine has also succeeded in reaching an agreement with Poland, Romania, and Bulgaria to simplify the visa process (Leoncikas and Zibas 2009: 13). When viewed from the perspective of relationships among individual nations, these agreements can be seen as compensation for Ukraine for having signed the readmission agreement with the EU. However, these agreements may have also come into being out of consideration for not hindering activities within the Euroregions Bug and Carpathian.

Meanwhile, Russia grew apprehensive of the EU's involvement in border control in its neighboring regions. Ukraine's seemingly pro-EU stance worried Russia, especially as Ukraine is on the railway path between Moscow and Sevastopol, where the Black Sea Fleets were based. Ukraine being allowed to join the EU would be an enormous hit to Russia's security. Russia therefore began putting pressure on Ukraine as soon as the latter showed certain pro-EU tendencies using the price of natural gas as leverage. Russia, however, shares common interests with the EU, including tightening measures to fight organized crimes and terrorism as well as energy trade activities. On the economics side, the EU is Russia's largest trade partner, and the EU relies on Russia for more than 50% of its energy resources, including natural gas. From Russia's viewpoint, establishing Euroregions in the region along the border with Ukraine would allow Russia to control the Ukrainian borders without being in direct conflict with the EU. These Euroregions would also provide a venue where Russia can always take a strong stance when dealing with Ukraine. The latter was Russia's most probable reason for supporting the establishment of Euroregions along its own border. Thus, Euroregions in Western and Eastern Ukraine, although similar in their form, differ from one another in their characteristics.

Therefore, sub-regionalism cannot always be explained by its own interest and efforts. Further, the influence of major regional powers cannot be ignored.

Meanwhile, sub-regionalism has its own logic. In the case of Ukraine, the advantage of establishing Euroregions along its western and eastern borders is that they would allow Ukraine to maintain a relationship with both Russia and the EU. The Euroregions would also satisfy both Western and Eastern Ukraine's stand: the western region favors the EU, whereas the eastern region leans toward Russia. Further, having Euroregions within their borders gave Ukraine and Moldova an opportunity to call in the EU as a mediator to deal with the Russian Army stationed within their territories by accepting EUBAM.

Russia and the EU, both involved in the Euroregions situated between them, have widely differing intentions and expectations. The leadership and self-interests of the regions, which are evident in regions within the EU, are not at all discernible in these Euroregions. As such, the creation of Euroregions almost seems to serve only the interests of the EU and Russia. Critics have pointed out that Euroregions are merely there to provide the EU and Russia with means to be involved in the region. Nonetheless, Euroregions in former "Eastern Europe" have certainly gone through a lengthy and winding process of becoming capable of taking initiative independently and have succeeded in raising awareness in these regions. Therefore, the Euroregions in the border regions between Russia and Ukraine need time until they will be able to acquire the capability to realize their regional interests. Further, as registered members of AEBR, they are supported to continue developing cross-border regional cooperation. This process of interaction among members of AEBR may also serve as an opportunity to build new relationships with other actors.

Notes

1 http://www.aebr.eu/en/members/list_of_regions.php, accessed July 24, 2017.
2 http://beleuroregion.by/index.php?option=com_contact&view=article&id=97&lang=en, accessed October 5, 2013.
3 This expression is used in EU official documents.
4 The EU signed the "EU–Russia Strategic Partnership and Cooperation Agreement" with Russia in 1994 and continued to discuss strategies. Between 2003 and 2005, the EU and Russia agreed to cooperate on four common spaces, namely, economy, freedom/security/justice, foreign policy, and research. The construction of the North Stream gas pipeline is also moving forward based on the bilateral agreement between Germany and Russia (Zurawski vel Grajewski 2012: 152).
5 Former Polish Minister of Foreign Affairs Bronislaw Geremek first proposed the concept of Eastern Dimension in 1998.
6 The natural gas pipeline from Russia to the EU goes through either Belarus to reach Poland or Ukraine to reach Slovakia.
7 According to this article, except for Euroregion Donbas where a conflict occurred, three of four Euroregions established with Russia still maintain a cooperative relationship.

References

Association of European Border Regions (AEBR) (2012) Presentation of Euroregion Yaroslavna in Congress of Local and Regional Authorities of Council of Europe, Strasboubg, March 2012 (http://www.aebr.eu/pdf/fmanager//Regionen/Y/Yaroslavna__RU_UA_/5_Yaroslavna.pdf, accessed May 10, 2013).
Association of European Border Regions (AEBR) (2013) Fact Sheet Euroregion Donbas (RU/UA) (http://www.aebr.eu/pdf/fmanager//Regionen/D/Donbass/Fact_sheet_EN.pdf, accessed October 13, 2017).

Association of European Border Regions (AEBR) (2015) A Delegation of the Krusk Region (Russian Federation) visited Euroregion Spree-Neisse-Bober from 2nd to 5th September 2015 (http://www.aebr.eu./en/news_detail.php?news_id.467, accessed January 23, 2016).

Delcour, Laure (2011) *Shaping the Post-Soviet Space?: EU Politics and Approaches to Region-Building*, Farnham, Surrey: Ashgate.

European Union (2012) EU Cooperation for a Successful Eastern Partnership, EU Publication office (http://ec.europa.eu/europeaid/sites/devco/files/eastern_partnership_flyer_filanl_en.pdf, accessed July 15, 2018).

Gower, Jackei, and Graham Timmins (eds.) (2011) *The European Union, Russia and the Shared Neighbourhood*, London: Routledge.

Herrschel, Tassilo (2011) *Borders in Post-Socialist Europe: Territory, Scale, Society*, Farnham: Ashgate.

Hill, Ronald J. (2012) "Russia, the European Union, and the Lands Between," in Elena Korosteleva (ed.) *Eastern Partnership: A New Opportunity for the Neighbours?*, London: Routledge, pp. 144–164.

Inoue, Naoko (2005) "Cross-Border Cooperation: A Case Study of Gorizia on the Italian/Slovenian Border," in Kibata Yoichi (ed.) *European Integration and International Relations*, Tokyo: Nippon Keizai Hyoronsha, pp. 173–204 (in Japanese).

Korosteleva, Elena (2012) *Eastern Partnership: A New Opportunity for the Neighbours*, London: Routledge.

Leoncikas, Tadas, and Karolis Zibas (2009) Migration Trends 2006–2008 Soderkoping Process Countries (http://www.migreurop.org/IMG/pdf/soderkopig_20migrations_20 trends_202006-2008_1_2pdf, accessed August 14, 2018 accessed July 13, 2009).

Oshima, Miho (2007) *EU Studies 3:Nation/Region/Race*, Tokyo: Keiso Shobo (in Japanese).

Popescu, Gabriel (2006) "Geopolitics of Scale and Cross-Border Cooperation in Eastern Europe: The Case of the Romanian–Ukrainian–Moldovan Borderlands," in James Wesley Scott (ed.) *EU Enlargement, Regional Building and Shifting Borders of Inclusion and Exclusion*, Aldershot: Ashgate, pp. 35–51.

Zurawski vel Grajewski, Przemyslaw (2012) "Russia and the EU's Neighbourhood Policy Template," in Elzbieta Stadtmuller and Klaus Bachmann (eds.) *The EU's Shifting Borders: Theoretical Approaches and Policy Implications in the New Neighbourhood*, London: Routledge, pp. 149–165.

Scott, James Wesley (ed.) (2006) *EU Enlargement, Regional Building and Shifting Borders of Inclusion and Exclusion*, Aldershot: Ashgate.

Sengoku, Manabu (2007) "Limitations of Euroregions: A Case of Polish/German Border," in Takashi Miyajima, Kunihiro Wakamatsu, and Hiromi Komori (eds.) *Europe of the Regions*, Kyoto: Jinbun Shoin, pp. 248–272.

Shiba, Riko (2007) "Regional Integration in Poland and Resident Awareness: A Case of Polish/German Border," *Journal of Tokyo University of Information Science*, 7 (1): 39–50 (in Japanese).

Stadtmuller, Elzbieta, and Klaus Bachmann (eds.) (2012) *The EU's Shifting Borders: Theoretical Approaches and Policy Implication in the New Neighbourhood*, London: Routledge.

Stegniy, Oleksander (2012) "Ukraine and the Eastern Partnership: 'Lost in Translation'?," in Elena Korosteleva (ed.) *Eastern Partnership: A New Opportunity for the Neighbours?*, London: Routledge, pp. 52–74.

Takahashi, Kazu, and Mariko Akiba (2010) *How Eastern Europe was Transformed: Micro-Analysis of Politics and Economy*, Hirosaki: Hirosaki University Press (in Japanese).

Takahashi, Kazu (2012) "Development of Micro-Level Regional Cooperation in Europe: Challenge for the Modern State System," in Hiroshi Momose (ed.) *Changing Power Politics in International Relations and Resistance*, Tokyo: Sairyu-sha, pp. 151–172 (in Japanese).

Velychko, Valerija Vasilivna, "The Future of Functioning Euroregions in Ukraine," *Economika and Region*, 4 (35): 131–134.

Wakamori, Fumitaka, Kiichiro Yagi, Koichi Shimizu, and Shinichi Nagao (eds.) (2007) *Regional Dimension of EU Economic Integration: Frontline of Cross-Border Cooperation*, Kyoto: Minerva Shobo (in Japanese).

9 The parallel evolution of functional macro-regions and cross-scale regional governance as emerging political instruments in the North Sea Region

Hideo Kojimoto, Yoshitaka Ota, and Ann Bell

Introduction

The need to cope with the quickening pace of globalization has led to structural changes in the European Union (EU)'s regional policy arena. Furthermore, with increased EU integration, complicated transborder issues—including natural resource management, the deterioration of the environment, and economic disparities—have emerged. Moreover, the state, long considered the container best suited to deal with political and economic issues, has proven less than able to deal with these and other transborder problems. Indications of this lack of suitability can be observed in the funds that have been established to deal with transnational development, including the European Regional Development Fund (ERDF) and the INTERREG Community Initiative, both launched by the European Commission. Some of these supranational funds and programs have been adopted and utilized by regional authorities who have subsequently gained the capacity to independently coordinate policies with Brussels and have precipitated initiatives that have occasionally run counter to the intentions of their central governments.

It has been shown that pressing transnational issues cannot be effectively handled through trilateral or quadripartite state agreements that rely on and sustain a state-centric paradigm. As a result, the macro-region has emerged as an alternative policy container to the state. The macro-regional perspective arose, informally at first, as a new, although *de facto,* instrument of EU policy during the process of rectifying disparities among regions. Macro-regions were subsequently identified as geographical locations that demonstrated the simultaneous emergence of new issues, requirements, and policies in the borderlands of neighboring states, including sea rim areas.

The concept of region has been remarkably successful in advancing our understanding of the social, economic, and political aspects of geographical units, with the EU emerging as the paradigm. The generative power of the macro-region can be further grasped by studying the multi-dimensional characteristics intrinsic to current EU polity, wherein region is found to enhance concepts of cross-border, cross-scale, cross-function, and cross-norm—all of which are useful and have proved to be useful tools in contemporary political science in general and governance theory in particular.

The term region has taken on several meanings in the field of EU integration studies. One meaning is found in the EU Nomenclature of Units for the Territorial Statistics 2 (NUTS 2) geo-code standard area. NUTS 2 is the fundamental unit used to configure a "Europe of the Regions" and includes the designation of regional governments, such as the county in the United Kingdom (UK). As a transnational policy container, region is also used to indicate the scope of a sphere through the use of prefixes such as "mega," "macro," or "micro." As indicators of relative size, these prefixes can be operationally defined and point to the particular nature of the relationships among scales. As Agnew suggests, one scale only makes sense in relation to others (Agnew 1997: 100), and each functional macro-region has a particular inter-scalar construction as well as inter-scalar power configurations. For the purpose of this study, the term 'macro-region,' situated between the EU mega-region and the transnational micro-region, implies an area where regional authorities' jurisdictions transcend, or operate externally to, national boundaries or authority. One such macro-region would be the North Sea Region (NSR).

Before the EU macro-regional strategy was put into place, a functional macro-regional approach had been implemented through the INTERREG transnational cooperation program, carried out under the EU Regional Policy, and by the Regional Advisory Council (RAC) situated under the Common Fisheries Policy (CFP). These early approaches addressed the functional role of each region. DG Regio, under which transnational spatial planning was accelerated, established INTERREG functional regions. The RAC functional regions were placed within the International Council for the Exploration of the Sea's (ICES) regional units in an effort to improve maritime resource management practices.

These early macro-regions were single function-oriented units that complemented certain EU-wide policies. Unlike the later macro-regional approach, introduced in the European Union Strategy for the Baltic Sea Region (EUSBR) to implement comprehensive, holistic, and functionally crosscutting management approaches, these earlier INTERREG regions and RAC regions were function-specific units. More importantly, the EU term 'macro-region' was not yet in use when implementing these early programs.

In the process of building the North Sea Macro-region, regional administrative bodies such as the Aberdeenshire Council of Scotland, the former Viborg County Council of Denmark, and the Telemark County Council of Norway, increased their capacity to coordinate their respective macro-regions by introducing norms and regulations for macro-regional governance. These authorities not only maintained their identities as clients of their respective central governments but also took on other identities, such as that of transnational coordinator (CEC 2001).

As Paasi has indicated, the erosion of the authority of one scale initiates a decline in its political power and he goes on to argue that the birth of a new scale indicates the emergence of new political power or leads to the growth of new identities for existing political actors (Paasi 2002). Accordingly, the advent of a new scale alters the relationships among existing scales as well as the power dynamics of actors within the governance structure.

The process of macro-region building

Spatial changes that impacted the instruments of state governance occurred simultaneously in the 1990s in European and Asian sea rim areas. In Asia, the Japan Sea Rim Zone Concept, which was introduced to promote the development of the Sea of Japan coastal region, helped bring on an increase in economic, social and cultural exchanges between local entities in Japan, South Korea, and China. Before this time, Japan's coastal region facing the Pacific Ocean had always been referred to as *Omote Nihon* (the front end of Japan), while the coast facing the Sea of Japan was commonly called the more derogatory *Ura Nihon* (the back end of Japan). According to Hook, as the more positive-sounding term *Kan-Nihonkai Chiiki* (the Japan Sea Rim Region) began to be used by the media, businesses, and academics, it came to replace the negative-sounding '*Ura-Nihon*' discourse, and the sub-region as a symbolic space came to be incorporated into the wording of regional policies (Hook 1997).

Focusing his attention on the construction of the Japan Sea Rim Region, Hook created a model for region-building that identified three necessary stages. Hook employed the word "sub-region" to identify the region as a constituent of the larger region of East Asia. Hook's stages are as follows:

- **First stage:** Promotion of objective linkages within the space
- **Second stage:** Attachment of subjective meanings to the space
- **Third stage:** Creation of symbolic space by attributing a name.

During the first stage, objective linkages are promoted through the accumulation of political, economic, and social interactions. This is followed by the attachment of subjective meanings to the space, together with the establishment of mutual acceptance. In the third stage of Hook's model, the space is designated with a name that distinguishes it as a distinct entity.

In the case of the EU macro-region building process, a fourth stage must be added to Hook's model in order to account for the DG Regio's attempt to implement the early macro-regional approach as an instrument to accelerate the establishment of the INTERREG IIC transnational cooperation endeavor that commenced in 1997. This fourth stage can be interpreted as a formalization of the region (Schack 2000).

- **Fourth stage:** Formalization ("EU-ization") of the regional policy container

With the formalization within the EU of the early macro-regions through the advances of INTERREG IIC, the macro-regional scale has taken on the role of an arena for territorial administrative actors such as the EU, EU member states, as well as regional and local authorities. Within this playing field, regional authorities negotiate directly with EU institutions to determine where and how to allocate EU funds. The active participation of actors within different scales has added another dimension to the governance of transnational issues, issues that require long-term and sustainable perspectives to achieve effective resolution (Table 9.1).

Table 9.1 Comparison of the 'Functional Macro-region' and the 'Comprehensive Macro-region'

	Functional Macro-region		Comprehensive Macro-region
Programme/project	INTERREG IIC	Regional Advisory Council (RAC) under the Common Fisheries Policy	EUSDR
Contents/container Address term	Contents first, container second Name of the program (e.g. North Sea Region of INTERREG IIC Program)	Contents first, container second Name of the RAC (e.g. NSRAC)	Container first, contents second Name of Macro-region
Function	Spatial planning	Marine resource management	Crosscutting, streamlining, efficiency Harmonization of differing interests for stakeholders of different functional areas
Network of actors	NSC, CPMR, CoR	Fish producers' organizations, green NGOs	Mixed; comprehensive diversification of stakeholders
Involvement of EU	Funds from the EU Commission and regulations	Funds from the EU Commission and regulations	Coordination by DG Regio of the EU Commission
Who determines the realm?	DG Regio of the EU Commission	DG Fisheries of the EU Commission based on the ICES division of the sea	DG Regio of the EU Commission
Norm/rule decision-making	Rules of the INTERREG Steering Committee (EU, Member States+ regional governments) Norms of the Grand Designs (VASAB2010, NorVision): agreement among Member states	Only advice received by the Commission concerning the particular region EU Council of Ministers on TAC and Quotas	Agreements in the EU Council Method of OMC
Interactions among territorial government actors	Cross-Scale Regional Governance	Cross-Scale Regional Governance	Multi-Level Governance
Institutions	INTERREG Steering Committee and Secretariat Possibility of European Grouping of Territorial Cooperation (EGTC)	Executive Committee and Secretariat (Company under the Scottish Law)	Three NOs (Three YESes) Possibility of EGTC
Overlapping the territories	Overlap	Not overlapped (coordination of Inter-RAC in some policy areas)	Overlap

Source: Created by the authors.

The emergence of the macro-region in the case of the North Sea

A case study will be conducted in order to illustrate the role of a functional macro-region through cross-scale regional governance (CSRG) (see Chapter 1). To verify the scaling up of actors' intentions to the macro-regional scale, the NSR's fisheries policy will be discussed from the perspective of the Aberdeenshire Council in Scotland, which is one of the leading regional authorities in the NSR. The NSR fisheries sector developed its macro-regional approach by establishing a functional macro-region and implementing the CSRG mechanism. Fisheries governance in the NSR is considered to be one of the models for the regionalization of the CFP. The EU Directorate General Fisheries at that time started to utilize the functional macro-regional approach to customize the CFP along each sea area in the EU EEZ. The NSR's successful partnership model was subsequently adopted by other macro-regions through the establishment of RACs for four other seas, including the Baltic Sea, the Mediterranean Sea, the North-Western Waters, and the South-Western Waters.[1]

As stated earlier, the Aberdeenshire Council led the development of a sequence of fisheries platforms in the NSR, including platforms for the fishing ports of Peterhead and Fraserburgh. From the perspective of economic development and the maintenance of fishing communities, it was of critical importance for the Council to meet these challenges together with counterparts around the North Sea. The Council developed a coordination strategy with the North East Scotland Fisheries Development Partnership (NESFDP), thereby forming the North Sea Regional Advisory Council (NSRAC). The Aberdeenshire Council's strategy involved the following:

- NESFDP (North East Scotland Fisheries Development Partnership);
- NSCFG (North Sea Commission Fisheries Group);
- NSCFP (North Sea Commission Fisheries Partnership);
- NSRAC (North Sea Regional Advisory Council).

The NESFDP was the initial component of the Aberdeenshire Council's fisheries development platform strategy. Before the NESFDP, the Grampian Regional Fisheries Committee was responsible for fisheries-related issues in North East Scotland. This arrangement changed once institutional reform divided the Grampian Regional Council into Aberdeen City, Aberdeenshire, and Morey.

The Aberdeenshire Council applied to PESCA, which was the EU funding program to assist with the development of regional fisheries cooperation. PESCA funds were allocated directly from the EU to each PESCA program. The Grampian PESCA program was administered by four local committees: Fraserburgh, Peterhead, Aberdeen, and Buckie. Although the NESFDP covered the ex-Grampian region, it was not allowed to use the appellation "Grampian" since the Grampian County Council had been dissolved and, in due-course, the term "North East Scotland" was adopted. The NESFDP addressed not only fisheries issues but also those that were indirectly relevant to fisheries, such as the problems of boat builders and seaport security.

The Aberdeenshire Council's secretariat wrote a 'memorandum of understanding' for all members of the NESFDP, identifying the objectives of the partnership. Furthermore, it was decided that the location of the meetings should be rotated to ensure equal distribution among the partners.

During the initial stages of the partnership, the Aberdeenshire Council attempted to incorporate marine scientists within the framework of the NESFDP. At first, this suggestion was opposed by the fisheries sector due to concerns about the participation of scientists and the potential for conflicting interests. Hence, neither mutual understanding nor the opportunity for stakeholder consultation existed in the initial phase. Eventually, however, the Aberdeenshire Council successfully recruited Professor Tony Hawkins, Director of the Aberdeen Marine Laboratory, as a representative of the scientific community. This meant that the participation of scientists had already been arranged prior to the formation of the North Sea Commission Fisheries Partnership (NSCFP). This was a critical first step in the establishment of stakeholder participation, which has been institutionalized in the series of stakeholder conferences that were convened within the NSR.

When the ICES recommended in 2003 that a moratorium be implemented to save Atlantic cod stocks in the North Sea, the Shetland Oceans Alliance (SHOAL) asked the NESFDP to fight against Brussels as a "united front." The Aberdeenshire Council recognized that a network at the macro-regional level was necessary to deal with the challenges faced by the NSR, which subsequently led to the development of a fisheries network in the North Sea Macro-region.

The next stage involved the establishment of the North Sea Commission Fisheries Group (NSCFG). The NSCFG Platform was important as it allowed the Aberdeenshire Council to gain access to networks of regional authorities in the North Sea, while also enabling access to and opportunities for political lobbying activities through the Conference of Peripheral Maritime Regions in Europe (CPMR). As a result of these activities, the council acquired a leading role in the coordination of political actions in the NSR.

Trina Samberg, Executive Secretary of the North Sea Commission (NSC), coordinated an *ad hoc* group that addressed fishery issues at the Lincoln CPMR Conference in 1996. In October 1996, the NSC Executive Committee (NSC ExCom) appointed Ann Bell of the Aberdeenshire Council as coordinator of the NSC Fisheries Working Group (NSCFWG); the NSCFWG held its first meeting at Malloy in Norway. Aberdeenshire representatives increasingly moved to leverage different platforms in order to convey their intentions at the European-scale level. For example, the NSC ExCom supported the controversial "Who's Eating Who" conference, which addressed food chain issues.

The third stage involved the establishment of the NSCFP, which offered a roundtable meeting for fishing industry representatives and marine scientists to work out a mutual understanding of their different perspectives. The NSCFWG thereby completed the preparatory stage required to establish a continuous roundtable for stakeholders.

As stated earlier, the Aberdeenshire Council originally applied to the PESCA program only for the NESFDP, which was a program that was nested within state-defined national boundaries; however, when applying to the program the council cleverly added "transnational activity" as one of the items for future use. Thus, in the fourth year of the allocation of PESCA funds, the Council began to implement these through the NSCFP, which became the first transnational fisheries roundtable for both industry and scientists. During the second year of the Partnership, the Council started to utilize INTERREG funding programs, since PESCA had expired.

Through the networking activities of the NSC, the Aberdeenshire Council gained expertise in dealing with European funding programs such as PESCA and INTERREG IIC and IIIB. The NSC worked with the INTERREG North Sea Program Secretariat and the Viborg County Council in Denmark managed to enhance its strategic position by hosting both secretariats at that time. Bent Hansen, Political Leader of Viborg County Council and President of the NSC, supported the Fisheries Partnership project in its aim to receive funding from INTERREG.

During the transition period, two institutions—the NSCFP and the NSRAC—acted together. The NSCFP's last meeting was in February 2005, at which point it became the foundation for the NSRAC. In September 2004, the Interim ExCom was held in Copenhagen and a draft proposal was sent to the European Commission. The first meeting of NSRAC was held in Edinburgh Castle in November 2004.

The Partnership offered not only a platform for scientists and persons in the fishing industry to consult one another, but also provided a transnational platform for representatives of national fisheries. The macro-region thus became the functional playing field for the actors who were originally separated by state borders but who subsequently became embedded into multilayered structures.

Jumping scale

In terms of territoriality, each geographical place is situated within the hierarchies of several scales. For example, the town of Peterhead is under the jurisdiction of the regional government of Aberdeenshire; this region, in turn, is under the jurisdiction of the Scottish government, which is part of the UK. Furthermore, Peterhead can also be considered part of the EU. However, with new scales such as macro-regions, power hierarchies in some cases are no longer absolute. These shifting or realigned hierarchies are enabled by scale jumping activities ("jumping scale") and other strategic actions by actors that are examined in political geography (Smith 1987; Smith 1992; Brenner 2001). Jumping scale by regional actors has nurtured the dynamic natures of macro-regions. With jumping scale, central governments, which previously played essential roles in budgeting and legal hierarchies, can now be disregarded, allowing regional governments to

220 *Hideo Kojimoto et al.*

engage in direct political engagement with supranational organizations such as the DGs of the European Commission.

The Aberdeenshire government illustrates the benefits of jumping scale and has used the North Sea Macro-region to pursue its agenda. In other words, it has initiated cross-scale regional governance in this macro-region (see Chapter 1). As a result, it has been successful in getting approval for the establishment of the NSRAC,[2] which submits advisory opinions to the EU on such important issues as the Total Allowable Catch (TAC) for cod fisheries in the North Sea. It is a permanent EU advisory council, of which forty seats are held by commercial fishermen and twenty by environmental non-governmental organizations (NGOs) and others. The EU is obliged to respect the decisions taken by this advisory body.

Viewed from a different perspective, it appears that a new cross-scale arena of political decision-making has arisen between international actors at different levels: the Aberdeenshire Council, the Scottish government, the UK government, and the EU. The political resolutions that have emerged from within the cross-scale arena help explain the new forms by which political resources are being allocated among scales (Tables 9.2).

Aberdeenshire, Peterhead and Fraserburgh are key harbors for North Sea catches of cod and haddock. In 2006, Peterhead and Fraserburgh brought in 135,127 tons of fish, or 89.0% of the total catch for the northeastern region of Scotland. When the 16,710 tons brought in at the Aberdeen harbor landing, under the jurisdiction of the city of Aberdeen, is included, the total catch for North East Scotland's three fishing harbors was 151,837 tons. As stated before, the Aberdeenshire government has established the NESFDP, a political platform for fisheries, and has developed a cooperative relationship with the city of Aberdeen, and they have developed a joint fisheries policy.

Fisheries under the NESFDP account for 52.5% of Scotland's total catch. The governments of Aberdeenshire and the city of Aberdeen use the NSC, a political platform within the North Sea Macro-region that promotes regional government linkages, to obtain the cooperation of the Shetland Islands' government. This enables them to engage with groups representing Scotland and to promote the formation of a fisheries working group and to successfully advance NESFDP

Table 9.2 Landings by scale (unit: tons)

Landing Harbor	1995	2005	2006
Aberdeen	27,942	25,164	16,710
Peterhead	112,376	117,490	104,998
Fraserburgh	39,833	46,705	30,129
North East Scotland	180,151	189,359	151,837
Scotland	481,872	366,260	289,200
UK	723,800	491,700	416,500

Source: Aberdeenshire government statistics materials published in January 2008 (http://92.52.88.74/statistics/economic/fishing/fishland_volval_jan2008.pdf, accessed October 10, 2015).

policy goals with the NSC. Moreover, the local discourse and political positioning of Aberdeenshire has not only supplanted that of Scotland, but as part of the UK's move toward devolution, it is also skipping over the UK central government to engage directly with the DG Fisheries regarding the establishment of the NSRAC as a policy voice for the North Sea Macro-region.

The political discourse regarding Peterhead or Fraserburgh fishery issues has moved from North East Scotland to Scotland, and from there to the North Sea Macro-region, gaining negotiating strength in the process. Furthermore, the Aberdeenshire regional government has successfully skipped over the UK government to promote the conversion of the EU's joint fisheries policy to a regionally based fisheries policy. This discourse conversion, as well as that found in other political platforms, is an important feature of what we have referred to as jumping scale. The Aberdeenshire government adopted this method deliberately and continued its jumping scale strategy until it reached a governance level that could satisfy its political and strategic ambitions. This stratagem was introduced over the course of the formation of the North Sea functional macro-region and has fostered political competition across scales (Figure 9.1).

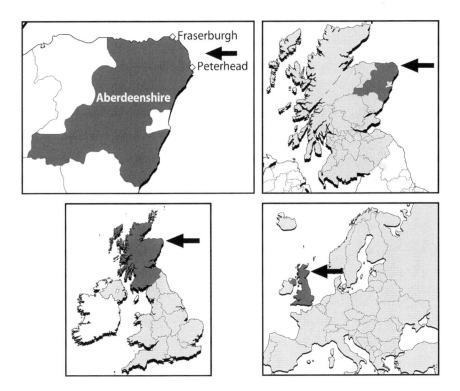

Figure 9.1 Mapping to understand jumping scale in stages
Source: Prepared by the authors.

222 Hideo Kojimoto et al.

This represents a process by which the handling of disputes and other policy issues has been moved up or down to non-state levels and serves as the means by which regulatory powers and control over resources that were previously dominated by the state can be transformed into a shared form. In other words, as argued by Swyngedouw, this is a process of extracting functions from the state, and a hollowing out of state functions (Swyngedouw 1997a; Swyngedouw 1997b; Swyngedouw 2004; Jessop 2004a).

Once macro-regions become soft spaces, the roles of stakeholders are revised and their respective positions are taken into consideration at conferences, meetings, and other venues where heterarchical political negotiations between actors are conducted (see Chapter 1). Here, in addition to territorial governance actors such as the European Commission and national and regional governments, functional actors such as commercial fishery groups, environmental NGOs and other issue-oriented actors, and even corporations that handle gas and natural resources, all participate in North Sea management. By participating in the drafting of regional governance rules, which are matters related to meta-governance (Jessop 2004b), these actors are exceeding the authority and capacity of delegated norms. Meta-governance here is a political form of governance based on comprehensive normative governance that involves not only actors such as territorial actors but also commercial fisheries groups, scientific organizations, and environmental NGOs whose positions and actions reflect different and sometimes conflicting norms.

Meta-governance can offer new possibilities for policy decision-making in the EU. This can be done by not limiting participation to territorial government actors, but incorporating civil society or market-driven stakeholders as well. In this way, unlike governance systems where the behavioral norms of the respective actors are given priority, the pattern of adjusting and harmonizing norms between actors is a major characteristic of meta-governance. When a new scale is created, and a new region is formed, macro-regional boundaries will differ for each governance arrangement. Therefore, a meta-governance agenda will include questions such as where to position a macro-region boundary, how far the region should extend, and what should be excluded.[3]

Allmendinger and Haughton have discussed fuzzy boundaries in relation to soft spaces, which relates to the earlier discussion of boundaries (Allmendinger and Haughton 2009). It follows that governance patterns in macro-regions can be adjusted, depending on the nature of the discourse, on issues related to sustainable development and environmental protection and on the normative positions of the actors involved. At the same time, the actual demarcation of the regional boundary becomes a subject for negotiation during the norms adjustment process.

Although boundaries are absolute and fixed in hard spaces, they can become fuzzy after spaces become soft. Within such a context, negotiations can overlap, leaving open the possibility for new political configurations. However, through EU-ization, a governance pattern in such a soft space will eventually be transformed into a hard space, and become fixed as a macro-region (see Chapter 1).

In recent years, we could say that the concept of macro-regionalization or macro-regionalism has made this hardening process of macro-regions, resulting in an "EU-ization" of political frameworks that emanate from the macro-regional strategy. In the macro-region creation process, use of the soft space concept helps us understand this secondary hardening process of the macro-region.

Conclusion

The development of a macro-regional approach within the EU policy arena has stimulated political activity between scales and has changed the nature of governance through the introduction of cross-scale processes. The macro-region has emerged to address the EU's need for new policy containers, as well as to offer an alternative for those diverging from the traditional paradigm of the MLG regional approach.

As the example of the North Sea Macro-region has shown, new actors, as well as newly identified actors who existed during the era of MLG (see Chapter 1), have facilitated the simultaneous development of the macro-region and of cross-scale regional governance. The involvement of new actors in regional governance does not necessarily remedy the weaknesses of the traditional policy structure but rather offers an alternative approach to the "scale down" demands of new EU policy modes such as territorial cohesion, sustainable development, and stakeholder participation.

Ironically, from the perspective of the MLG analytical framework, this infiltration of policy modes into other scales appears akin to the "top-down" approach; however, this infiltration actually indicates that the MLG structure, which is comprised of existing static, geographical scale units, does not offer a sufficient policy accommodation system under these new EU modes. Therefore, it can be argued that this historically embedded disjuncture was one of the primary stimuli in the production of the current dynamic CSRG within the NSR.

In order to explain the rationale for the development of the macro-regional approach and CSRG, we first discussed the historical and functional background of the macro-region, particularly from the perspective of delimiting state policy containers. An analysis of the functional macro-region approach was also undertaken using case studies of the NSR, with CSRG emerging as a result of transborder, trans-scale, and trans-norm processes.

While it can be argued that the North Sea Macro-region is a unique case that validates the application of CSRG, it can also be argued that the simultaneous development of the functional macro-region approach and CSRG can be applied to new developments in macro-regions that involve candidate states seeking EU entry. This diffusion has been observed with RACs and in early INTERREG initiatives.

The macro-regional approach fosters a multiplicity of identities for territorial actors who participate in CSRG. The actors strategically choose identities that are most suitable for the macro-regional mode in order to maximize their gains on a cross-scale, level playing field. In contrast, actors within a fixed-scale hierarchical governance system try to maximize their gains using their traditional embedded subordinate position. Flexible regionality has thereby made it possible to depart from multi-level embeddedness.

The macro-regional approach and CSRG are particularly useful in that they allow EU norms to be extended to other stakeholders, especially in the fields of marine resource management and spatial planning. In this sense, the macro-regional approach and CSRG can be considered predictably effective for future marine spatial planning, particularly in situations where the interests of the stakeholders diverge and the jurisdictions of both geographical and functional authorities are complex. Moreover, the changing nature of the identities of involved actors is enhanced through the political dynamics that occur among scales.

Finally, the potential for this analytical framework must also be validated in newly established EU macro-regions, particularly in terms of the changing permeability of EU norms.

Acknowledgements

Prof. Victor Lee Carpenter of Hirosaki University has helped us with English proofreading and Ms. Naoko Sato of Aomori Chuo-Gakuin University tidied up figures. We would like to thank both of them.

Notes

1 This advanced stakeholder participation model can be seen in Civil Society Dialogue in the EU transportation policy and Global Compact in the UN.
2 NSRAC has changed its name to the North Sea Advisory Council (NSAC).
3 Jessop (2004b) has proposed the concept of multi-level meta-governance to manage the governance of both MLG and meta-governance.

References

Agnew, John (1997) "The Dramaturgy of Horizons: Geographical Scale in the 'Reconstruction of Italy' by the New Italian Political Parties, 1992–95," *Political Geography*, 16 (2): 99–121.

Allmendinger, Phil, and Graham Haughton (2009) "Soft Spaces, Fuzzy Boundaries, and Metagovernance: The New Spatial Planning in the Thames Gateway," *Environment and Planning A*, 41 (3): 617–633.

Brenner, Neil (2001) "The Limits to Scale?: Methodological Reflections on Scalar Structuration," *Progress in Human Geography*, 25 (4): 591–614.

Commission of the European Communities (CEC) (2001) European Governance: A White Paper, COM (2001) 428 final (Brussels: CEC, 25 July 2001), European Commission, Brussels.

Hook, Glenn D. (1997) "Japan and Subregionalism: Constructing the Japan Sea Rim Zone," *Kokusaiseiji*, 114: 49–62.

Jessop, Bob (2004a) "Hollowing Out the 'Nation-state' and Multi-level Governance," in Patricia Kennett (ed.) *A Handbook of Comparative Social Policy*, Cheltenham: Edward Elgar, pp. 11–25.

Jessop, Bob (2004b) "Multi-Level Governance and Multi-Level Metagovernance," in Ian Bache and Matthew Flinders (eds.) *Multi-Level Governance*, Oxford: Oxford University Press, pp. 49–74.

Paasi, Anssi (2002) "Place and Region: Regional Worlds and Words," *Progress in Human Geography*, 26 (6): 802–811.

Schack, Michael (2000) "On the Multicontextual Character of Border Regions," in M van der Velde and H van Houtum, (eds.) *Borders, Regions and People*, London: Pion, pp. 202–219.

Smith, Neil (1987) "Dangers of the Empirical Turn: Some Comments on the Curs Initiative," *Antipode*, 19 (1): 59–68.

Smith, Neil (1992) "Contours of a Spatialized Politics: Homeless Vehicles and the Production of Geographical Scale," *Social Text*, 33 (33): 54–81.

Swyngedouw, Erik (1997a) "Excluding the Other: The Production of Scale and Scaled Politics," in Roger Lee and Jane Wills (eds.) *Geographies of Economies*, London: Arnold, pp. 167–176.

Swyngedouw, Erik (1997b) "Neither Global nor Local: 'Globalization' and the Politics of Scale," in Kevin R. Cox (ed.) *Spaces of Globalization: Reasserting the Power of the Local*, New York: Guilford, pp. 137–166.

Swyngedouw, Erik (2004) "Scaled Geographies: Nature, Place, and the Politics of Scale," in Eric Sheppard and Robert B. McMaster (eds.) *Scale and Geographic Inquiry: Nature, Society, and Method*, Oxford: Blackwell, pp. 129–153.

Conclusion

Future challenges in the study of sub-regions/sub-regionalism

Hidetoshi Taga and Seiichi Igarashi

With the end of the Cold War and the spread of globalism across the world, the sub-region is now attracting unprecedented attention as a transborder social unit. The emergence and expansion of the sub-region, whether artificially or naturally occurring, compels us to review a social unit that has been presupposed by conventional international relations (IR) theories and demands that we reconstruct these theories by incorporating the sub-region as a new social unit.

At the beginning of the current volume, we suggest the importance of the following four analytical perspectives in examining sub-regions/sub-regionalism using Asia (the Mekong region) and Europe as empirical cases: sub-regions and state strategies, the bottom-up dimension of sub-regions, sub-regions and borders, and relativization of the Eurocentric approach.

In current state strategies, for example, if a region is located at the very front of a group of states that have a competitive or hostile relationship, the "enclosure" of said region would have significance in the international order. This implies that changes in interstate relationships can be explained by carrying out a reverse interpretation that focuses on the formation of sub-regions. As Chapters 2 and 3 reveal, the Mekong region, in which state strategies are entangled and complex, can also be considered as a sub-region with such a nature. Chapter 8 shows that the easterly expanding Euroregion is rejecting regional autonomous movement and witnessing interstate conflict among Russia, Ukraine, and Poland. The "dangerous" side of international politics is being revealed through the relationships between sovereign states and sub-regions. Chapter 7 demonstrates that the expansion of normative politics by the European Union (EU) as a regional organization is implied in the formation of a sub-region, through which the EU is encouraging neighboring countries to accept EU norms.

When focusing on sovereign states, the United Kingdom (UK)'s recent withdrawal from the EU, the so-called "Brexit," created a considerable stir. Here, the kind of influence that a sovereign state can exert on the sub-region through its actions is worth noting. The UK Government has repeatedly said, "We are leaving the EU, not Europe." If this is true, the UK's participation in Europe—as part of the EU instrument INTERREG—with an identity, would continue; however, INTERREG Europe expressed concern in June 2016 that "the next steps are uncertain until the UK and the EU have negotiated a position which will then be discussed within the Interreg Europe monitoring committee" (INTERREG Europe Joint Secretariat 2016). The INTERREG North-West Europe Programme also said that, until further notice, it would continue operating as usual on the following basis: The UK is still a full member of the EU, with all the associated rights and obligations this entails; all project contracts are still valid for UK beneficiaries as well as for all other beneficiaries; the Programme Manual and procedures are still in place and will remain in place until a new decision is made (a process that may take years to complete); the next Monitoring Committee where Call 3 projects will be decided will take place as planned.[1] It is evident that the UK's withdrawal from the EU would exert influence on INTERREG Europe, though it is difficult at the moment to accurately predict the kind of influence it would have, which creates the need for further research.

In North America, the rumors of the United States (US) attempt to withdraw from the North American Free Trade Agreement (NAFTA) and the NAFTA renegotiations that would accompany it are attracting global attention. In this case, it is highly likely that the San Diego–Tijuana region, as a sub-region, will be influenced by the actions of the US as a sovereign state. The San Diego–Tijuana region has largely benefited from NAFTA, particularly in the manufacturing sector. In March 2017, Mexico's deputy economy minister told a delegation of San Diego and Baja California leaders that during the NAFTA renegotiations, Mexico would not accept any new deal that might limit trade. In addition, the delegation of about 90 business leaders and politicians, led by the San Diego Regional Chamber of Commerce, is advocating cross-border collaboration at a time of tension in the binational relationship, due in part to President Donald Trump's threats with regard to NAFTA. The chamber signed a memorandum of understanding with Mexico's Senate, allowing the San Diego–Tijuana border region leaders to collaborate on federal legislation south of the US border on issues of trade, immigration, and border infrastructure.[2] This is a case in which actors related to a sub-region have taken subjective action to mitigate the negative impacts brought about by a sovereign state's actions.

As for the bottom-up dimension, there is an insufficient accumulation of empirical and theoretical research in the conventional study of regionalism; however, regardless of scale, it is not only states and international organizations that are involved in forming regions. As Chapters 3 and 4 show, in the Mekong region, civil society actors are constructing a Mekong public sphere with a Mekong identity in the bottom-up direction. Civil society has issue-orientation; consequently, the development of transborder networks in civil society results in a hegemonic struggle among actors in the Gramscian sense, regarding various issues. Currently, in many regions, "development-oriented regionalism" and "neoliberal regionalism," which prioritize the economy and development, are achieving hegemony. As this type of hegemony becomes dominant, it is predicted that civil society will strengthen counter-hegemony from the "third position," which differs both from the state and the market. Meanwhile, some organizations in civil society have already participated in the process of formal policymaking related to a sub-region. The expansion of this type of "participatory regionalism" would encourage the growth of "multi-stakeholder governance" in the sub-region. Needless to say, not all sub-regions have active civil society networks, as this varies depending on the region and field.

We cannot forget the role of local governments, which are non-state actors just like civil society. In IR, in the mid-1970s, researchers began investigating the influence of domestic politics on international politics ("the second image"), as well as the reverse vector of influence ("the reverse second image") (Gourevitch 1978; Keohane and Milner 1996). While there has been little interest in local governments as new international actors in these studies, as Chapter 9 reveals, in the North Sea in Europe, a sub-region has been developed, largely by local governments. Further research would encourage more local government studies, which are underdeveloped compared to investigations on civil society in the field of IR.

As the European case shows, in sub-regions, local governments often act as agencies to implement policies and the local administrative unit often constitutes a policy container or policy space. In the Mekong region, the Mekong Basin Disease Surveillance (MBDS) is one example. The MBDS is a self-organizing consortium of six countries along the Mekong River that form a sub-regional framework of cooperation, with a view toward collaboration in regard to infectious diseases led by the health ministries of the participating countries. What is unique about the MBDS is the fact that the policy space is comprised of two local administrative units that transcend borders. Unlike in Europe, however, local autonomy is extremely underdeveloped in the Mekong region. This is largely due to the fact that all six member states adopt a nondemocratic regime. Still, there is a possibility that the center–periphery relationship could change with the formation of a sub-region. In fact, China's Yunnan province, which is partly free from the influence of the central government, has been actively involved with the Greater Mekong Sub-region (GMS) (Li and He 2011: 20–27). This implies that even under a centralized regime, local governments can enhance their autonomy by developing sub-regions.

As for the relationship between sub-regions and borders, it is easy to imagine that the emergence of a sub-region relativizes borders, and that this relativization would encourage the creation of a sub-region. In order to disentangle the relationship between sub-regions and borders, however, thorough and continuous fieldwork is essential. Findings from the tripartite relationship of sub-regions as "planes," borders as "lines," and border crossing-points as "points" are very interesting. Chapters 5 and 6 use comprehensive fieldwork to shed light on changes in borders, along with the formation of sub-regions. Stationary measurements were used during this fieldwork, either as a team or by assigning the work to one of the team members in December 2007, December 2009, December 2010, August 2013, March 2014, March 2015, February–March 2016, and September 2017. We have shared findings within the team and witnessed changes in the field in real time as a result.

It is meaningful to examine changes in borders with the formation of a sub-region in regards to the "route" as well. In the Mekong region, there are three

Conclusion: future challenges 229

such routes, which are complexly entangled: (1) the old trade routes, or sometimes nodes in the old tribute routes, which are being revived by the modernization process under the Asian Development Bank (ADB)'s GMS vision; (2) dedicated entry/exit points for freight vehicles in addition to the main national roads, which distinguish the movements of people from those of goods; and (3) "unofficial," everyday routes that freely crisscross an area that has been divided because borders were imposed on the preexisting "living sphere" (Taga 2015: 59).

In order to achieve the relativization of the Eurocentric approach, it is essential to escape from the teleological thinking of previous studies, which regard Europe as "the model" or "point of arrival." Regrettably, many existing IR theories are produced in Europe; however, there should be limits on investigations of Asia by way of Western IR theories, which have developed from Western tradition (Ikenberry and Mastanduno 2003). Acharya and Buzan query why there is a lack of non-Western IR theory (Acharya and Buzan 2007). While this current volume does not wholly construct a non-Western IR theory, it does manage to reveal the limits of the Western-centric approach and relativize them. In fact, Chapter 1 clarifies the limit of the existing Eurocentric approach, and introduces new concepts such as "cross-scale regional governance" and "soft space." Although this chapter mainly focuses on Europe, these analytical concepts will enable us to overcome Eurocentric teleology and investigate sub-regions in East Asia.

In addition to the Mekong region discussed in the current volume, sub-regions on a more diverse scale have been formed or proposed in East Asia since the latter half of the 1980s: in Southeast Asia, the Indonesia–Malaysia–Singapore Growth Triangle (IMS-GT, which involves Singapore, the state of Johor in Malaysia, and the province of the Riau Islands in Indonesia), the Indonesia–Malaysia–Thailand Growth Triangle (IMT-GT, which involves 14 southern provinces of Thailand, 8 states of Malaysia, and 10 provinces on Sumatra Island of Indonesia), the Brunei–Indonesia–Malaysia–Philippines East ASEAN Growth Area (BIMP-EAGA, which includes Brunei; four provinces in Kalimantan; the provinces of Sulawesi, Maluku, and Papua of Indonesia; the states of Sabah and Sarawak; the Federal Territory of Labuan of Malaysia; and Southern Mindanao and the province of Palawan of the Philippines), and the Cambodia–Laos–Vietnam Development Triangle Area (CLV-DTA, which involves Mondulkiri, Rattanakiri, and the Stung Treng provinces of Cambodia; the Attapeu, Saravan, and Se Kong provinces of Laos; and Dak Lak, Dak Lai, and Kon Tum of Vietnam), and in Northeast Asia, the Greater Tumen Initiative (GTI, which involves the provinces of Liaoning, Heilongjiang and Jilin, and Inner Mongolia of China; Eastern Mongolia; port cities in the eastern part of South Korea; Rason Special Economic Zone of North Korea; and the coastal regions of Russia), the Northern Economic Sphere (made up mainly of regions and provinces surrounding the Sea of Okhotsk), the Northeast Asia Economic Zone (made up mainly of regions and provinces surrounding the Sea of Japan), the Yellow Sea Economic Zone (made up mainly of regions and provinces surrounding the Yellow Sea), the East China Sea Economic Zone (made up mainly of regions and provinces surrounding the East China Sea), the Horai Economic Zone (made up mainly of the Fujian province, Taiwan, and Okinawa), and the South China Economic Zone (made up mainly of the Guangdong, Fujian, and Hainan provinces, Hong Kong, Taiwan, and Macao).

It is impossible to model these East Asian sub-regions on Europe, where sub-regions are institutionally formed under the EU as INTERREGs and Euroregions; in contrast, these East Asian sub-regions were created freely and without hierarchy. We need new analytical tools and approaches to investigate Asia. By reconceptualizing these East Asian sub-regions—which tended to be treated as "economic zones," "market zones," or "reproduction zones" in previous studies—as new social units within international society, as in the case of the Mekong region, and by approaching them from a political science perspective, we should be able to obtain rich findings (Igarashi 2016). The future research agenda in sub-region studies should include investigation, not only into the reality of sub-regions on a diverse scale, but also the interactions among them.

We are currently engaged in research into these sub-regions, with the aim to understand state strategies, regional institutions, normative discourses, and the characteristics of the actors involved. We also seek to shed light on the reality of sub-regions as functional spaces through detailed fieldwork in each sub-region, as well as comparative analyses. By way of this continuing study, we aim to extract the security functions of the sub-region, which mainstream theories have thus far ignored, and to provide new findings for security policies in East Asia.[3] A new horizon for peace studies will be opened through sub-region studies.

Notes

1 http://www.nweurope.eu/news-events/latest-news/how-does-brexit-affect-nwe-projects/, accessed October 13, 2017.
2 http://www.kpbs.org/news/2017/mar/29/top-mexican-official-reassures-san-diego-tijuana-r/, accessed October 13, 2017.
3 The Japan Society for the Promotion of Science (JSPS), Grant-in-Aid for Scientific Research (B) (Grant No. 16H05700, FY2016-FY2019, Multi-Layer Sub-Regions and New Security Architecture in East Asia).

References

Acharya, Amitav, and Barry Buzan (2007) "Why is There No Non-Western International Relations Theory?: An Introduction," *International Relations of the Asia-Pacific*, 7 (3): 287–312.
Gourevitch, Peter (1978) "The Second Image Reversed: The International Sources of Domestic Politics," *International Organization*, 32 (4): 881–912.
Igarashi, Seiichi (2016) "Re-creation of Peace in East Asia," *Peace Studies*, 46: i–xx (in Japanese).
Ikenberry, G. John, and Michael Mastanduno (2003) (eds.) *International Relations Theory and the Asia-Pacific*, New York, NY: Columbia University Press.
INTERREG Europe Joint Secretariat (2016) Statement on UK Referendum, June 27, 2016.
Keohane, Robert O., and Helen V. Milner (1996) *Internationalization and Domestic Politics*, Cambridge: Cambridge University Press.

Li, Chenyang, and Shengda He (2011) "China's Participation in the GMS Cooperation: Progress and Challenge," in Mingjiang Li and Chong Guan Kwa (eds.) *China-ASEAN Sub-Regional Cooperation: Progress, Problems and Prospect*, Singapore: World Scientific, pp. 15–36.

Taga, Hidetoshi (2015) "The Position of Myanmar in GMS," *Waseda Studies in Social Sciences*, 16 (1): 41–94 (in Japanese).

Index

Note: Page numbers in italics refer to figures and in bold refer to tables. Page numbers followed by 'n' with number refer to endnotes.

Acharya, Amitav 75, 229
ACMECS *see* Ayeyawady-Cho Phraya-Mekong Economic Cooperation Strategy
ADB *see* Asian Development Bank
ADD *see* Arrest, Detention, and Deportation
AEBR *see* Association of European Border Regions
AEC *see* ASEAN Economic Community
Agreement on the Cooperation for the Sustainable Development of the Mekong River Basin 80, 86
AICHR *see* ASEAN Intergovernmental Commission on Human Rights
Aksyonov, Sergey 207
AMBDC *see* ASEAN Mekong Basin Development Cooperation
AMEICC *see* ASEAN-METI Economic and Industrial Cooperation Committee
Arrest, Detention, and Deportation (ADD) 91, 92
ASEAN *see* Association of Southeast Asian Nations
ASEAN Economic Community (AEC) 108, 120, 134
ASEAN Intergovernmental Commission on Human Rights (AICHR) 120, 121
ASEAN Mekong Basin Development Cooperation (AMBDC) **57, 64, 79**, 80–3
ASEAN-METI Economic and Industrial Cooperation Committee (AMEICC) 64, **79**, 80, 82
ASEAN way 80, 81, 83
Asian Development Bank (ADB) 53, 63, 66, 71, 78, 82, 85–7, 92–3, 96, 161

Asian Migrant Center (AMC) 90
Asia's local economic zones 5
Association of European Border Regions (AEBR) 189, 200, 208, 210
Association of Southeast Asian Nations (ASEAN): economic cooperation 120; Laos's integration into 58, 60, 61, 63, 65; multilateralism 53, 60; power politics 56; regional cooperation frameworks 59, 63; regional integration 54–9, 66
Atlantic Arc Region 190, **191**
Ayeyawady-Cho Phraya-Mekong Economic Cooperation Strategy (ACMECS) 63, **79**, 81–3

B7 Baltic Islands Network 32
Balassa, Béla 72
Baltic Sea Commission (BSC) 32
Baltic Sea Macro-region *see* macro-region
Basin Development Strategy (BDP) 95, 97
BCPs *see* border-crossing points
BDP *see* Basin Development Strategy
Bell, Ann 218
Black Sea Region 190, 201
border communities 128; under economic reform and political changes 132–3; and emergence of GMS 133–5; under ideological conflicts in Indochina 129–31; in mainland Southeast Asia (1975–1986) 131–2
border-crossing points (BCPs) 160, 161–4, *162*; Daluo (China)- Mongla (Myanmar) 175, *175*; Houayxay (Laos)-Chiang khong (Thailand) 171–3; Mohan (China)-Boten (Laos)

169, 169–71, *170, 171*; Myawaddy (Myanmar)-Mae Sot (Thailand) 175–7, *176*; positive and negative outcomes at 167–8; Tachileik (Myanmar)-Mae Sai (Thailand) 173–4, *174*
border pass system 167
border towns of GMS: Aranyaprathet (Thailand) 127, 151, 152, *153, 154*; Boten (Laos) 127, 135, 138, *139*, 140–1, *169–71*; Chiang khong (Thailand) 127, 131, 135, 136, *137*, 138, *172, 173*; Dansavan (Laos) 127, 141, 142, 144, *145*; Houay Xay (Laos) 127, 131, 135, 136, *137*, 138, *172*; Lao Bao (Vietnam) 124, 125, 127, 141, 142, *143*, 143–4, *144*; Mae Sot (Thailand) 126, 141, 147–9, *148, 149*, 151, 152, *176*; Mohan (China) 127, 139, *140*, 163, *169, 170*; Mukdahan (Thailand) 127, 141, 142, 144–6, *147*; Myawaddy (Myanmar) 126, 141, 147–52, *148, 150, 176*; Poipet (Cambodia) 127, *151*, 151–2, *152, 154*; Savannakhet (Laos) 127, 141, 142, 144–6
border trade 126, 131, 132, 134, 136, 143, 145, 147, 148, 151, 155, 156
Boten Special Economic Zone 141
Brexit 20, 226
Brunei–Indonesia–Malaysia–Philippines East ASEAN Growth Area (BIMP-EAGA) 229
buffer state 53–6, 61–5, 67n2
buffer system/buffer systems 58–61, 68n10
business and human rights (BHR) 120

Cambodia, Laos, Myanmar, and Vietnam (CLMV) 54, 63
Cambodia–Laos–Vietnam (CLV) 63, 65, 67
Cambodia-Laos-Vietnam Development Triangle (CLV-DTA) 79, 81, 83, 229
Carpathian Region 190, 200, 209
cartographic scale *see* scale
casino 138, 139, 146, 149, 152, 168, 169, 175
CBC *see* cross-border cooperation
CBTA *see* Cross-Border Transport Agreement
CFP *see* Common Fisheries Policy
Chao Phraya River 86
Chiang Khong community 131
Chiang Khong–Houay Xay route on Road R3A 138

Chiang Saen Port 136
China: Boten (Laos)–Mohan (China) route 138–9; cooperation project with Laos 140, 141; economic reform and political changes 133; Four Modernizations 133; relationship with Laos 57, 60, 61–2; Yunnan province 62, 65, 71, 135, 228
Choonhavan, Chatichai 71, 132
civil society 12, 117–21, 227, 228; Dawei 112–13; Mekong Region 83–92, **84**; and regionalism 72–6
CIS *see* Commonwealth of Independent States
CLMV *see* Cambodia, Laos, Myanmar, and Vietnam
CLV *see* Cambodia-Laos-Vietnam
CLV-DTA *see* Cambodia-Laos-Vietnam Development Triangle
Committee for Coordination on the Lower Mekong Basin (MC) *see* Mekong Committee
Committee of the Regions (CoR) 30, 39, 41
Common Customs Area (CCA) 166
Common Fisheries Policy (CFP) 214, 217
Commonwealth of Independent States (CIS) 205
Comprehensive National Development Plan (Japan) 11
Conference of Peripheral and Maritime Regions of Europe (CPMR) 39, 41, 218
connectivity 55, 81, 126, 134–6, 138, 140, 142, 143, 148, 155, 161, 162
constructivism/constructivist 2, 27, 46, 68n18
CoR *see* Committee of the Regions
corporate social responsibility (CSR) 120, 121
corporatist regionalism *see* regionalism
Council of Europe 197
Council of the Baltic Sea States (CBSS) 32
counter-hegemony *see* hegemony
Cox, Robert 74, 75
CPMR *see* Conference of Peripheral and Maritime Regions of Europe
cross-border cooperation (CBC) 9, 12, 19, 183, 185, 187–90, 197, 199, 209
Cross-Border Transport Agreement (CBTA) 19, 65, 160, 164–9, **165, 167**, 174, 175, 177
cross-scale regional governance 30, 36, **40**, 45–6, 217, 223, 224; definition 37; MLG model 36–7; types of 39–41
CSR *see* corporate social responsibility

Daluo (China)-Mongla (Myanmar) BCP *see* border-crossing points
dam construction 78, 85, 86, 88, 89, 97, 98, 108, 109, 115–19
Danube Region 39, 41, 42
Daoroung, Premrudee 86
Dawei Deep Seaport Development and Industrial Estate 109, 110
Dawei Deepwater Port Project 109
Dawei Development Association (DDA) 112, 113
Dawei Special Economic Zone Project: Dawei civil society in 112–13; development 109–11, *110*; impact of 110; international non-governmental organizations in 113
DDA *see* Dawei Development Association
development-oriented regionalism *see* regionalism
Doi Moi 125, 132, 133, 154
dominant hegemony *see* hegemony
Don Sahong Dam (Laos) 108, 116, *117*, 117–19
Don Sahong Power Company Limited (DSPC) 118
double movement 73
DSPC *see* Don Sahong Power Company Limited

EaP *see* Eastern Partnership
East China Sea Economic Zone 229
Eastern Europe, EU/Russian regional policy in 201–5
Eastern Partnership (EaP) 183, 201–4
East-West Economic Corridor (EWEC): BCPs 175–7; of Road No. 9 141–54
ECAFE *see* Economic Commission for Asia and the Far East
Economic Commission for Asia and the Far East (ECAFE) 76, 77
economic corridors 71, 133–5, 161–4 *see also* East-West Economic Corridor; North-South Economic Corridor
ecosystem 86, 98, 114–16
Électricité du Laos (EDL) 118
Emerald Triangle (ET) 79, 80
ENI CBC *see* European Neighborhood Instrument's Cross-Border Cooperation
ENP *see* European Neighbourhood Policy
ENPI *see* European Neighbourhood and Partnership Instrument
ERDF *see* European Regional Development Fund

ET *see* Emerald Triangle
ethnic minority/ethnic minorities 125, 135, 142, 144
ETOs *see* extra-territorial obligations
EU *see* European Union
EU Border Assistance Mission to the Republic of Moldova and Ukraine (EUBAM) 203, 206
EU Commission 39, 42, 194
EUBAM *see* EU Border Assistance Mission to the Republic of Moldova and Ukraine
EU-ization 34, 41, 215, 222, 223
EUREGIO 188
Eurocentric approach 15–16, 229
Euro-Mediterranean Partnership (EUROMED) 183, 195, 202
EUROMED *see* Euro-Mediterranean Partnership
European Coal and Steel Community (ECSC) 30
European Neighborhood Instrument's Cross-Border Cooperation (ENI CBC) 183; EU norms in 187–92; political significance of 192–4
European Neighbourhood and Partnership Instrument (ENPI) 203, 209
European Neighbourhood Policy (ENP) 12, 183, 192, 193, 202–4; normative politics 184–6
European Regional Development Fund (ERDF) 187, 188, 213
European Union (EU): cross-border cooperation 12, 187–90, **189**; cross-scale regional governance 30, 36–42, **40**, 45–6; deviation from state borders 43–4; hard spaces 34, **35**, 36; integration process 9; macro-regional strategies 190–2, **191**; macro-regions and macro-regionalism *31*, 31–4, **40**; MLG model 30, 36–7, 39, 44–5; power reallocation process 44–5; regional integration 213, 214; regional policy 30, 32, 201–4; soft spaces 34, **35**, 36, **38**; state re-scaling process 30–1, **38**, 44–5
Euroregions 14, 19, 183, 197, 208–10, 230; between Russia and Ukraine 198–201, *199*
EU Strategy for the Adriatic and Ionian Region (EUSAIR) 32, 190
EU Strategy for the Alpine Region (EUSALP) 190

Index 235

236 Index

EU Strategy for the Baltic Sea Region (EUSBR) 32, 190, 214
EU Strategy for the Danube Region (EUSDR) 32, 190
EWEC *see* East-West Economic Corridor
extra-territorial obligations (ETOs) 120, 121

FDI *see* foreign direct investment
feudal state 127
Five-Year National Socio-Economic Development Plan (Laos): 2011–2015 63; 2016–2020 62
foreign direct investment (FDI) 18, 107, 109, 132
Foundation for Ecological Recovery (FER) 85
free trade agreement (FTA)/free trade agreements (FTAs) 16, 205
Friendship Bridge 136, 138, 144–5, *148, 171–7, 172, 174, 176*
functionalism 72
functional macro-region *see* macro-region
fuzzy boundary 222

geographical scale *see* scale
Gill, Stephen 74, 75
GMS *see* Greater Mekong Sub-region
Goh Chok Tong 80
Golden Triangle 136, 168, *168*
Greater Mekong Sub-region (GMS) 8, 8–9, 59; and border communities 133–5, 154–5; Economic Cooperation Program 53, 63, 65, 66, 71, 78, 80, 82, 92–3, 97; on-site surveys in border areas of *161*; organizational framework 93
Greater Tumen Initiative (GTI) 5, **6**, 229

Haas, Ernst 72
Hansen, Bent 219
hard regionalism *see* regionalism 21n8
hard spaces 34, **35**, 36
hegemony 72, 74–6, 92, 97, 98, 227; and civil society 74–76; counter-hegemony 18, 74–76, 98, 229; dominant hegemony 18, 74–76, 97–98; hegemony in realism 74; hegemony in neo-Gramscian 74–76
Helsinki Commission (HELCOM) 32
Hettne, Björn 7, 12, 20n3, 73
Hook, Glenn D. 215
Horai Economic Zone 229
Houayxay (Laos)-Chiang khong (Thailand) BCP *see* border-crossing points

human rights 18, 90, 98, 109, 112–14, 118, 120, 121, 204
human trafficking 90, 93, 98, 160, 168, 178
hydropower 18, 77, 87, 97, 107–9, 114–16, 119

IICBTA *see* Initial Implementation of CBTA
IMC *see* Interim Mekong Committee
Indonesia-Malaysia- Singapore Growth Triangle (IMS-GT) 2, 229
Indonesia-Malaysia-Thailand Growth Triangle (IMT-GT) 229
Initial Implementation of CBTA (IICBTA) 160, 166, 169, 170, 173
Interim Mekong Committee (IMC) 78, 79, 80, 86
International Centre for Environmental Management (ICEM) 97
International Commission of Justice (ICJ) 113
International Council for the Exploration of the Sea (ICES) 214, 218
International Energy Agency (IEA) 98
international law 113, 121, 128
INTERREG 2, *3, 4, 7,* 12, 31, 42, 183, 187, 188, 190, 198, 213–15, 219, 226, 227
issue-oriented regionalism *see* regionalism
Italian-Thai Development Public Company Limited (ITD) 109, 110, 112

Japan 11, 80–2, 130, 131, 142, 155, 215
Japan Sea Rim region 7, 46, 215 *see also* Pan-Japan Sea Region
Japan Sea Rim Zone Concept 215
Jintanakarn Mai 125, 132, 133
jumping scale *see* scale

labor migration 90, 95
Lancang-Mekong River Dialogue and Cooperation (LMRDC) 79, 82
Lao Bao Special Economic-Commercial Area 142, *143*
Laos: bilateral relationships 60–5; as buffer state 60–5, 67n2; dam projects in 114–17; economic reform 56, 57, 61, 63; integration into ASEAN 58, 61, 63, 65; international relations 54–8, **57**; political and economic history 56, 57; regional formation 59–65; relationship with China 57, 60, 61–2; relationship with Vietnam 60, 62–3; relations with Thailand 55, 61–3, 65; small states 56–9; state formation in 55, 61

Lengsavad, Somsavat 62
Li Peng 61
liberal institutionalism 72
Lipponen, Paavo 202
LMI *see* Lower Mekong Initiative
LMRDC *see* Lancang-Mekong River Dialogue and Cooperation
local community 115, 120
local government 7, 12, 13, 15, 17, 20, 81, 130, 189, 197, 198, 228
Lower Mekong Food Security Database 95
Lower Mekong Initiative (LMI) 79, 81

macro-region: Baltic Sea Macro-region 39, 41, 42; building process 215, **216**; EU macro-region 31–4; functional macro-region 214, **216**, 217, 221,223; North Sea Macro-region 39, 41–3, 47, 217–19
macro-regionalism 31–4, **40**
macro-regional strategy (MRS) 31, 185, 187, 190–2, **191**
Malaysian Human Rights Commission (SUHAKAM) 118
Mannheim, Karl 59
Maputo Development Corridor (MDC) **6**
MC *see* Committee for Coordination on the Lower Mekong Basin
Mediterranean region 183, 190, 202
Medvedev, Dmitry 204
Mega First Corporation Berhad 118
Mekong Basin Disease Surveillance (MBDS) 228
Mekong Committee (MC) 77, **79**
Mekong Congestion 71, 72, 78–83, **79**, 92, 98
Mekong Energy and Ecology Network (MEE Net) 87–8, **88**
Mekong Institute (MI) **79**, 80, 95–6
Mekong-Japan Summit (MJS) **79**, 81–3
Mekong Migrant Network (MMN) 90–2, **91**, 95
Mekong region 65; civil society networks in 83–92, **84**; development of 71, 76–8, 81; memorandums of understanding (MOUs) 90, 91; multilateralism of **64**
Mekong River 62, 71, 76, 78, 108, 114, *137*
Mekong River Commission (MRC) **64**, 77, **79**, 80, 86, 93–5, **94**, 96, 97, 108, 116–18
Mekong spirit 77, 78
Mekong Watch 87
Merkel, Angela 208
meta-governance 31, 36, 43, 222
methodological scale *see* scale

Mexico 227
MI *see* Mekong Institute
micro-region 2, 12, 14, 15, 20
migration 13, 29, 90, 95, 96, 111, 147
Minh, Ho Chi 130
Mitrany, David 72
Mittelman, James 73, 74
MJS *see* Mekong-Japan Summit
MLG *see* multi-level governance
MMN *see* Mekong Migrant Network
Mohamad, Mahathir 80
Mohan (China)-Boten (Laos) BCP *see* border-crossing points
MRC *see* Mekong River Commission
MRS *see* macro-regional strategy
multi-level governance (MLG) 9, 13, 15, 30, 36–7, 39, 44–5, 73, 187; Type II 37
Myanmar: Dawei Special Economic Zone Project in 109–13, *110*; economic development 107, 108
Myanmar Investment Law 107
Myawaddy (Myanmar)-Mae Sot (Thailand) BCP *see* border-crossing points
Myawaddy Special Economic Zone 148, 149

NAFTA *see* North American Free Trade Agreement
Nam Theun 2 Dam (Laos) 87, 115
National Human Rights Commission of Thailand (NHRCT) 120
Ne Win 132
Neighboring Countries Economic Development Cooperation Agency (NEDA) 109
neofunctionalism 72
neo-Gramscian approach (NGA) 72, 74, 75
neoliberal institutionalism 17
neoliberal regionalism *see* regionalism
NESFDP *see* North East Scotland Fisheries Development Partnership
new regionalism *see* regionalism
New Regionalism Approach (NRA) 12, 13, 15, 72–6
new social unit 1, 14, 15, 226, 230
NGA *see* neo-Gramscian approach
NGOs *see* non-governmental organizations
Nomenclature of Units for the Territorial Statistics (NUTS) 214
non-governmental organizations (NGOs) 12, 31, 85–7, **89**, 90, 92–7, 108, 109, 113–14, 118–21, 197, 220
Nordic Council 32, 39

238   Index

North American Free Trade Agreement (NAFTA) 125, 227
Northeast Asia Economic Zone 229
North East Scotland Fisheries Development Partnership (NESFDP) 217–20
Northern Economic Sphere 229
North Sea Commission (NSC) 39, 218–20, 221
North Sea Commission Fisheries Group (NSCFG) 217, 218
North Sea Commission Fisheries Partnership (NSCFP) 217–19
North Sea Macro-region *see* macro-region
North Sea Region (NSR) 19, 20, 34, 214; fisheries sector 217; jumping scale 219–25, **220–2**, *221*; North Sea Macro-Region 39, 41, 47, 214, 217–19
North Sea Regional Advisory Council (NSRAC) 217, 219, 220, 221
North-South Economic Corridor (NSEC) 151, 156; BCPs 169–75; of Road R3 135–41
NRA *see* New Regionalism Approach
NSC *see* North Sea Commission
NSC Fisheries Working Group (NSCFWG) 218, 219
NSEC *see* North-South Economic Corridor
NSR *see* North Sea Region
NSRAC *see* North Sea Regional Advisory Council
Nye, Joseph S. Jr. 1

ODA *see* official development assistance
official development assistance (ODA) 85, 86, 108, 109
One Belt One Road Initiative 156–7, 169
Orange Revolution 203, 205, 206
Organization for Security Co-operation in Europe (OSCE) 208

Pak Beng hydropower project (Laos) 119, 120
Pak Mun Dam (Thailand) 115
Pan-Japan Sea Region 7, 8, 11
Paris Peace Accords 61, 71, 78
participatory regionalism *see* regionalism
PCP *see* prior consultation process
People's Revolutionary Party (Laos) 57, 59–63
PESCA 217, 219
Phomvihane, Kaysone 61

PNPCA *see* Procedures for Notification, Prior Consultation, and Agreement
Polanyi, Karl 73
political geography 7, 14, 17, 28–30, 47, 219
Poroshenko, Petro 208
postclassical realism 11, 83
poverty reduction 80, 82, 87, 92, 114, 115
power geometry 27, 28, 36, 37
prior consultation process (PCP) 116
Procedures for Notification, Prior Consultation, and Agreement (PNPCA) 119, 120

rationalism 72–4
realism/realist 17, 74, 68n18
reflectivism 72–4, 98
Regional Advisory Council (RAC) 20, 214
regional corporatism *see* regionalism
regional hegemony *see* hegemony
regionalism: and civil society 12–13, 74–76; corporatist regionalism 75, 96–7; development-oriented regionalism 83; hard regionalism 21n8; issue-oriented regionalism 76, 83; neoliberal regionalism 12, 72–5, 83, 85, 98, 227; new regionalism 1, 73, 74; participatory regionalism 75, 86, 96–8; regional corporatism 75; soft regionalism 17; state-centric regionalism 72, 74, 76, 96; theoretical approaches to 72–6
Regional Stakeholder Forum 119
regionness 20n3
Russia: regional policy 204–5; relationship with Ukraine 205–6
Russia–Ukraine border region 198–201

Samberg, Trina 218
San Diego–Tijuana region 227
Save the Mekong Coalition (SMC) 88–90, **89**, 96, 118, 119
Savon-Seno Special Economic Zone 145, *146*
Sayasone, Choummaly 62
scalar turn *see* scale
scale: cartographic scale 28; geographical scale 28, 37; jumping scale 29, 39, 41–2, 219–25, **220–2**, *221*; methodological scale 28; mobilization 28, 37; politics among scales 17, 33, 37, 39, 41–2, 46; relationship between politics and 28; re-scaling 30–1, 33, *33*,

34, 36, **38**, 39, 41, 42, 44–6; scalar turn 27; struggle between scales 31
Schengen area 207, 208
SEA *see* Strategic Environmental Assessment
Seinsverbundenheit 58–60
Sen, Hun 81
SEZs *see* Special Economic Zones
Shetland Oceans Alliance (SHOAL) 218
Shinawatra, Thaksin 81
Singapore–Kunming Rail Link (SKRL) 80
single-stop inspection (SSI) 144, 166
single-window inspection (SWI) 144, 164, 166
Sinohydro 118
small states 53, 56–9, 66, 67
SMC *see* Save the Mekong Coalition
soft regionalism *see* regionalism
soft spaces 32, 34, **35**, 36, **38**, 41, 229
South Asia Sub-Regional Economic Cooperation (SASEC) **6**
South China Economic Zone 230
Southeast Asia: borders in 129–33; nation-states in 128, 129, 133–4
Special Economic Zones (SEZs) 109–11, 113–14, 142, 145, 146–9, *162*
special purpose vehicle (SPV) 109
SPV *see* special purpose vehicle
SSI *see* single-stop inspection
stages of economic integration 72
state-centric regionalism *see* regionalism
State Law and Order Restoration Council (SLORC) 132
Strategic Environmental Assessment (SEA) 97, 116, 118
straw effects 160
sub-regions: Asia 5, **6**; and borders 13–14; bottom-up dimension of 12–13; challenges in study of 226-30; definition 2; Europe *3, 4,* **5**; in international society **6**; and state strategy 11–12, 226
supranational institutionalism 39, 41, 46, 72, 193
SWI *see* single-window inspection

Tachileik (Myanmar)-Mae Sai (Thailand) BCP *see* border-crossing points
Tennessee Valley Authority of Asia 77
Ten-Year Socio-Economic Development Strategy (2016–2025) (Laos) 62

TERRA *see* Towards Ecological Recovery and Regional Alliance
territoriality 2, 14, 29, 30, 219
Thailand: border trade **126**; relations with Laos 55, 61–3, 65
Thai National Human Rights Commission 114
Towards Ecological Recovery and Regional Alliance (TERRA) 85, 86–8
transformative regionalism 74–6, 83, 96
Trump, Donald 227
two plus principle 78

Ukraine 198–201, *199*; Orange Revolution 203, 205; relationship with EU 206–7; relationship with Russia 205–8
UN Human Rights Committee 121
Union of the Baltic Cities (UBC) 32
United Nations Guiding Principles on Business and Human Rights (UNGPs) 113, 114, 120, 121
United States (US) 12, 20, 77, 81, 82, 125, 129–31, 149, 155, 157, 227
U Nyun 77
US Agency for International Development (USAID) 95

Viêt Minh Movement 130
Vietnam: relationship with Laos 55, 60–3; relationship with USSR 60
Vietnam National Mekong Committee 119, 120
Vision 2030 (Laos) 62
Vorachith, Bounnhang 62

water catchment area 7, 11, 43
World Wildlife Fund (WWF) 92, 93, 96
WWF *see* World Wildlife Fund

Xayaburi Dam (Laos) 107, 108, 116, *117,* 118
Xi Jinping 156

Yali Falls Dam (Vietnam) 115
Yanukovych, Viktor 205–7
Yellow Sea Economic Zone 229

Zambia-Malawi-Mozambique Growth Triangle (ZMM-GT) **6**
Zhou Enlai 122